ROAD FROM SINGAPORE

John Dodd

Road from Singapore

by
DIANA NORMAN

HODDER AND STOUGHTON
LONDON · SYDNEY · AUCKLAND · TORONTO

British Library Cataloguing in Publication Data

Norman, Diana
    Road from Singapore.—Revised ed.
    1. Dodd, John   2. Rehabilitation of criminals
    I. Title
    364.8'092'4   HV9346

ISBN 0 340 23483 0

FOR MY MOTHER
WITH LOVE AND GRATITUDE

ACKNOWLEDGEMENTS

In writing this book it has been impossible to name all the people whose lives have affected and been affected by John Dodd, and to them I apologise.

On the other hand, I received time and consideration from so many others who *are* mentioned that I can only give a general thank you and list a few.

My admiration and affection to Mme. Marquita Bischoff for her hospitality and help, and my thanks to Geoffrey Howard of the B.B.C. for the notes of interviews with John he so generously gave me along with his advice, and to Alyson Dodd whose judgement has remained constantly good.

Mr. Ronald Searle kindly gave permission for his drawing of John Dodd in Changi to be used.

As anybody who knows them will see, I have imbibed background material from the following books: *The Fall of Singapore*, by Frank Owen, *The Singapore Story* by Ken Attiwill, *Sinister Twilight* by Noel Barber, *The Story of Dr Wassell* by James Hilton, *The Naked Island* by Russell Braddon, *The Unknown Citizen* by Tony Parker and *Safe Lodging* and *A Pretty Sort of Prison* by Merfyn Turner.

I should mention that in every case the names and places that might identify the men of Langley House have been changed but that in all other respects their stories are true.

Above all, although he'll hate the cliché, my love and gratitude to my husband, Barry Norman, without whom this book would not have been written.

FOREWORD

Time and again in the history of humanity our whole attitude to a social problem is changed because a man comes along with a concern. He has to be a particular kind of man, with enormous resilience, courage and persistence. He must know his subject from the inside. He must know how to enlist the aid of others whose experience and skills go beyond his own. He makes faster progress if he charms people and makes friends quickly. But above all he must be able to communicate his own compassion and concern and help other people to feel as he feels and to see the issues for what they are.

John Dodd is such a man and when the social history of our time comes to be written he will be remembered as one of the men who opened the eyes of the British public to the needs of the recidivist, the habitual offender, the fellow who, unless he is given the help he so desperately needs, will certainly return to prison.

Gradually the battle is being won and people are beginning to realise that society itself often creates the criminal. Many of these offenders are bruised and hurt in mind and in their social attitudes. Defective home life, deprivation, alcoholism and general inadequacy have led to crime. They need remedial treatment both in prison and especially on release as surely as any other injured person. These are the people John Dodd longs to help. These are the men for whom he cares and wants us to care. Many of them will never be able to live an ordinary civilian life. They will want constant care, support and understanding. This is what he sees so plainly and what he has made others see.

In the New Testament that he carried with him through those appalling years are the words 'I was in prison and you visited me'. Only those who have been prisoners can know what that condition means and what it does to a man—the shame and humiliation, the physical and mental degradation, the feeling of helplessness, the hatred it breeds, the struggle it is to retain one's self-respect.

Because John Dodd has been in prison he knows what it feels like. He knows what prison does to a man. And he knows what Christian love can do.

Here then is the story of one who is every inch a man—a man with a great concern. His one desire is that the telling of this story will draw many readers to share in that concern.

Leslie Davison

Westminster, S.W.1.
February 1970

CONTENTS

ILLUSTRATIONS

(between pages 96–7)

[1] B.B.C.
[2] Ronald Searle
[3] Alan D. Baker

'The mood and temper of the public with regard to the treatment of criminals is one of the unfailing tests of the civilisation of any country . . . We must not forget that when every material improvement has been effected in the prisons, when the temperature has been rightly adjusted, when the proper food to maintain health and strength has been given, when the doctors, chaplains and prison visitors have come and gone, the convict stands deprived of everything that a free man calls life.'

Hansard, July 20, 1910

Winston Churchill
(Home Secretary)

'He brought me to the banqueting house,
and his banner over me was love.'
SONG OF SOLOMON, chapter 2, verse 4.

PROLOGUE

AN UNSUNG VILLAIN

Early in the morning of December 21, 1959, a man walked out of Durham Prison where he had just finished a three-month sentence for larceny and went straight into a transport café.

He bought himself a cup of tea and a box of matches and took them to a table by a window. He drank his tea, picked up the matches, lit one. Then, with extreme care, he held the flame to the café curtains.

Within seconds the greasy material was burning.

It took only a little longer for the angry café owner to put out the fire and call the police. While he did so the man stood quietly waiting, and when the police came he went away with them, just as quietly.

At the next Assizes the judge, commenting on Terence Fenby's long record of petty crime, sentenced him to three years. So, only a few weeks after he'd left it, Terence Fenby re-entered Durham Prison having been at liberty for just thirty-five minutes.

The case was closed. There was a paragraph about it in the local paper and that was all. Nobody seemed to wonder what it had all been about.

Ten years ago when I first wrote this book I started it, as I have here, with the case of Terry and what later happened to him because then he was the archetypal criminal. Bigger and nastier crimes grabbed the headlines but it was the Terence Fenbys who were silting up the magistrates' courts, shuffling in and out of prison to form the largest proportion of its population and costing the taxpayer hundreds of times more than the goods they stole or damaged.

The more things change the more they stay the same. Hooligans, vandals, muggers and political terrorists are grabbing the headlines now. But still they aren't typical. Many of the muggers and vandals will, as Sir Robert Mark once said, 'grow out of it'. For all sorts of reasons connected with adolescence, social deprivation and unemployment, it is a dreadful stage they pass through before becoming, more or less, respectable men with families. Political terrorists are a phenomenon and, thank God, a tiny minority.

It is still the Terence Fenbys who cause magistrates their biggest headache, although now the problem is how to keep them out of prison rather than chuck them in. This is partly because prisons are filled to overflowing with them already and partly because at least one lovely thing has happened in these last ten years; there has been a growth in understanding and, therefore, compassion. Terence Fenby wouldn't be described as a criminal now, perhaps not even as an inadequate. The current word social workers use about people like him is 'damaged'. It is an exact description. Somewhere along the line something so awful has happened to them — usually in childhood—that they have become emotionally disabled.

They drift into crime not because they want to but because they're incapable of doing anything else. Asking them to hold down a marriage, a job, and make the hundreds of decisions necessary to lead an ordinary life is like asking a legless man to run the mile. If some well-meaning person offers them a chance they're likely to bite the hand that feeds them and throw the chance away. They even fail at crime. They are frightened, exasperating, lonely men.

Prisons, grim as they are—and only those who haven't seen one think prisons have become holiday camps—make refuges for the damaged personality because there you're told exactly what to do and you do it.

As one elderly ex-con, now in sanctuary at one of the Langley Houses, said: 'It gets so's the most frightening thing about prison is when they open the gate to let you out. And if you've nowhere to go they might as well not bother; you'll be back.'

Anyway, in 1959 the judge trying Fenby's arson was con-

cerned with none of this. He didn't clog up the issue by asking for a social inquiry report. He just gave him three years.

Only at the end of those years did Terry Fenby get what
was probably the first lucky break of his life. He was ordered
to the welfare office where a tall man called John Dodd was
waiting to talk to him.

It was a productive talk. Terry learned that John Dodd
ran an after-care set-up called the Langley House Trust which
had houses in various parts of the country where men coming
out of prison could live in a home atmosphere until able to
face life outside.

John learned that Terry had been born in Middlesbrough,
one of seven children. He had been rejected by his family. He
was thirty-two years old, he had never held a job for more
than a fortnight and his longest time out of prison since he
first entered it had been six months.

He was a model prisoner, liked and trusted by the prison
staff and, yes, he would like to go to the Langley House at
Bradford on his release.

John Dodd was not deceived. Inside the security of prison
Terry might be at ease, but outside he would be a different
proposition.

And so he was. The Terence Fenby who walked up to the
door of Box Tree Cottage at Bradford on October 1, 1962,
seemed to have withered. He held himself rigid and spoke, if
he spoke at all, in monosyllables.

Box Tree Cottage made him uneasy. It seemed noisy and
undisciplined after prison and the fourteen other ex-prisoners
astonished him by moving about freely and talking and laughing as if they were at home. There were no notices telling
him what to do. He couldn't understand the friendliness of
the young couple who were houseparents, and when the housefather mentioned that in the morning he would help him find
a job, Terry became very frightened indeed.

That night he walked to a car park in Bradford and lurked
in it, knowing that sooner or later somebody would call the
police. But when they came and found his address was Box
Tree Cottage they merely told him to go back and not do it
again.

The next night he did better. He walked again to the car

park and set fire to one of the cars.

It never occurred to John Dodd to give up trying, and let Terry stew in his own juice. He has built up the Langley House Trust to become the largest and most professional organisation of its kind in the field of rehabilitation and he learned long ago to abandon concepts like success and failure, as an amateur thinks of them anyway.

Told of Terry's re-arrest, he said: 'Next time we'll change our tactics.'

A plea was made on Terry's behalf by the housefather and instead of receiving a long sentence of preventive detention, for which he now qualified, he was given a year's imprisonment.

At the end of that time, in August 1963, he returned to Box Tree Cottage. Although it was then one of Langley's strict rules that men should find immediate outside employment, they were beginning to realise this wasn't always feasible. Instead, Terry was allowed to stay in the Cottage doing odd jobs until his houseparents felt he could bear contact with the world outside.

After two months he went to Mary Calwell, having rarely spoken to her in that time, and offered to help with the washing-up. By the end of five months he was taking part in conversations. Then and only then was the question of a job brought up. It was obvious he couldn't cope with strangers yet, perhaps he never could. But what sort of job didn't involve meeting other people? Bill Calwell came up with the perfect, if macabre, solution ... he found Terry employment with the Parks Department as a cemetery gardener.

On that first day when Terry went to work Bill Calwell went with him. In fact, for that first week Mary Calwell packed two lunch boxes and waved both of them off to catch the bus to the cemetery where, side by side, they worked all day and came home in the evening, still together.

By the second week Terry was able to go to work by himself and continued to do so.

It wasn't the greatest rehabilitative success story in the world, but it wasn't a bad one either. Terry was secure, working hard, paying his tax and insurance, a useful and relatively happy man.

It would have been nice, from a selfishly journalistic point of view, if he had stayed there, neatly frozen in his landscape. But real people insist on spoiling literary patterns. They change and move on.

When I began to update this book I asked about Terry. For thirteen years, apparently, he had gone on living at Box Tree and working in his cemetery. Then, two years ago, an older sister persuaded him to leave Bradford and go and live with her. They were sorry to see him go, but Terry was a free man, and it was worth a try.

What happened is not clear. Terry just says that he and his sister 'didn't get on'. However it was, after about a year Terry went out and set fire to a sports pavilion.

This time—a sign of greater understanding—he was put on probation and returned to Langley; not to Box Tree, but to one of the Trust's working communities. For Langley House has changed a great deal in ten years, and five of its houses are now sanctuaries where men who can't cope with outside work have jobs in protected workshops or on the Trust's farms and gardens.

It was there, after all this time of just hearing about him, that I actually met Terence Fenby. For me it was like meeting someone from a storybook. For Terry it was obviously less than thrilling. He had read *Road from Singapore* and had, I think, resented my use of his story although of course, I'd changed his name. I can't blame him. Still, he was courteous and showed me the greenhouses where he grows plants and produce to take to market. He is fifty-one now, although he looks older, a quiet, gentle man whose loneliness can be felt, if you stand near him, like the chill from a cold store.

Neither of us mentioned the book or his past. He only showed bitterness once, when I asked if he thought he would leave Langley again. 'I hope so,' he said, 'I don't want to feel I've done nothing with my life.'

As far as the housemother, Elizabeth Prior, is concerned he's doing a good deal with it. He and she are very fond of each other and sometimes quarrel accordingly.

'He works twice as hard as anyone else and then he'll complain because he hasn't had a day off, and I say: "Well, take one then." But he's really progressing. There are friends in the village who invite him out to tea because they like him very much. Sometimes he says he can't go, he's got a sore throat or something, but more often he does, and enjoys it.

'Peter (her husband) wants him to go to a music society he belongs to—Terry's very fond of music. He hasn't gone yet, but he says he'd like to one day.'

Going out to tea occasionally doesn't sound like the greatest social achievement to you and me, perhaps, but it's not bad for a man who, at the age of thirty-one, was so unable to cope with society that he committed a crime in order to go straight back into prison.

I am truly sorry if Terry has been hurt by my use of his story—but my job is to tell the story of Langley House and in so many ways Terry, achievements and defeats, is what Langley has been about.

It was created for the emotionally legless. It is the home, John Dodd likes to think, for the Mephibosheth. He was the crippled son of Jonathan to whom, for his father's sake, David showed mercy and kindness . . . 'So Mephibosheth dwelt in Jerusalem, for he did eat continually at the king's table and he was lame on both his feet.'

But Langley is more even than that. In its twenty years it has learned a very great deal about offenders, most of it the hard way, and it has passed on that precious knowledge, as the Home Office will tell you. It has contributed enormously to the new insight and the compassion which the authorities are now bringing to the damaged in our society.

And how it came to do that is a very strange story which began in 1941 when an unconcerned young corporal in the R.A.F. stepped off a troopship on to the doomed soil of Singapore . . .

PART ONE

THE WHITE MONKEY

CHAPTER ONE

'WASH THOROUGHLY AND OFTEN, TAKING CARE TO DRY BETWEEN THE TOES'

If you were white, an officer, and not gifted with second sight, Singapore in the summer of 1941 was as pleasant a base as anywhere in the war zone.

It offered unlimited sun, unlimited sport and some of the finest hotels in the world where—if you were white and an officer, of course—you could eat a good dinner and dance with pretty English girls to orchestral selections from Ketelby beneath real palm trees.

Open to you also were the arms of the girls' families, the Singapore colonists. It wasn't that they were grateful to you for coming to defend them since there was nothing to defend them against; the Japs were a comic nuisance and a long way off and, as everyone knew, Singapore with its great fortress guns facing out to sea was impregnable. No, you would never see action. But, since you *were* white *and* an officer, you might be eligible to marry the pretty daughter.

So they took you home for stengahs, and on Sundays you played golf, cricket and tennis or went yachting, or were taken over the causeway into Johore to see a native festival or puppet show—just as in London they might have taken you to the Zoo.

To other ranks, however, Singapore was less welcoming. For them the city was a jig-saw of off-limit areas. The best hotels, the Adelphi, Seaview and Raffles, and most of the clubs, were out of bounds. So, in practice, were the English girls. On the other hand there was discouragement about fraternising with the natives.

At every reception camp the other ranks were given more or less the same lecture. It started off with instructions on how to survive the humidity—'Wash thoroughly and often, taking care to dry between the toes, fingers and around the crutch or you'll get a fungoid that'll turn you into a walking mushroom. And change your underclothing regularly.'

The few who did survive were to remember that lecture with grim amusement.

The instructor would then launch into a talk on how to get on with the native population. They were not, it appeared, to get on at all. The Chinese were cunning and rapacious to a man and would skin you alive for a Straits dollar. The Malays were easy-going and shiftless. The Tamils, who formed the lowest grade of labour on the Island, were beneath attention. All of them had odd religions, with easily outraged taboos and super-stitions. And anyway, ninety per cent of the Malay women had V.D.

Thus instructed, the other ranks were turned out to spend their off-duty hours in the streets of Singapore.

Rebuffed by the colonial English and alienated from the natives a high proportion of servicemen turned, not surpris-ingly, to Lavender Street, the centre of the red light area. There, if you got V.D., you at least got a friendly smile with it.

So when R.A.F. Corporal John Dodd stepped off a troopship in July he was, due to his rank or lack of it, stepping on to one plane of a multi-strata society in which he could move neither up nor down.

It didn't worry him at first. He was twenty-five, a fairly class-less product of the William Hulme Grammar School in Man-chester whose parents ran a nursing home. His politics, so far as he thought about them, extended only to disapproving of Mr. Chamberlain and supporting Mr. Churchill, and he had volun-teered on that basis. He had been vaguely disappointed when, having more bodies than planes, the R.A.F. had refused to make him a pilot, but now looked forward to a short, enjoyable war after which he would return home, marry perhaps, get on with his job and, most important of all, play cricket and golf at the weekends.

With the rest of his outfit, a radio-location unit, he was sent to R.A.F. Seletar, an airbase on the eastern coast of the Island, listened to the lectures with half an ear and, on his first duty-free day, caught a taxi into the city.

Even to other rankers, Singapore city was a very attractive place with the wide streets and impressive buildings of the colonial era, the teeming shops and stalls of the Chinese quarter, the junk-bedecked waterfront and even the exotic squalor of the Indian section. John Dodd found it all new and exciting. Incurably English, however, he managed to find a restaurant in Stamford Road that offered roast pork, potatoes, mushrooms, peas, three pancakes with jam, jelly and ice cream—all of which he described in detail in his next letter home. (The rationing that applied in England was never enforced in Singapore.)

He emerged into Stamford Road lacking only one thing to complete his euphoria. He looked around, spotted a nice-looking blonde, walked up to her and said: 'Excuse me, I'm lost. Can you direct me to . . .'

It was a simple approach but back home, used as it was by a six-foot, well-built young man in uniform, it had always proved effective, leading to a date and an invitation to meet the family.

This girl, however, might have been propositioned by an orang-outang. She gave a swift glance at the two stripes on his sleeve, and walked away.

He tried two or three others with the same result, decided it wasn't his day and went, alone, to the cinema.

The cinemas of Singapore waxed rich that summer and autumn out of lonely other-rankers like John Dodd. When the Cathay cinema advertised 'A Rowdy, Racy, Riotous Comedy. Fling Your Troubles Away And Have A Fling At Love And Laughter. See Ray Milland And Claudette Colbert in "Skylark" ' a queue of khaki and air force blue stretched down the street. It was a lousy film.

They queued to see Greta Garbo and Ramon Novarro in 'Mata Hari' at the Alhambra, and Laurel and Hardy at the Pavilion. They queued to see anything that would take their minds off their isolation for an hour or two.

Apart from the cinema and Lavender Street, the only other recreational activity for the non-commissioned defenders of Singapore lay on the sports field. The sports facilities for servicemen on the Island were superb; every game that involved hitting a ball was catered for, and John Dodd played them all.

If anything distinguished him among the thousands of other young men on Singapore it was his energy. His need to be constantly up and doing had always been a feature of his life, and the bane of everybody else's. As a small child he had run his

mother nearly ragged; at school his untiring ability for organising devilment was remembered by his masters with awe.

The humidity which had his friends flaked out on their bunks
beneath their mosquito nets or lazing on the beach, left him
unaffected. When he wasn't wielding a bat, a racquet or club, he
was watching other people do so. When he wasn't doing either,
he was betting. An inveterate gambler, he only had to see a race
track, a poker game or two flies crawling up a wall and he
would start to bet, as if his life depended on the outcome.

This often left him so short of money that he was reduced to
walking the streets in his free hours, watching a newly-emerging
sport—the fights between the Argyll and Sutherland High-
landers and the Australians. The Argylls had been based in
Malaya for years and regarded Singapore as their preserve, an
outlook strongly contested by the Australian servicemen who
were beginning to arrive in strength.

As the year went out, however, relationships improved, partly
because the streets were becoming so crowded that there was
hardly room to swing a punch. Besides the British and Australians, Singapore was filling up with other soldiers, Moslems,
Sikhs, Dutchmen from the Netherland East Indies, Gurkhas,
Malays and Dogras, most of them inexperienced in jungle war-
fare, most of them due to die violently and soon.

All the Dogras stationed at Kota Baru, ten miles from the
Siamese Border, did die, crumpled around their guns in the first
big engagement of the war for Malaya.

The first gong of their death knell had, in fact, sounded by
November, when a convoy of landing craft made off from the
Japanese occupied ports of China to 'destinations unknown'.

The talks Washington was having with Tokyo to prevent
any further advance of Japanese troops into south-east Asia
were breaking down. Most dangerous of all, a top-level confer-
ence held in Singapore to investigate the whole Far East situation decided that the threat to the Naval Base was exaggerated
because the Japs were concentrating their strength against Russia and, anyway, no invasion of Malaya was likely during the
monsoon period, which was due to start in October.

John Dodd had some worries at this time but, like nearly
everybody in Singapore, the Japanese weren't one of them. His
letters home never mentioned them. 'Yes,' he wrote, 'you might

as well send on all my accumulated mail. We'll take a chance on the war being over before it gets here.'

He asked for newspapers to be sent on from home, but only ... 'So that I can see what chance Camperdown has got in the St. Leger.'

His letters were fluent and chatty—English had been his best subject at school—and were full of the meals he had eaten, the films he had seen, the games he had played and his problems.

'The girls here are so snooty,' he wrote, 'that I'm wondering whether I oughtn't to haul down my flag after all this time and learn to dance.'

He mentioned his teeth often. The dental surgeon at R.A.F. Seletar had said that two of the front ones must come out, and John was worried about the length of time before he could be fitted with a plate to replace them. The effect on his looks didn't worry him, but he was afraid the end of the war might come, and he would be demobbed before he could get his plate. The R.A.F. were taking them out. The R.A.F. could put them back.

He harped, too, on his financial troubles. Once when the mail from England failed to arrive, he sent a telegram home: 'Are you all right? Worried about you. Please send me ten pounds. My thoughts are with you. Dodd.'

He refrained from explaining that he'd put every dollar he'd got on a horse that turned out to have three legs at Bukit Timah racecourse, and had to walk half across the Island home to Seletar and then pawn his watch to get him through the rest of the week. He was never to redeem it.

His parents would not have approved. His mother particularly, a deeply religious woman, regarded her favourite son's gambling impulse as his only weakness.

Before he and his brother, Terry, had left for the war she had presented them both with a Moffatt's New Testament and asked them to read a portion of it at midday every day so that at that time the family could be together in thought at least. John, busy with his own cares and enjoyments, never opened it but, as a sop to his conscience, carried it everywhere.

In October, two nice things happened to him. The first was meeting Irene Symons.

Most of the boys at Seletar had abandoned hope of meeting a

'decent' girl who would admit them into social life on the Island, and had turned to Lavender Street or resigned themselves to celibacy for the duration. John, however, refused to give up. Not for nothing had he been a salesman in civilian life.

One afternoon, pausing drearily between the attractions of the Cathay and Alhambra cinemas, he saw a pretty, fair-skinned girl looking in a shop window. He straightened his uniform, went up to her and into the old routine. 'Excuse me, but can you direct me to . . .'

She not only gave him his directions, but lingered to admit that the weather was good for the time of year and to accept his invitation to walk her home.

The Symonses lived in a pleasant white house in a be-palmed outskirt of the city. At the gate Irene stopped and explained that, owing to the strict colonial etiquette, she could not invite him in. 'My parents are at their bungalow up country,' she said, 'but perhaps, when they come back, you could come to dinner. Once you've met them you can take me out.'

They exchanged phone numbers and John raced back to camp to tell his friends of his good luck.

The Symonses, who were nice people, completely changed his outlook on Singapore. The cinemas lost a good customer and the Symonses gained a welcome guest who spent all his off-duty evenings with them, talking, playing bridge and mahjong, and practising cricket with the boys of the family.

Mr. Symons was a top-drawer colonial of an old army family that had scattered colonels and captains all over the Empire. His job as Investigations Officer in the Land Office was a good one. He had served King and country well in the hotter outposts for many years and was now nearing retirement. He had, however, alienated himself from the best society in marrying, during a term in Ceylon, a Singhalese woman. They'd had six children, two girls and four boys with ages ranging from twenty-three to ten.

Up to that point John Dodd had never considered the race problem. Like most young Englishmen of his age and upbringing he thought, if he thought about it at all, that wogs began at Calais. Now, through the Symonses eyes, he saw the ludicrous prejudice which kept Mr. and Mrs. Symons out of so many clubs and homes, and put petty restrictions on their good-looking, intelligent but Eurasian children.

When Terry Dodd arrived in Singapore early in November he found his brother changed. The old ebullience was there, but John had become more thoughtful, more liberal.

Terry's arrival was the other nice thing that had happened.

The two brothers had never been close. John was the elder by five years and the taller by several inches. He had been the cleverer at school and unquestionably the more difficult; as such, he had always commanded more of his mother's attention. They'd had different friends, different interests and Terry had always regarded John as the authoritarian big brother. Their mother had been too overworked and their father too remote to amend the relationship. At the age of seventeen Terry had run away from home and joined the R.A.F. as groundcrew, and the breach between the two had widened. So, all in all, John was surprised at how pleased he felt to get the news of Terry's posting. He looked forward to introducing him to the Symonses.

The two had a happy, but brief, reunion. The night after his troopship docked Terry, a corporal armourer, was put in charge of a party of groundcrew and sent straight up country to join No. 62 Squadron of short-nosed Blenheim bombers stationed at Alor Star in the north-west Malay state of Kedah, near the Siamese border.

John Dodd pulled every string he knew to get his brother posted back to Singapore. 'Alor Star, from all accounts, is rather primitive and far removed from civilisation and entertainment,' he wrote to his parents.

It was also dangerous, but as neither he nor anybody else was thinking in war terms at this point, he didn't consider this.

CHAPTER TWO

'OUR DEFENCE IS SURE'

On the night of November 29 a notice was flashed on to the cinema screens of Singapore and other key Malayan towns: 'All British and Australian Imperial Forces to report immediately to their units.' A War Office cable had been received warning of the complete breakdown of the Washington talks. 'Second Degree Readiness' was the order of the day.

Everybody dashed about looking efficient and confident. And when, three days later, the Navy's most modern battleship, H.M.S. *Prince of Wales*, with the battle-cruiser *Repulse* and four destroyers sailed regally into the Naval Base harbour, confidence boomed into jingoistic certainty.

From then on, just to make sure nobody missed the point, the cinema newsreels showed shots of Hurricanes being unloaded on to the Singapore quayside. It was only if you looked carefully that you realised they were always the same Hurricanes photographed from different angles.

Troops being poured into the Fortress from parts of the world where they took the war seriously were mildly surprised to find the English tuan still dressing for dinner at his club, still escorting pretty women to dances.

At midday on December 6 a solitary reconnaissance Hudson, flying through the monsoon, spotted Japanese troop transports in convoy moving due west on a course from Indo-China, bound either for Siam or North Malaya.

The tuan went on dancing.

In the first few minutes of December 8 the shore defences at Kota Bharu, the north-eastern tip of Malaya, saw transports and warships steaming fast towards them over the horizon and were soon under heavy shellfire.

The tuan went on dancing. The streets of Singapore were brilliantly lit.

They were still lit at four-thirty a.m. when Japanese bombers came roaring overhead, and they remained lit during the entire raid which killed sixty-three people and injured one hundred and thirty-three.

Nobody could find the man who had the only key which operated the central switch that would black out the city.

Ken Attiwill in *The Singapore Story* tells of the English-woman who, woken by the explosions, rushed to the window in time to see a direct hit on an import house near by and watch it topple to the ground. She telephoned the police.

'There's a raid on. Why doesn't somebody put out the lights?'

'Don't be alarmed,' a reassuring voice told her, 'it's only a practice.'

'Well, tell them they're overdoing it,' she shouted.

The Order of the Day that greeted the people of Singapore when they emerged next morning to view the damage is a superb example of what a High Command can say if it is stupid enough and is prepared to tell sufficient lies.

'We are ready; we have had plenty of warning and our preparations are made and tested. We are confident. Our defences are strong and our weapons efficient.'

'What of the enemy? We see before us a Japan drained for years by the exhausting claims of her wanton onslaught on China.'

Up at Alor Star Terry Dodd was wishing somebody would tell the Japanese how exhausted and drained they were so that they would stop bombing his airfield. Incendiaries and high-explosives were coming down from 1200 feet, thick as the monsoon rain, followed by low-flying machine-gun attacks.

When the raid had finished there were only two serviceable Blenheims left.

By a miracle, both brothers got a Christmas Day pass. Terry emerged into Singapore to spend it with his brother at the hospitable Symonses' house, with the dazed look of someone coming out of darkness into light. John thought he looked ill.

The inconceivable had happened. The *Prince of Wales* and *Repulse* had been sunk; those floating symbols of British invincibility had gone down, taking confidence with them. North Malaya was lost. Our troops had 'fallen back to prepared positions'—a phrase that was repeated so often it became terrifying.

Independent thinkers had dragged their minds away from general belief and were making plans against the invasion of Singapore, or, at least, were begging to be allowed to do so.

But the tuan went on dancing. The Adelphi, Seaview and Raffles were still advertising their dinner-dances, shops—those which hadn't been bombed—were doing good business, people were still buying houses. As an American newscaster broadcast to the United States: 'This is a grim Christmas in Singapore, because the British are getting *ready* for war, with the war going on.'

At the Symonses' house, over a traditional Christmas lunch, the Dodd boys pulled crackers with the children and listened to Mr. and Mrs. Symons's argument over evacuation. Tragically, there had been no directive from High Command on the matter. 'Useless mouths' could go or stay as they pleased and too many women, even young ones with children, were to agonise indecisively until it was too late.

Mrs. Symons was insisting that she would not go and the children were agreeing with her. Mr. Symons was saying they should go and leave him—if it ever came to that.

The argument, however, was academic. Like all good Singaporians, the Symonses believed the Fortress to be invulnerable.

Both John and Terry had weighed in, urging Mrs. Symons to go; John because he'd heard enough now to know that the enemy were not short-sighted clowns, but crack troops with first-class modern armoury; Terry because he knew what the others didn't—that the R.A.F. had begun to blow up its own airfields.

They could envisage an uncomfortable siege of the Island. But even they, even then, never dreamed that it could fall.

In mid-January John got an urgent message to go to Johore Baru, just over the causeway, where his brother was dangerously ill.

By now Allied troops had fallen back so far that not even the High Command could pretend that all was well.

What was left of Terry's outfit had been pulled back with the rest and were in the front line at Kluang. In the complete disorganisation, the fact that Terry was ill had been overlooked until in the middle of the night; too much in pain to notice the bombs and shelling, he had wandered away from his own camp and into the Australian lines where he had been picked up semi-conscious and operated on immediately for appendicitis at the Australian casualty clearing station.

Then he and the wounded were rushed down through chaotic roads jammed with troops withdrawing for the defence of Johore, to Johore Baru.

Somehow, through the now intensified bombing, the dis-organisation and the general panic, John struggled over the causeway to visit his brother and returned to Singapore a very worried man.

He was concerned about Terry who had, of necessity, been moved too soon after his appendectomy and now faced another operation for peritonitis. The boy looked weak and ill and very slight, especially in contrast to the huge, six-foot-five Australian orderly, 'Tiny' Parker, whose special concern Terry was. But Tiny had been a comfort. 'Don't worry about him, cobber. We got to take care of him. He's the only Pommy we got here.'

On the wider scale, though, there had been no comfort at all in Johore Baru. John had been shocked by the number of wounded. They lay on stretchers between the beds and flowed out of the wards into the corridors. Nurses and doctors were blurred streaks of movement who, when they did stand still, looked fit to collapse. Ambulances, private cars and comman-deered taxis were queuing up to deliver their loads of untidy men patched with reddening field dressings.

It took John two hours, coming back to Singapore, to get over the 1100-yard causeway jammed, as it was, with wounded being taken on to the Island and fresh troops, a Pioneer bat-talion that had recently disembarked, going off it to swell the troops on the mainland. The contrast between the white, hollow faces of the injured men and the unmarked confidence of the outgoing soldiers looked like a before-and-after advertisement for Hell.

The Pioneers had been trained for the Middle East—most of them had only just enlisted—and had no more idea of the jungle than an Eskimo. All they were fit for was to die in it, and that most of them were to do.

As far as the critical eye could see, and John's had suddenly become very critical, there were still no prepared defences along the north side of Singapore Island. He supposed that, if the worst came to the worst, the causeway would be blown up. But he could see, and the Japs with their miraculous intelligence system would surely know, that just here the Straits were shallow, not much more than four feet at low tide.

For the first time he faced the fact that Singapore could and in all probability would fall. He went back to Seletar and wrote to his parents. 'I've just seen Terry,' he said, 'and he's fine. Everything's under control, so don't worry.'

About this time Churchill away in Whitehall was facing the fact that had stared John Dodd in the face. 'I ought to have known,' he wrote in *The Second World War*. 'My advisers ought to have known and I ought to have been told, and I ought to have asked. The reason I had not asked about this matter, amid the thousands of questions I put, was the possibility of Singapore having no landward defences no more entered into my mind than that of a battleship being launched without a bottom.'

The great Fortress guns could not be turned round. They had been emplaced to defeat a gentlemanly attack from the sea, not unsporting advances from Malaya. Singapore had been caught not only with its pants down, but with its backside invitingly exposed to the Nippon boot.

The explosion that heralded the fine, sunny morning of January 31 struck more fear into the demoralised people of Singapore than any of the daily air raids had done. The causeway, road and rail, had been blown up. Singapore was once more in truth an island, over-crowded, panic-stricken, on which half the population milled around with no orders at all while the other half moved mechanically to obey conflicting orders.

As at Johore Baru, wounded were everywhere, silting up the hospitals, church halls, warehouses and schools, while doctors, nurses and orderlies worked miracles of improvisation, less worried by the constant bombardment than by the shortage of food, water and medical supplies.

The final retreat over the causeway had been well organised and Terry had been brought over in time and was now in a girls' school turned into an emergency hospital.

There on February 10 his brother went to say goodbye to

him, accompanied by the unusually subdued Symons family.

Some days before John's unit had been shipped out bound for Burma; John had been left behind until his dental treatment was completed, and had been very glad to be so. It had seemed dreadful to him to be leaving the Island now that the Japs had landed on it—by February 10 they had three divisions on Singapore and the Allied troops were withdrawing to a perimeter round the city—leaving his friends and his brother to the mercy of Nippon.

But now General Wavell had ordered that all remaining Air Force personnel must be evacuated immediately, their usefulness having ended when Kallang, the last remaining airfield in Singapore, became unusable because of bomb craters.

To the sound of gunfire and mortar shells John and the Symonses stepped through the more immediate noises of pain, threading their way through stretchers that blocked every conceivable space. Behind the smell of antiseptic and vomit was the background smell of chalk, reminding them of the schoolgirls whose domain this had been only a few days before.

They found Terry in one of the dormitories. The rough journey during the retreat from Johore had been too much for him and he was now critically ill. He lay in an overcrowded room, looking slighter than ever, with a saline drip in his foot and death all around him.

It was his twenty-first birthday.

'Happy birthday, Terry,' said John, not knowing what else to say.

'Many happy returns,' feebly echoed the Symonses. Mrs. Symons showed Terry the gift they had brought him, some hand-cut Chinese teaspoons. Terry's eyes moved slowly down to them and he smiled.

John said: 'Well, it's Goodbye, Dolly Grey. General Wavell wants me to go tonight.' Terry nodded and smiled again.

John felt that his brother was dying; would die here, alone, without him. He went off to find the Australian M.O. Major Nairn who, with hundreds of lives in his care and countless problems on his mind, still found time to listen to John's pleas for his brother.

'I'm hoping to get him away on a boat tomorrow,' said Major Nairn, 'but I can't promise. Invalids and wounded aren't priority just now.'

Actually, the day before Major Nairn had put the wounded
on stretchers in the quadrangle in the hope of getting them all
on a hospital ship that was leaving for Australia. The men had
lain there all morning in blistering sun as the stretcher bearers
worked, carrying them on to lorries that would take them to the
docks. There had been only two men to go before Terry when
the news came that there was no more room on the ship. Major
Nairn had realised that was it. From that point on ships leaving
Singapore would be carrying only the able-bodied.

'Don't worry,' the Major told John, 'we'll look after him.'

Both knew that the Japanese had no use for their own
wounded, let alone anybody else's. At the Parit Sulong bridge
where the 45th Brigade had eventually dragged itself in retreat
only to find it held by Japs, every single wounded man who'd
been left behind was bayoneted or beheaded.

John went back to Terry. Tiny Parker was with him, as big
and optimistic as ever. 'Don't you worry, cobber,' he kept saying. 'Old Doddy here can do an impression of Stanley Holloway that's better than Stanley Holloway. We won't let anything
happen to him.'

John walked out of the school, his usual energy and briskness
dissipated by a sense of betrayal.

Outside he said goodbye to the Symonses, feeling more of a
traitor than ever. He went down the row, kissing the girls and
shaking hands with the boys, wondering what would happen to
them all.

That evening, in a rushed little ceremony at R.A.F. Seletar,
the Last Post was sounded and the R.A.F. flag lowered. Only a
few men were there to watch it come down and they were impatient to be off. Nobody seemed to want the flag so John took
it, folded it carefully and stuffed it into his kit bag.

The next evening, February 11, he stood among the remnants of
the R.A.F., pressed against the rail on the deck of the cargo
steamer *Empire Star*, looking down at the crowds of women,
children, nurses and soldiers packed on to the Keppel dockside,
hoping that the ship, which was crammed, could still take a few
more. He and the others had spent the night on the docks and
had been among the first to file aboard in the morning. A steady

stream of people had been coming up the gangplank all day.

It was the turn of a young European woman clutching her child, a boy of about three, and two suitcases. Having made the decision between leaving her home or staying she was now desperate to get away. The checkers were ordering her to leave her luggage behind. Confused and bewildered, she was crying.

Out of the crowd behind her suddenly surged about twenty armed Australian soldiers. It took a minute or two for John to realise that they were deserters, as desperate in their way as the young woman. But they were armed. The checkers, who tried to stop them, were knocked out of the way with rifles and they marched up the gangplank.

In order to avoid any more incidents like that the Captain of the *Empire Star* ordered the gangplank to be raised immediately. He had 1254 souls on board a ship which, in peacetime, had accommodation for sixteen passengers.

John saw clearly—he would always see it—the face of the young woman as they told her she could not now go aboard. He comforted himself with the thought that the *Vyner Brooke* was due to sail the following day and that she would probably get accommodation on that. Long after he heard that the *Vyner Brooke* was bombed and sank off Banka Island. Many passengers, mostly women and children, were drowned and the rest slaughtered by the Japanese after they had struggled ashore.

It was a glorious evening with a pink, gold and emerald sunset such as only occurs in the Far East. The sea was calm and very blue, but every eye was turned on Singapore to see the last of its city. Greasy black smoke from burning oil tanks hung heavily over it; pierced by flashes of exploding shells and bombs. There was a particularly fierce flame to the north-west where the Indian Base Hospital at Tyersall and most of its patients were burning.

As they passed Pulau Blakang Mati, the island south of Keppel Harbour, a crashed Hurricane was being washed against the shore by the lapping waves; a futile symbol of a futile situation.

At that moment John Dodd felt as much hatred for the British High Command as he did for the Japs; their idiocy had done this to him, making him run away leaving his brother, the Symonses and the girl on the dockside. 'The able-bodied first,' he said to a companion, 'women, children and wounded last. If at all.'

There and then he became the complete individualist, never again to trust the apparent infallibility of authority. He would make his own decisions in future, based on his own observations because they were as good as anyone else's and certainly better than the bluffers who had run things until now. Security was a chimera. Security had been Singapore and its invulnerability, its caste system, the British way of life, the *Prince of Wales* and the *Repulse*, and it had gone like a mist.

He never sought after security again.

BOMBS AND BETJAS

The next morning, out of an eggshell-blue sky, two rapidly moving dots appeared astern. Somebody with binoculars on the bridge yelled out: 'Junkers eighty-eights.'

The order came: 'All those with armaments remain on deck. Everyone else below.'

Like a clamp John's hand came down on his tommy-gun as the decks cleared with magic swiftness. He'd often wondered how he would react in action and was pleased to find himself breathless but moderately calm.

On his part of the top deck only two others remained with him, both R.A.F. men he knew—Corporal Evans and L.A.C. McDermott. As the Junkers came swooping down all three fired until the planes were so low they could see the markings on the bombs in the open bays. Then Evans leaped for the port side and took cover behind a lifeboat, McDermott dived for the lifeboat to starboard and John, for no reason he could think of, made a rugby tackle for the ship's spare propeller which had been lashed to the deck. It afforded the least cover of the three. The noise became appalling, the ship lurched and the sky went red and black.

John opened his eyes. His propeller was buckled and twisted but intact. Over on the port side, blood was pouring out of the corporal's legs. Where the starboard lifeboat had been there was a hole and the only recognisable thing left of McDermott was his identity tag.

And that was the beginning of a series of situations which John Dodd got into and came out of, amazed, uncomprehending, but alive, while other men died; as if an invisible finger were prodding him along the only safe path through a maze of death. At the time he thought it was coincidence.

The Junkers kept up their attack all that day and the next, and John remained on deck the whole time. At one point, during a lull, one of the Australian nurses tried to persuade him to go below. 'No thanks,' he told her, 'I get frightened down there.' It was true. A non-swimmer, he found the bombs and bullets that swept the deck healthier than the effect of the near-misses down in the hold.

If the deserters had lowered the image of Australians, the Aussie nurses who stayed on deck also through the attacks, bandaging and comforting, getting killed, put it right back up again. John heard afterwards, with great sadness, that most of them were massacred later by the Japanese on a small island off Sumatra.

When, on February 14, a blackened and torn *Empire Star* limped into Batavia harbour on Java, the 1240 people who filed ashore—fourteen had been killed during the voyage—felt that they had survived through a miracle, and looked forward to a more well-ordered war.

For most of them it was only the beginning.

Batavia seemed slightly more tawdry than Singapore, but it had the same frenetic gaiety and disorganisation that prevailed in the Fortress city. All incoming air force personnel were billeted in a big office building near the dock area in a compôte of nationalities.

Tired Australians camped down between the beds of Dutch flyers. British queued for the washroom with Americans. Orders were posted up on boards and then countermanded. Equipment, rifles and canned food lay in disorganised piles on the barrack floors. Discipline was lax and men wandered in and out of the building more or less at will.

Most of the R.A.F. who had been evacuated from Singapore were moved out almost immediately, some to rest stations, leaving only a minimum in Batavia, of which John Dodd was one.

One evening the sort of quiet that only means bad news fell over the building. 'What's the matter?' John asked of a Dutchman who had gone to find the cause of the lull.

'Singapore has fallen,' he was told, 'and the Japs have crossed over to Sumatra and are beginning an invasion of Bali.'

Java was bracketed.

Trying not to think of Terry and the Symonses John stood up.

'Where are you going?' asked the Dutchman.

'To find a dentist.'

He marched crossly out into the streets of Batavia. He dared not think about Terry so ill and at the mercy of the Japs; the way things were going he would soon be at their mercy himself. It had been idiocy to have sent them all to Java which was obviously next on the list for invasion by the unstoppable Imperial Army. They should have been taken to Australia, regrouped and then brought back to have a properly organised crack at the Nips.

He had lost all faith in High Command whose inefficiency in Singapore had forced him to run out on his brother and friends and whose same inefficiency would send him skeltering like a rabbit into more degradation.

He wanted desperately to get to Australia and into a force that would be of use so that he could wipe out his sense of shame.

But before this happened he was damn well going to get his plate made, if he had to fight off the entire Japanese army to do it. He had, he felt, been mucked about enough.

The dentist he eventually found was an elderly Dutch civilian speaking good English who lived over his surgery in one of the main streets. The old man agreed to make the plate and took the impression there and then. It was a lengthy process for he was nervous and kept questioning John over and over about the possibility of an invasion and the fate of the Singapore civilians under the Japanese, about which John was as wise as he.

(Later the news filtered through about the Jap occupation of the Alexandra Military Hospital in Singapore when they had swept in, bayoneting patients including one on the operating table, raping nurses and herding two hundred assorted patients, doctors and orderlies into queues to be shot. From then on, realising that if they could do it in one hospital they could do it in all, John thought of his brother as dead.)

Once outside the dentist's, John hailed a betja—the bicycle version of the rickshaw—and rattled off to see the sights while there were still sights to be seen.

Clashing music came from the dance halls, bars and restaurants, the band of Henry Hall mingling with the jangle of the traditional gamelan.

John noticed that there were more Dutchmen to be seen out walking with a native or Eurasian girl on their arm than would have been permitted by the raised eyebrows in Singapore. He was not surprised; he had frequently admired the beauty of the Eurasian girls before, but here in Batavia they seemed breathtaking.

At that moment another betja glided up alongside his own, containing what he describes as 'a couple of smashers'. Both women in it were pretty, well-dressed and sophisticated. They looked fresh and gay. One was somewhat older than the other, probably, thought John, who was a lousy judge of feminine age, in her late twenties, while the younger girl looked about eighteen. He put them down as sisters.

A few seconds later both betjas were waiting, side by side, at a stop light. John went into his well-tried routine.

'Excuse me,' he said, leaning over the side, 'but can you direct me to the Sahari canal.' He knew there was one and it was the only place he could think of.

Both women looked amused. If he'd needed directing he had only to ask his betja driver.

The elder spoke: 'I don't know why you want to go there. We are going to a tea dance if you would like to come with us.'

Marquita never did have any truck with ceremony.

Within seconds John had swapped betjas and was driving off with his new acquaintances.

He had just met one of the most extraordinary women to come out of the Far East. She was to save his life several times over at the risk of her own but, besides that, she was to widen his horizons about people so that ever after he evaluated them differently. Morality, because of Marquita, became not a judgement by a society which is how he had thought of it, but a matter of how one human being treated another.

Marquita Bischoff was born in Java, the granddaughter of a Javanese princess whose son became a naturalised Dutchman and married a Spaniard, the result being Marquita.

By the time John met her early in 1942 she had made an early and disastrous marriage, had a daughter called Phiphine—who was the other girl in the betja—been divorced and married again, this time to a Frenchman who had been swamped somewhere in Europe by the German advance.

She spoke German, Spanish, Javanese, Malay, Dutch, French and English fluently and could get by in half a dozen other languages. She was utterly classless, cosmopolitan and completely without fear.

John Dodd's life has been strongly influenced by three women. The first was his mother. When he got into that betja on February 16, 1942, he had just met the second. He was to meet the third, years later, outside a cemetery.

By the time they had gone to the tea dance and back to their cool pretty bungalow on the outskirts of Batavia with its two monkeys, a parrot, a cat and a dog—Marquita was mad about animals—they were all old friends. Marquita and John had humour and, although they didn't know it then, courage in common, and John was already half in love with Phiphine.

She was less forceful than her mother, but very beautiful with pale skin and a perfectly oval face. He tried to find out how old she was, but Phiphine merely laughed and Marquita said that was a lady's secret. Old enough, he presumed, since that evening a young man called for her to take her out on a date.

Burma had been invaded and John's anger against the High Command had increased. He thought of all the friends in his unit who had arrived in Burma just in time to be killed or herded into prison camps. That clinched it for him. He would act on his own, make Australia on his own and, if necessary, come back and fight the Japs on his own.

But first he *must* get his plate. Those two teeth had become a symbol of personal order in a disorganised world. He had left behind too many things undone in Singapore; his watch, for instance, had never been redeemed and was now, presumably, adorning some Jap's wrist. It became a matter of the first importance to him that at least he didn't leave without his plate.

As more and more men left Batavia, equipment and weapons were strewn on the floor of the R.A.F. billet, thick as autumn leaves. John began to collect his own personal armoury, keeping a tommy-gun, a couple of revolvers and a stack of ammunition underneath his mattress. It made the bed decidedly lumpy but nevertheless he slept easier.

On February 26 his acting C.O. called him into an office to

have a quiet chat and explain that the R.A.F. remnants would pull out next day for Tjilatjap in the south where boats were still getting away, despite heavy bombing by the Jap air force.

'Request permission to stay on medical grounds,' said John, promptly.

'What medical grounds?'

'Getting my dental plate, sir.'

'And how long will that take?'

'Tomorrow, sir, the dentist says. Or the next day.'

The C.O. was a busy man and had more important things to worry about than a madman who would risk his life for a couple of teeth. John's record, however, was a good one.

'All right, Corporal, make Tjilatjap on your own. Most of us will have to anyway. But for God's sake don't leave it too long. The Japs will invade any day.'

John divided the next two days between harassing the poor dentist and playing cards with Marquita and Phiphine. He had given up trying to persuade them to leave; Java was Marquita's home, it seemed as secure to her as Singapore had seemed to the Symonses. Nothing John could say convinced her that the Japs would invade her island and she refused to consider leaving it if they did not.

The bungalow had a new visitor, an American fighter pilot Master Sergeant 'Smudge' Smith, another of Marquita's tea dance acquaintances. Despite Marquita's evident liking for him, John didn't take to the American who was ebullient, hard-drinking and hard-swearing.

John's upbringing had been such as to regard swearing before women as a cardinal sin, but the ground was cut from beneath his feet by Marquita who just laughed and Phiphine who took no notice. In spite of her youth, Phiphine's education had, thanks to her mother, been in many ways broader than John's.

On one point, however, the two men were in complete agreement. Smudge had taken Pearl Harbor as a personal affront and hated all Japs, a fact which he told everybody volubly and often.

'And I'll tell you something else,' he would say, 'I'm not going to be herded into no prison camp like an arse-licking sheep by a lot of bum-sucking Japs.'

And there John was with him all the way. Just as soon as he

got his plate he would make for Tjilatjap as fast as possible and thence to Australia where, he hoped, somebody with a bit of sense was making plans to hit back at the Nips with success.

On the last night in February John Dodd took Phiphine to see Abbott and Costello in 'Hold That Ghost'. The next morning they met again at Marquita's home and John was relating the most immediate chapter in the saga of the dentist.

The shock of the front door being kicked open brought them all to their feet, to see Smudge staggering through the doorway. His clothes were steaming and his eyes were bloodshot. There were holes in his flying jacket.

'The Nips have landed at Bantam,' he managed to say.

They stared back at him. Bantam was the north-westerly state of Java and Bantam, the port, was only one hundred kilometres away as the crow flies.

They calmed him down, got him a drink and dry clothes and listened to his story.

He had been on flying patrol off the north coast when he'd caught sight of landing craft just off Bantam. He had gone down to strafe them and been hit by flak. Losing height, he'd managed to keep airborne until well away from the invasion force. Then he'd hit the water. The next thing he remembered, he was being hauled aboard a native fishing boat only a few hundred yards away from land.

Once ashore he'd stopped only to telephone his base and then, wet and shocked as he was, he'd commandeered a car and made straight for Batavia and Marquita. 'You've never seen so many goddam Japs,' he kept saying.

They turned on the radio to listen to the news. The Dutch had declared Batavia an Open City. All troops must leave at once.

John and Smudge held council. There was nothing to do but, in Smudge's words, 'get the hell out of here'.

It was arranged that John should return to his billet, get his weapons and ammunition and then come back. In the meantime Smudge was to buy, borrow or steal a car.

'And make it a big one,' Marquita interrupted. 'We're coming, too. I do not want Phiphine raped by a lot of filthy little Japs.' (It was a general assumption that invading Japanese soldiers raped every woman on sight. In some captured towns that assumption had not been far wrong.)

It was a complication but, as John realised, an inevitable one. When it came to it, he could no more have left the two women behind to the mercies of Bushido than he could have left his mother or sister if he'd had one. By protecting Marquita and Phiphine he could perhaps make up in part for his enforced desertion of Singapore. It occurred neither to him nor to Smudge that the boot might be on the other foot; that the women they were so gallantly saving from a fate worse, than death would, in fact, turn out to be saving them.

Late that afternoon the four regathered outside Marquita's bungalow.

John had found an almost deserted billet, picked up his armoury, added another tommy-gun for luck, shoved his mother's New Testament, the flag from Seletar and some clean clothes into a kit bag and left.

While Phiphine had done some hurried packing, Marquita had gone to her bank manager's home demanding, and eventually getting, her savings. She had then spent the rest of the afternoon trying to find homes for her menagerie of animals which John had told her forcefully, would not be allowed to go with them.

Outside the bungalow Smudge was holding a pistol to the head of a sullen Javanese taxi driver, sitting in a Ford that had seen better days nearer the turn of the century.

'You tell Charlie here,' he told Marquita (all natives were Charlie to Smudge), 'that all we want is for him to drive us to Tjilatjap in his taxi.'

There was a long and impassioned exchange of words, then Marquita explained: 'He doesn't want to be seen with you and Johnny in your uniforms, he says the Japs might shoot him.'

'Tell him we'll shoot him if he doesn't.'

Bitterly, the taxi driver started up his engine, and they loaded up. Before getting in Smudge traded his U.S. Army Air Corps Elgin wristwatch for one of John's tommy-guns, thereby replacing the watch John had pawned another age ago.

Then Smudge with the gun on his knees, pointing into the driver's groin, got into the front seat while John held open the rear door for the two women. 'After you, Claud,' he said to Marquita. And to Phiphine: 'After you, Cecil.' Marquita and Phiphine exchanged shrugs. This Johnny was always saying things like that and had tried to explain why such catch-phrases made him roar with laughter, but they had abandoned all hope of understanding English humour.

They set off. It wasn't until they had reached the southern outskirts of Batavia that John remembered his plate.

'My teeth,' he howled. 'We've got to go back for my teeth.'

'We're not going back for any goddam teeth,' Smudge said.

'Oh yes we are,' said John firmly. He'd waited too long for that plate to abandon it now.

Marquita and Phiphine both sided with John. 'I want to see what he looks like with them,' said Phiphine.

Wearily, Smudge jerked his gun at the driver. 'Turn, Charlie. We're going to the dentist.'

The streets of Batavia seemed even more ghoulish going in than they had coming out. The natives to a man had disappeared to sit tight and wait for the co-prosperity programme the Japs had promised them. Here and there frantic Dutchmen loaded cars with luggage. Through everything ran a monotonous trickle of jungle green as the last remnants of an army hurried away.

The dentist, to John's great relief, was still there, shouting orders to his elderly wife, grabbing ornaments off sideboards, taking down Queen Wilhelmina's picture and asking himself and everyone in earshot what would become of them all. John had to shout to attract his attention.

Eventually, after much searching, the old man unearthed a package, thrust it at John, who paid him and went.

'Let's see these pearly wonders,' said Smudge.

Everybody sat and waited in a dying city as John turned his back and seemed to go into a convulsion.

Then, for the first time in the presence of women, John Dodd swore. 'Hell, the bloody things don't fit.'

There was a roar of laughter from the taxi and John, grinning his gap-toothed grin, got in and, with tremendous ceremony, dropped the plate out of the window.

Still laughing, they drove off, and the two teeth grinned out of the dust after them as they went.

CHAPTER FOUR

ENTER KOLMES

They saw a lot of Java, but they never got to Tjilatjap. It was like a dream in which one runs and runs but never moves forward and, as time went on, the dreamlike quality became accentuated as friendly faces evaporated and they seemed to be left alone, surrounded by fear and hate.

At first the roads had been packed and noisy, jammed with ambulances, military lorries and the gaily-painted ox carts of the Javanese. There was intensive bombing of the roads and several times they had to make wide detours to avoid craters and broken bridges. They struggled on through Soekaboemi, Tjianrjoen, Bandoeng.

On the second day at the government rest station near Sitoe Goenoeng in the mountains of central Java they had lost the taxi. There had been nothing but women there; scores of nervous Dutch women and children and a terrified old man who seemed to be in charge who'd taken one look at John's and Smudge's uniform and told them they couldn't stay. 'We want no trouble when the Japanese come.'

While they'd been arguing with him, Charlie, the driver of the taxi, had taken the opportunity to start the engine and drive away in the direction of Batavia.

Smudge was furious and John had to knock up his tommy-gun to stop him shooting after the disappearing vehicle. Then, leaving the women at the rest station, the two men had split up to look for alternative means of transport. John had no luck. But Smudge came back driving a new, smart-looking light-green convertible.

He had picked it up, he told them vaguely, 'down the road'. It had been abandoned, he said, and nobody wanted it so he'd taken it. In the back seat of the car was luggage and clothing belonging to a Dutch naval officer. There was also a bullet hole through the windscreen which Smudge ascribed, equally

vaguely, to 'snipers'. Judiciously, nobody asked questions and
they went on their way.

Had they known it, they were hot on the heels of Dr. Wassell, that intrepid American, and his company of wounded from
the U.S.S. *Marblehead*. In fact, Dr. Wassell had started his trek
about the same time as John Dodd and his party, but he had
begun it considerably further inland and therefore nearer the
requisite coastline. And as the U.S. Navy doctor had shep-
herded his little band into Tjilatjap, the approaches to the port
had been blown up behind them—severing John's hopes of getting out that way.

After that they headed south and west, hoping to find a port
with a boat in it on which they could buy or bludgeon a passage
to Australia. The roads became clearer as the military escaped
the island or set up pockets of resistance, but they remained
noisy and eventful. After three days their smart green convertible had aged considerably in appearance, having survived a dive-
bombing attack at Tjiadej, pro-Jap snipers at Tjiboeni and
crashed a road barrier guarded by armed Javanese at Bengbreng.
The Japanese army was still in the north, but it was clearly only
a matter of days before it overran Java and the nationalists who
saw in it their chance of liberation from the Dutch were beginning to show their colours.

Yet none of this had perturbed John nearly as much as
Smudge's recklessness; the American had found a pot of red
paint from somewhere and had painted 'U.S.A.' in giant letters
all over the bonnet of the car—unnecessary bravado in John's
eyes, attracting the attention of an increasingly hostile native
population. 'We're supposed to be running away from the
Nips,' he pointed out to Smudge, 'not blazing a trail for them.'
Elementary caution, it appeared, was equated with arse-licking
in Smudge's eyes, and John, having no paint remover, had to
shrug his shoulders and allow the letters to stay.

Compared with Smudge's driving, however, this piece of
rashness was as nothing. With predictable panache and disregard of safety—his own or anyone else's—the American persisted in driving on the right like they did in 'God's own country'. This led to heart-stopping encounters on the twisting
roads since in Java they drive on the left. Gradually, however,
as they emerged unscathed from each crisis, John ceased to

worry. The whole situation had gone beyond his control, they were being whirled along by some mad Fate and all a poor human could do was sit back and await his destiny. He became as calm as Marquita and Phiphine who, with true Eastern acceptance, sat and chatted in the back seat as if being driven at seventy miles an hour along the convoluted roads of a war-torn island were a mundane matter.

Strangely enough, the further west they got and as the roads became quiet and deserted with signs of population and war becoming fewer, their spirits rose. Marquita in particular became positively joyful. The weather was superb and the speed and the perfumed air of Java that rushed in through the open windows seemed to intoxicate her.

'Isn't this the most beautiful country in the world?' she would shout over the noise of the engine, and John had to admit that it was very lovely. Every corner of those blistering roads which rose and fell like enormous switchbacks, presented a glorious view of mountainous country, lush with brilliant shrubs and trees, with an awe-inspiring volcano or two ever-present on the horizon. Such cultivation as there was wriggled insidiously against these breathtaking backgrounds in soft terraces, waterfalls and curiously shaped paddy fields.

Despite the discomforts—during those five days and nights on the move they slept in bed once; the other nights being passed on the floors of warehouses and sheds—John was homesick only once; in one of the colourful little roadside pasars, the Javanese markets, where they had stopped to buy food and he spotted among the rich vegetables a cauliflower. It had seemed to him a very English thing to see among all that fecundity and he had a moment of pain, remembering the cool, restrained fields of England.

Back in the car Marquita had seen he was subdued and told them an old Javanese legend. 'The white monkey will be driven out of Java by the yellow monkey,' she shouted to him from the back seat. But after a hundred days the white monkey will return and chase out the yellow monkey. You are the white monkey, you see Johnny. So we have only to wait for a hundred days and all will be well.'

He knew it was ridiculous but Marquita's certainty and gaiety were infectious and within a few minutes a booming English baritone was wafting out of the car windows in a rendering of 'Begin the Beguine'.

On the fifth day, however, even Marquita was subdued. Prices for food and petrol, especially petrol, were becoming prohibitive. At every stop they seemed to have soared. Both Smudge and John had spent all their money and Marquita was paying for everything. Worse, they were wasting gallons of fuel in exploring roads that seemed to lead to the sea, but petered out just short of it.

As John said, irritably: 'If this is an island, where's the blasted coast?'

Marquita explained that the Javanese have a distrust of the sea and turn their sights—and their roads—inland. 'There is a fishpool in every kampong,' she said, 'so they do not have to go out to sea for fish.'

The previous evening they had managed to get to Genteng, a port on the extreme south-west, but it had been bare of shipping of any kind. This morning they had travelled seventy kilometres over dreadful roads in an attempt to find Palaboehan Ratoe which meant 'the anchor dropping place', and which, on the map, promised to be a sizeable harbour further north and west. The map proved less useful, however, in leading them to it. Signposts seemed to have been obliterated, whether by pro- or anti-Dutch factions they were not sure. Tempers were becoming frayed and Smudge's language explosive when, quite suddenly, the road dropped steeply in front of them, falling down to a large village and then ending on the edge of a large, speedwell-blue bay. They had found Palaboehan Ratoe.

They all got out of the car to look at the incredible view of geysers splashing like fountains along the honeycombed cliffs. But by far the most beautiful thing about it that day was the stained and ragged oil tanker that lay alongside the disused jetty.

Involuntarily they all cheered and Smudge kissed Marquita while John picked up Phiphine and swung her round. 'How would you like to marry me in Australia?' he shouted, 'because that's where we're going.'

And Phiphine laughed up at him and said she would marry him anywhere.

The pipe-smoking elderly Dutch captain, who was the only person on board, listened carefully to their request and took several puffs of his pipe before answering them. There was, he explained, nothing he would like better than to take them to Australia, but unfortunately only a few days before, after hearing of the Jap landings and seeing a Japanese submarine in the bay, his native crew had deserted.

'We'll be the crew,' John said.

The old man, rugged and stained as his ship, puffed some more. Unfortunately, he said, the crew had done an efficient job of wrecking the engines before they left. 'About the only time they've ever done a job properly,' he added bitterly. He was only awaiting orders from the owners before abandoning her himself.

'Haven't you got anything? A lifeboat?'

The captain removed the pipe from his mouth once again. Unfortunately, he said—and Smudge nearly hit him—his last lifeboat had been taken only a few hours before by a party of English and American war correspondents who had been desperate to get away. 'One of them was from the B.B.C.,' he said proudly. He didn't know where they were making for but personally he didn't fancy their chances of getting there.

Too shocked to talk, the four stumbled back to the jetty. In the five days' flight from Batavia not one of them had doubted that, in the end, they would get away. John realised that he had been savouring the excitements of that wild ride to tell as anecdotes when he got back home.

But he wasn't going to get back home. To go further north would bring them face to face with the advancing Japs, to the west and south lay the shark-infested sea and behind them in the east lay the coastline that had already proved shipless. They had nowhere to run to any more, and within a fortnight or less the Japs would reach this part of Java and he, Smudge, Marquita and Phiphine would be in the hands of Nippon. In all likelihood the grab would prove fatal.

They panicked. They went straight to the palm-thatched hut with the petrol pump up in the village, and asked if there was somewhere they could stay. They realised they were taking a risk. With U.S.A. blazed all over the car it meant that if the Japs came tomorrow the natives of the kampong could tell them precisely where to lay their hands on a uniformed Britisher and

American. But they were suddenly incredibly tired and, like animals, needed a hole to crawl into while they recouped.

It was even more dangerous than they knew, for talking to the proprietor of the petrol pump was a tall Eurasian whose heavy-lidded eyes fell on the brooch that Marquita was wearing and he wanted it and schemed to get it and, eventually, betrayed them because of it.

The brooch was extremely valuable, a gift from her French husband who was a jeweller and was made from platinum set with sixty-eight diamonds. John and Smudge had urged her to take it off more than once during the drive from Batavia but Marquita had refused.

Despite their preoccupation, they all saw the man staring at the brooch and he made Marquita so uncomfortable that she took it off there and then and put it in her handbag. Then they drove off to follow the directions they had been given, and forgot all about the incident.

Their objective was a pasang grahan, a holiday home for Dutch civil servants, now deserted, that lay ten kilometres outside Palaboehan. It was a complex of small, neat chalets and a main building that served as kitchen and dining-room, the whole being set into an uninhabited curve of Wijnkoops Bay, high up on a cliff with a path leading to a rocky beach below. Ordinarily they would have been delighted with such luxury, now they hardly noticed it. All of them—with the possible exception of Marquita who thrived on irregularity—were beginning to show signs of slow shock. Stepping into deserted houses, moving to no programme, feeling constant fear, regulated by no laws, abandoning old standards and behaviour, these things had a cumulative effect. They found that they acquired information without being sure where they had got it; they became inert and tired easily while the threat of the Japanese became increasingly unreal, leading them to carelessness. By the afternoon, the events of the morning were remembered as distant flashbacks.

It took great effort that night to sit down and decide what to do. Smudge was for bribing somebody with a fishing boat to take them out to sea. Ignoring the fact that they hadn't seen a fishing boat, he said: 'There are thousands of islands out there, the Nips can't occupy them all.'

John on the other hand was for taking to the jungle which

matted inland Java. 'Can't we go and live there until the Allies counter-attack? The Japs would never find us.' But, as Marquita pointed out, neither would anybody else. 'We'd need reliable help from a native. Nobody can live in the jungle on their own.'

Every plan they thought of depended upon the co-operation of at least one native—and the natives weren't co-operative. Marquita, however, was certain of her ability to find a friendly Javanese and persuade him to help her. Knowing her charm, the men were inclined to agree with her and it was decided that next morning they would go into the nearest kampong and see what good looks and personal magnetism could do.

But the next morning, on the sortie, they heard about the Wilhelmina plantation, an estate in the mountains about thirty kilometres away where white refugees were converging. John was aware that the fact of the Japanese not having shown up yet must be due to considerable resistance by somebody somewhere; having a low opinion of the Dutch that he'd met, he thought that it must be small pockets of British and Australians who were slowing up the advance. But if the natives knew of such fighting they weren't letting on about it and turned blank faces to any questioning about the war.

So, partly to get news, but mainly in the hope of finding some sort of organisation, they drove out to the Wilhelmina, only to find a situation similar to the one at Sitoe Goenoeng.

There were white and Eurasian women in plenty, most of them with children, but very few men and certainly no organisation. Even the overseer of the estate was a woman ... 'In a way', said John. Her hair was cropped, she wore jodhpurs and cracked a whip against her high boots as she walked. 'The Lesbia' as Marquita insisted on calling her greeted them kindly enough however. They could stay, she said, as long as they foraged for food; she was sheltering thirty souls and supplies had run out. They had been unable to get milk for two days and one of the women had a young baby.

They stayed: the Wilhelmina had a radio and they were desperate for news.

At that point they spotted the big Eurasian who'd been so interested in Marquita's brooch at the filling station. He was introduced by Lesbia as: 'My cousin, Kolmes.' The eyes evaluated them as if they were merchandise, but the tongue was smooth and charming, offering sympathy and help.

Foraging proved eventful. Open revolt had broken out against the Dutch but was directing itself, as always, against the shop-keepers, who were mainly Chinese. John had to wave a threatening tommy-gun at a crowd of looters who were doing a good job of stripping the local store before they would disperse—and immediately found himself a looter. The shop was deserted and there seemed little point in leaving money on the counter to be picked up by the pillagers who would swarm in the moment his back was turned. Guiltily, he transferred supplies into the car, trying to avoid the eyes of the small crowd who were being held at bay by Smudge's revolver. On the way back to the plantation Marquita spotted a nanny-goat tethered to the side of the road and the men hauled it into the back seat. It did nothing to enhance the car and added theft to their record, but at least the baby at the Wilhelmina got some milk.

At nine a.m. the next day—it was Sunday—a voice broke into the programme of music issuing out of the wireless, telling its listeners to stand by for an important announcement. In perfect silence everyone gathered on the verandah. Even the children were quiet. Then came another voice speaking in Dutch. John and Smudge could understand exactly what it was saying from the expression on the faces around them.

Java had surrendered. The Javanese were now citizens of the co-prosperity programme, thanks to their liberators, the Japanese. Remnants of resistance were ordered to lay down their arms. It would be a capital offence to harbour the enemies of the new regime.

The announcement was repeated in Javanese and the gamelan orchestra resumed playing. John and Smudge looked up from their thoughts to find that every eye in the place had swivelled round to them.

'All right, all right,' shouted Smudge, irritably. 'We'll go.'

The four of them left within the hour.

Both John and Smudge urged Marquita and Phiphine to stay behind at the Wilhelmina. It was, they pointed out, extremely dangerous to continue to be seen with two Allied servicemen, both still in uniform. The native population had orders to arrest and hand over any such men to the Japanese. Better stay where they were. As Eurasians—and Marquita had lately been introducing Phiphine as her sister since it was becoming risky to acknowledge Dutch parentage—they would probably escape internment.

Phiphine, however, refused to be parted from John and Marquita just said: 'What would you do without us? You wouldn't last a day.'

This was patently true; neither John nor Smudge could speak a word of the language and both were broke.

Not knowing where else to go they drove back to the limbo of the pasang grahan.

The next day Marquita and Phiphine, armed with a pistol apiece, drove into Palaboehan alone. Mission: buy or loot civilian clothes for the men and establish contact with friendly natives.

The argument whether they should or should not go had lasted far into the night, both men had felt it was too dangerous; the Japs might arrive at any moment and the native situation was unstable not to say unfavourable to anyone in European dress. Marquita, however, had eventually quelled opposition with common sense. 'Somebody's got to go. We speak the language. It's even more dangerous for us if you come too. So shut up.'

They shut up, but they didn't have to like it. And they didn't.

Smudge, in particular, watched the women drive off with a deep sense of shame. 'We sit here like bumps on a log while a coupla dames do our dirty work,' he said bitterly to John. John, too, was embarrassed that others were running into danger on his behalf, but the fact that they were women didn't trouble him as it did Smudge. He had his blind spots, but sex prejudice wasn't one of them, due to the fact that for as long as he could remember his mother had been the breadwinner in his family after an accident had disabled his father. He had a respect and admiration for women and accepted his dependence on these two more easily than Smudge who liked his women to be fluffy, clinging and, where possible, in bed.

Nevertheless, John was more than relieved when, later that

evening, the light green convertible drew up and the girls, highly pleased with themselves, got out.

Not only had they found a pair each of anonymous-looking boiler suits for the men to wear but, even more important, had made an ally.

'His name is Salih,' said Phiphine, 'he is the local taxi driver. We think he is also a bandit, but we trust him.' 'And he has relatives everywhere,' added Marquita.

Salih, it appeared, had been very struck with Marquita and even more struck with her money. He told her that the Japs were still in Central Java and moving south slowly, mopping up as they went. He had promised to find them a friendly kampong where they could hide when the Japs came and until then would drive out to the pasang grahan every night to report progress and give them the latest Jap position.

The arrangement worked well; Salih turned out to be a small, comic-looking Javanese with something about him that John Dodd trusted immediately. He was inordinately proud of his decrepit taxi which he drove with considerable risk at nights owing to it having no lights. For a Javanese he was punctual and turned up regularly each evening. Negotiations to hide the men in a kampong further inland were going well since the kepala, the head man, was his brother-in-law, but all negotiations in Java took time. Luckily they had time; the Japs were still some way away.

The only person who didn't like or trust Salih was Smudge. 'These wogs are all the same, all Jap arse-lickers,' he would say and, despite their warnings and protests, would insist on driving into Palaboehan every day to find out for himself. He became increasingly restless and his language became more foul. He and John quarrelled when John told him that his daily trips to Palaboehan were endangering all of them, but he couldn't be stopped.

On the fourth day he drove off as usual in a cloud of ill-tempered dust, saying he'd be back by lunchtime. They waited lunch until tea time, but he didn't return. John and Phiphine became worried: Marquita became frantic. By seven o'clock they had to face up to the fact that something drastic had happened. 'The Japs have come. They've got him,' moaned Marquita.

There was the sound of an engine drawing up outside. John put out the lights and picked up his tommy-gun, but it was Salih. And he had news.

Earlier in the day, he told them, a party of Australian wounded, retreating from the Japs, had limped into Palaboehan. Some of them were nearly dead, most lacked boots. They had asked at the petrol station for transport to take them to Tjikotok, a Dutch Army fortress high up in the mountains where there was a hospital. Nobody offered to take them; the Japs had broadcast that there would be a reward for any Allied serviceman turned over to them. Then Smudge had driven up and, after talking to them for a while, had piled them into the light-green convertible and driven them off in the direction of Tjikotok.

'But why hasn't he come back?' asked Marquita.

Salih explained that while it was easy to get *in* to Tjikotok, there was a road block to prevent anyone coming out. The Dutch colonel in charge of the fortress had orders to surrender to the Japanese when they came and, in order to keep the surrender ceremony as pleasant as possible, was discouraging all resistance in the area. To this end he was forcibly detaining such members of the Allied Forces who came within his grasp. Smudge would not be allowed to leave.

'They will keep him, too, if he goes,' he added, jerking his head at John.

Marquita turned a tear-stained face to John. 'You are not going, Johnny,' she said. 'We are alone now. We can't lose you too.'

They never saw Smudge again. Enquiries made after the war revealed that, with the rest of the men at the fortress, he had been put into a prisoner of war camp in Central Java and, one year later, had been shot while attempting to escape.

CHAPTER FIVE

NO WAY OUT

The Japs reached Palaboehan but, true to his promise, Salih whisked John, Phiphine and Marquita away in time.

Considering the bitterness in Java against the Dutch rule, the hope of liberation at the hands of the Japanese, the constant propaganda against the Allies and, most especially, the penalties imposed on anyone sheltering them, it was amazing that they found help at that time. But they did.

They travelled along what seemed to be an unspecified, directionless but efficient escape route, like the one in France for shot down Allied airmen, only this route wasn't going anywhere. As far as John could make out they had shuttled back and forth over the border between the states of West Priangan and Bantam several times and would continue shuttling over it until the war stopped.

They travelled independently. The women went first-class, staying sometimes one night, sometimes two in the houses of those Dutchmen who hadn't been interned, before being driven smoothly on to the next. Their hosts were courteous, but Marquita and Phiphine felt a sigh of relief go up when they said goodbye.

John travelled third, staying with the natives in atap palm-huts, but felt he had a better deal, preferring the all-out hospitality of the Javanese to the nervous politeness of the Dutch. In each kampong he was received as an honoured guest instead of a nuisance for whom the villagers were risking their lives. He would spend the day concealed and at night follow a guide to his next hiding place in another kampong. Since he and Marquita and Phiphine were travelling on separate, though parallel lines, they rarely met up, and communicated mainly through Salih who did a great job of liaison.

He was given no time to think of plan, even if there had been a plan to be made; events came in a cascade, confusing him, and running time together so that only isolated moments stood out clearly in his memory.

The Japs had nearly caught him this time. It would only need one of them to bend down and peer under this hut and they would see him, penned in by a little bamboo stockade with a dozen chickens and a small goat. By squinting through the stockade he could see their boots and puttees as they strutted back and forth. He counted five of them.

Although the Japs must have heard of his presence in the area this particular bunch weren't looking for him. They had come to requisition food; at this honeymoon stage of the occupation the Japs had only to request it politely and they were given it, equally politely. But not all of it—hence this little cache of livestock under the hut.

He was terrified of discovery, partly for himself, partly for the men and women of the village whose decision it had been to take him in. He had planned and rehearsed a series of panto-mime gestures which should indicate to the Japs that he had staggered out of the jungle unaided and hidden himself under the hut without anyone in the village being aware of him. He hoped very hard that, if it came to that, the Japs would believe him.

Nevertheless he felt somehow extraordinarily pleased with himself. Merely by lying in this rich, red mud with chickens' feathers tickling his nose and an over-affectionate and smelly goat standing over him, he was putting one over on the Nips as they walked around unconscious of his presence ten feet away. Some of his exultation faded when he found that he had be-come verminous. Whole clouds of fleas were jumping merrily back and forth between himself and the livestock.

Not daring to scratch for fear of flurrying the hens he pushed himself deeper into the mud and tried to discourage the goat from breathing down his neck.

He was spending the day in the hut of an old retired Chinese seaman, about the only person John had so far encountered in his series of hide-outs who wasn't one of Salih's inexhaustible relatives. He wondered how the little taxi driver had prevailed on the old man to take in such a dangerous guest as himself.

'Why are you helping me?' he asked suddenly.

Instead of answering him—or perhaps it was the answer—the old man had explained in good English that he was a convert to the Muslim faith, and spent the next hour in explaining to John the teachings of the Koran.

'If a stranger asks us the way,' he said gently, 'we must take him to the right path no matter how far it may take us out of our own way.'

Feeling duty bound to present something of his own, rarely remembered religion, John had produced his mother's Moffatt's New Testament. Marquita had his revolver and bullets and the flag from Seletar with her in the suitcases which, miraculously, she managed to get transported from one refuge to another. But John kept the New Testament on his own person.

He was disconcerted to find that the old Chinese seemed to know a good deal more about it than he did.

He was in the village where they wouldn't eat shark—one of the few kampongs he'd seen that was within sight of the sea. It was the usual collection of atap and banana thatched huts, but situated on some low cliffs leading out to coral reefs.

A shark—usually a prized delicacy—had been washed up and was lying dead on the beach below, but not a soul would touch it. A few days before some wounded Australians had been hiding in a cave just below the kampong, and with its consent. But they had been restless; two of them had climbed the cliff to the road and stopped a pedlar such as abound on Javanese highways and bought some cigarettes off him. The pedlar had gone away and informed the Japanese who had come, found the Australians and made them wade out to sea. Then they had shot at them until there was nothing left but a tangle of bloodstained water thrashed by sharks.

John was a great hit with the village children he met. Whenever the coast was clear they would swarm round him, all eyes and electric smiles, and he would wink and pull funny faces and sing 'Alexander's Rag Time Band' to them while they rolled in the dust with laughter. He was touched to find he had acquired a name.

'Ompong, Ompong,' the children would chant at him.

'What's Ompong?' he asked Marquita when they next met up.

'Gap-tooth,' said Marquita.

Things were getting too hot. The Japs, infuriated by guerilla bands who were still holding out, had intensified their patrols and searches, and Salih had decided that John's night marches were getting too dangerous. Marquita and Phiphine, too, had temporarily run out of Dutch families willing to help them. So Salih had brought the three of them to a kampong high in the mountains where he hoped to find them a more permanent refuge.

John sat on the floor of the cool, green hut while Marquita and Salih opened negotiations with the headman. He was tired, hot and dusty and longed to swig down the bowl of thin green stuff which had been set before him, a drink that Marquita said was called tjing tjao and was made from leaves; but he had learned enough of Javanese etiquette to know that he mustn't touch it before the host first sipped his. The only trouble was that the headman didn't seem to be thirsty.

He was younger than the usual run of kepala, about forty, quiet and dignified. Salih called him Ruslan. John wondered where the man fitted into the complicated structure of Javanese politics that Marquita had once tried to explain to him and Smudge back in Batavia in what seemed like another century, using a bewildering string of initials like the P.N.I. and the P.K.I. and the B.T.I., communists, nationalists and republicans. 'You can save your breath, honey,' Smudge had said, confused, 'they're all wogs to me.' Perhaps he was none of these things, perhaps he was just a Sundanese Muslim going out of his way, like the old Chinese seaman, to help strangers according to the Koran.

John shifted irritably, watching the kepala's hand like a hawk, willing it to make a move towards the bowl. Ruslan caught the look, smiled and immediately lifted his bowl to drink and, a split second behind him, John gulped down the green, refreshing liquid.

Then Ruslan stood up and went outside the hut. 'He's going to have a musjawarah to see if we can stay,' said Marquita.

John put his hands behind his head and settled down for a

snooze. He'd seen musjawarahs before: probably the truest form of democracy, allowing every adult in the kampong his say. No vote was taken but, eventually, a compromise was reached. Musjawarahs took a long, long time. This one took three hours, but in the end Ruslan returned to say that they could stay.

They stayed there for eight peaceful days. John became very fond of Ruslan and his people, but found the language barrier a constant irritation. The village was like any other mountain kampong, set on the side of a hill with terraces of sawah (wet rice) stretching above and below in carefully irrigated paddy. What distinguished it was that it was the site of a telephone exchange—the only stone building John had seen since he left Palaboehan—forming the only communication link between two Japanese garrisons, one forty miles away to the north and the other on the coast, thirty miles off.

One night when John and Salih were sitting talking together, Ruslan came in and spoke at length. 'He's been listening in to the Japs,' translated Salih. 'There are some Australians hiding out in the jungle north of here. He says the Japs are planning to ambush them at first light. Ruslan says he will get a note taken to them if you will write it.'

John wrote: 'I am an R.A.F. corporal hiding near by. I've had information you are to be ambushed tomorrow. Please destroy this note, and please get the hell out of there.'

The next day the telephone exchange connected up angry Japanese voices: when they'd swooped on the hide-out it was abandoned.

From the same source, Ruslan learned that his village was to be searched the next morning by Japs looking for 'a white spy' that had been reported in the area. He took it calmly enough, suggesting gently to Marquita and Phiphine that they put on Javanese dress and mingle with the women. At dawn he led John up the hill to a paddy field covered with three feet of muddy brown water and indicated that John was to lie down in it.

John stayed there for twelve hours, blue with cold and trembling from the pain in his arms which supported him while the rest of his body floated heavily behind. At no time could he stand or even crouch in case the sudden protuberance on the flat, neat field attracted an enemy eye.

The Japs came and went. He heard their lorry arrive and then the high shout of their voices which were like nobody else's and, after two hours, the sound of the lorry again as it drove away. But still he dared not move in case they made a sharp return—one of their favourite tricks.

He spent those two hours resolving that this would be the last time he involved anybody else; if he were caught the whole village stood to suffer. And as for Marquita and Phiphine he had been too dependent on them for too long. By now fifty people must be aware of their connection with him. He must try and get some control over events and go off on his own. He would revert to Smudge's original plan and try to find a boat that would take him to one of the uninhabited islands in the Indian Ocean. Salih must have a relative with a fishing boat; he had relatives everywhere.

At that point the crocodiles found him. They emerged out of nowhere ... long, slow ripples in the water that circled lazily round his body, showing only a knobbly crest out of which two alien eyes stared at him. He would have run then, Japs or no Japs, if he hadn't been terrified that any sudden movement would make the crocs attack him. So he stayed there rigid, balanced on his hands, eaten alive by water insects and only moving his head to follow those terrible eyes.

Later Salih told him that paddy field crocodiles have never been known to attack and are, in fact, very small. To John they looked ten feet long.

When Ruslan and Salih came to fetch him after dark, he was in a rigor of cold and they had to carry him back to the hut and force open his jaws to pour hot soup down his throat.

The next night he bade a tender farewell to Marquita and Phiphine and then set off for the coast with Salih going ahead as a guide. For what it was worth he had put on the long native sarong and a coolie hat. He was a foot too tall and several shades too light to pass as Javanese, but he had been practising walking with his knees bent and hoped he might just fool a Jap in the dark. He hated leaving the two women but they had proved more capable of looking after themselves than he had; they would be safer without him.

According to plan, Salih walked fifty yards ahead along an invisible path. They had passed through two villages and were approaching a third when two Japanese soldiers stepped out into the moonlight from some bushes and pointed a bayonet at Salih.

John dropped flat into the mud and lay like a rock. He could hear the violent outbursts which were Jap questions and long chatterings from Salih in answer. He felt sick and frightened for the little taxi driver; every move he made seemed to involve some innocent person in danger.

One millimetre at a time he raised his head so that he could see from under the big straw hat.

Whatever explanation Salih was making for breaking the strict curfew seemed to be good enough; he was actually going to get away with it. John saw one of the soldiers gesturing him on with the bayonet.

Wisely, without a glance back, Salih went.

Then John realised he was in considerable danger himself. He was right across the path; if the Japs came on they would fall over him. He couldn't understand why they didn't see him now, the moonlight was like a searchlight.

The flame of a match and a whiff of tobacco told him the Japs had lit a cigarette. Then, unhurriedly and chatting in their harsh voices they turned round and ambled off in the direction Salih had gone.

Wearily John picked himself up out of the mud. He seemed to be spending most of the war on his belly. He'd made a bid to go off on his own and he'd failed. Now he could only go back.

Two hours later a tall, muddy scarecrow with a gap-toothed grin appeared at the doorway of Marquita's hut and said: 'Here I am again, folks,' and Phiphine burst into tears and threw herself into its arms.

They went to stay at Kolmes's house. None of them liked the idea, but it had become about the only place to go, since John refused to endanger Ruslan's village any more.

It had seemed to Marquita that everywhere she went, at every house she stayed during her sojourn with the Dutch colonials, Kolmes would pop up sooner or later, smooth and charming as ever, offering her his friendship, help and—he kept stressing this—his house.

None of her Dutch hosts had liked him but had been forced to admit him; Kolmes, it seemed, had influence. 'But don't think it's his house he's inviting you to,' one of her hosts had told her when Kolmes had gone. 'He's just the estate overseer. His master was dragged off by the Japs as soon as they arrived— acting on information laid by Kolmes, I wouldn't be surprised.' The Dutch had definitely not trusted Kolmes. But just then the Dutch weren't trusting anyone very much.

Finally, she and John had consulted Salih on the subject of the suave Eurasian. 'Sure, you go to Kolmes, he's okay,' Salih had said. 'He is a bandit, but you can trust him. His mistress is my cousin.' This was good enough for them; the little Javanese taxi driver had become the arbiter of their lives.

It was a beautiful house, long, low and white with a green-tiled roof, and overlooking a great valley out of which the road wound up to the door. On all sides neat tea terraces moulded themselves against the mountains.

Kolmes greeted them with enthusiasm and introduced them to his mistress, a beautiful little Javanese village girl with delicate hands and features who rejoiced in the name of Fatmawati.

Their rooms were cool, spacious chambers containing four-poster beds and old, polished Dutch presses. Before they dressed for dinner Marquita went to John's room and handed over her jewellery, including the sixty-eight diamond brooch. 'You keep them on you, Johnny, just in case,' she said.

The next morning Kolmes disappeared, explaining that he had business to attend to and begging them to make themselves comfortable. He would, he said, be back that night. In the meantime Fatmawati would take care of them. (It came as a shock to John to find that Fatmawati was fourteen years old; he had thought her to be at least the same age as Phiphine. For the first time he began to wonder just how old Phiphine really was.)

Kolmes did not come back, a fact that worried John and Marquita considerably since they preferred him under their eye, but left Fatmawati unmoved. He often went away like this, she told them.

They decided to stay where they were—the luxury of being all together in comfortable surroundings, and of being able to stay in one place had got through to all of them. But the lotus-eating led to carelessness.

On the fourth day of their stay there John Dodd was lying on a chaise-longue on the verandah overlooking the magnificent view, listening to the Easter Sunday service from St. Martin-in-the-Fields coming from a wireless inside the house.

He knew the service so well; his mother and father had taken him and Terry to church on that day for as long as he could remember, and it brought back to him, through the scents of Java, the smell of polish from the pews and the trace of his mother's eau-de-cologne.

It brought too an almost intolerable vision of his parents sitting at this moment in the church at home, as he knew they would be, perhaps singing the very hymn he was hearing. They would be lonely without their two sons and anxious for news, but still worshipping the God they believed in. He wondered if they'd heard about Terry.

Another vision, as intolerable as the first, came to him of his brother, small and young in bed at the Singapore school with the saline drip in his foot. It led him on to other memories of Terry at other birthdays, blowing out the candles on his cake so that he could be a year nearer to dying in a hot, fly-ridden country surrounded by strangers.

The words of the epistle came blaring out: 'Set your affection on things above, not on things on the earth.'

His mother would bear up somehow. Her unshakeable faith would support her. He knew, as surely as he knew anything, that she would pray not that her sons should be kept safe but that, wherever they were, they should find God.

Well, he at least hadn't found Him. God was part of home, as built into routine as Yorkshire pudding on Sunday lunchtimes: not here with the Japs and the danger and the crocodiles. The risen Christ did not tread these exotic volcanoes; he belonged to the cool Easter streets of home and the Cheshire countryside where the Dodds spent their holidays.

He fell into a favourite daydream: 'Phiphine, when I take you back home after the war...' He never finished. In that moment he saw, they all saw, a trail of dust climbing up the road far below them. In a few seconds they could make out a green car with a pennant flying from the bonnet, too far away for the device to be seen, but they didn't need to. Only Japs had pennants on their cars nowadays.

It was coming up fast. They had three minutes at the most.

Marquita took charge. 'Phiphine, you turn off that wireless and then go for a walk among the tea bushes. And keep out of sight, your face would give us away.' Phiphine had gone grey.

'John, come with me.'

Phiphine ran off and Marquita and John hared through the house and out the back door, across the blistering gravel to the inevitable bath house that stood outside every Dutch-built house in Java. Scooped-out in its tiled floor was a sunken bath, now filled with dirty clothes. They belonged to Kolmes and, as Fatmawati hadn't bothered to do any washing since his disappearance, the smell from them was nauseous. Marquita scooped them up in armfuls and John lay down in the bath like a hare in its form while Marquita piled the clothes back on top of him.

Then she raced back through the house taking a desperate inventory as she went. Shaving tackle, underclothes—all those things could be explained away as belonging to Kolmes, and John had left the tommy-guns and uniform tucked into a hollow tree behind the pasang grahan at Palaboehan.

As she reached the front door she remembered—and nearly collapsed. Hidden among her linen in a cupboard in her room was John's revolver, Smudge's watch with U.S. Air Force issue written all over it, a Player's cigarette tin containing bullets for the revolver and the flag from Seletar which John had refused to leave behind. Enough evidence to have Phiphine, Fatmawati and herself tortured to death.

At that moment the car pulled up outside the front steps, doors banged and running boots sounded on the gravel. In slow motion, like a woman moving in heavy water, Marquita opened the door. There were three Japanese soldiers outside in the sunlight, one of them a sergeant, looking like all the anti-Jap posters Marquita had seen—squat, yellow and evil.

The sergeant, speaking pidgin Malay as the lingua franca, said: 'You have a spy here. We look.'

Marquita recovered her wits. They were only men, after all, and she could deal with men.

'A spy?' she shrieked. 'Why would I hide a spy? I am a good Javanese. Who has told you that? Kolmes? Kolmes is a crook.'

This was, apparently, such a generally known fact that the

sergeant seemed to accept the idea without surprise.

'We look,' he said, however.

One soldier had already run round the back, the other stood with fixed bayonet at the front, and the sergeant and Marquita went on a tour of the house—the sergeant with a pistol in his hand. It took half an hour before they reached the wash house.

Tethered to a stake just outside the doorway was a monkey, the pet of the former owner. The gravel around it was littered with its excreta which stank in the hot sunshine. The sergeant wrinkled his nose. 'Dirty animal. It smells bad.'

He motioned to Marquita to go into the building first and followed her in. Having kept up a constant flow of protest until now, Marquita suddenly found nothing to say and was terrified the Jap would suspect her silence. She tried to keep her eyes away from the pile of clothes in the middle of the floor.

In the humid atmosphere the clothes stank. Underneath them John was trying very hard not to breathe. He heard the Jap's boots on the tile and the flesh on his back moved involuntarily as the man came and stood to the right of his head. He waited for a bayonet thrust, feeling a tremendous urge to jump out and give himself up, like a child in a game of hide-and-seek when the tension gets too much.

But the sergeant had no bayonet; idly, he stirred the clothes with his foot. Marquita fought hard not to faint. Just then the monkey outside set up a screaming and the smell from the disturbed clothes rose up to attack the Jap's sensitive nose. 'It smells bad here,' he said disapprovingly. 'What that animal see?' And he walked out of the bath house.

The monkey had merely been screaming at the two soldiers who had come to report on finding nothing.

'Now we go search your things,' said the sergeant.

He turned out the house with the thoroughness of an expert. By the time he got to the danger point, the cupboard in Marquita's bedroom, she was limp with perspiration and tension.

Desperately she tried to think of stories to explain away an R.A.F. flag, a British revolver, ammunition and a U.S. Air-Force watch; she could think of nothing.

The man was taking linen off the shelves piece by piece. She could see the bulge that the cigarette tin of bullets was making underneath a sheet. On the next shelf down she could see the blue edge of the Seletar flag peeping out from between the blankets. She was immobilised. Then, by a miracle, she got her wits back.

She dashed to her dressing table and caught up a spray bottle of Worth perfume that her French husband had given her.

She began spraying it over the sergeant. 'You say everything smells bad,' she said hysterically, 'now I make you smell good.' The sergeant was cross and embarrassed. 'You stop,' he said, and took the bottle away from her. But at the same time he turned away from the cupboard and walked out of the room and out of the front door. Like a dream coming true she heard him call to his men, get into the car and drive away.

She watched them go all the way down into the valley before she collapsed into a crying, sobbing heap on the verandah.

Raised from his burial under the clothes, John was furious. He was angry with Kolmes, the Japs and, most of all, himself.

'That does it,' he said, 'tomorrow I'm going into the jungle to live on my own, and I'm going to stay there until the war's over or somebody finds me a boat—whichever comes first.'

They sent for Ruslan to guide him into the jungle and build him a hut, taking food and water to him every week.

John kissed Marquita and Phiphine who watched him go reluctantly. They stood on the verandah and waved until he was well into the hills, heading for the rain forests that covered the inland horizon in black.

CHAPTER SIX

THE FRYING PAN

Bradman was out for a duck. Wearily John Dodd put in Hassett. Now he had W. A. Brown at one end and Hassett at the other. Australia was thirty-five for two and Ken Farnes had taken both wickets.

At twenty-five he was playing a game he had played on dull days at the age of twelve. Never a boy to read when he could indulge in sport, even at second-hand, he had played the game then until he was sick of it. You took a book, any book, and used each letter of the alphabet as a situation in cricket; a=one run, b=bowled, c=caught, d=two runs, e=no score, f=a leg bye, and so on. You picked two imaginary elevens and went through the book, letter by letter, keeping a note of the bowling analysis.

Now he was playing the game in a clearing in the jungle, somewhere in south-west Java, using his mother's New Testament. And he was still sick of it. Its only value lay in the fact that it stopped him thinking.

His feet were still healing from the forced march to get here. They had travelled twenty miles that day when he left Kolmes's plantation, most of them over some of the most obstructive terrain in the world.

At first it hadn't been too bad. Ruslan had brought him a pair of woven sandals to wear—his R.A.F. shoes were buried with his uniform—but they had been too small and given way after a while from the pressure of his feet as they slipped down steep paths to slimy streams and then clambered up again, and he had thrown them away and gone barefoot. He was to go barefoot for the next three years.

He had clambered down to streams and up again, down to streams and up again until the world was a tormenting switchback. But when they left the paths that threaded the outskirts of the jungle and moved into the interior the going became worse.

Ruslan used his parang to cut through bamboo, grass, creepers and liane vines. At times they clambered over rotting tree trunks, at others waded through pools of stagnant water thick with leeches. Each step entailed a decision of where to put his foot. The kepala had warned him of snakes overhead by making an undulating movement with his arms and then had pointed down at his feet and made snapping gestures. John had no idea what he meant, but it was disconcerting, and his eyes became strained with jerking up and down.

Insects flew into his face while others made an incredible noise in his ears, a constant irritation, until at last his body was a misery that walked on bleeding, painful feet.

But the strong brown legs of the headman went remorselessly on, seeming to know exactly where they were going. 'If a Javanese can do it, an Englishman can do it,' was the only thought that stopped John begging for a rest.

At last they arrived in a natural clearing about the size of a large house. The headman motioned John to sit on a fungus-covered tree stump and then, without pause, began cutting down tall stems of bamboo and hacking off the leaves.

What happened then was a miracle of craftsmanship that almost made John forget the pain of his feet.

The man drove four large bamboo poles into the ground in an oblong about eight feet long by six wide and seven high. To these he lashed crosspieces, using creepers for rope—four about six inches from the top and four one foot from the bottom. Between the bottom crosspieces he built a floor of bamboo, then surrounding it with bamboo walls. On the top crosspieces he thatched a masterly, sloping roof of atap palm fronds, interwoven so perfectly that not a drop of rain, even the torrential rain of Java, could penetrate it. Finally, along one side of the hut, he built a sort of bamboo shelf to act as bed, table and shelf. On this he placed the pack he had carried through the jungle containing food, blankets, a tin cup and plate and an earthenware ewer. Then he stepped back, smiling, and with a bow invited John to enter.

It had taken him just under two hours to complete an adequate, dry and comfortable shelter.

For the first time in his life John questioned his own education. The William Hulme Grammar School, Manchester, and the R.A.F. had spent a lot of time cramming him with facts, but at no point had they thought it worth equipping him with a basic knowledge of survival. In that this uneducated Javanese was far and away his superior.

In the weeks that followed, after Ruslan had bowed and gone, the thought recurred more and more often.

Physically he just about managed. The average Englishman if he has courage—and John Dodd had that—is the most adaptable animal on earth. But mentally he was adrift, having neither the self-discipline nor the mental resources necessary to see him through the monotony of the days and nights.

This was not altogether the fault of his masters at school. From a toddler John had always rebelled against authority, and this had developed into what his family doctor described as 'one of the most difficult adolescences I've ever seen'. He had got brains but used them only as much as he wanted to. At one point the headmaster had asked Mrs. Dodd to come and see him and discuss the problem. 'It is difficult to understand a boy,' he said wearily, 'who puts in a brilliant history paper in the morning and gets sent off the football field for blasphemy in the afternoon.' He could have said nothing that would have hurt Mrs. Dodd more.

John's fifth-form master begged him to go on to the sixth and from there to university, but he refused. It would take too long. He didn't know what he wanted, but he wanted it immediately.

He tried sports journalism and gave it up when he found he would have to spend years on a local paper. He joined Shell but left when they demanded a seven-year course in pure chemistry 'just so I could get ulcers like all the other middle-aged men in their labs'. He walked out of an estate agents when they too demanded five years' qualification, and abandoned a career in an export firm because the clerk in the desk opposite him 'looked like an old crone'.

Eventually he had wandered into selling because it was something he could do well without effort.

All of which did nothing for him now; he couldn't swap Java or walk out on the jungle or trade in the Japs for a less dangerous enemy. Now, for the first time in his life he had to see something through, and he found it incredibly difficult.

He did not, for instance, have sufficient self-control to ration himself properly. Ruslan had left him large sections of bamboo stuffed with fried egg, rice, vegetables and fruit and brought more on his weekly visits. True it became a damp and sticky mess by the end of the week, but there was enough if he limited himself to three small meals a day. But as the boredom became ferocious he would start to think about eating.

Eventually, with the guilt of an adulterer, he would be forced to eat. These illicit raids, which were a great worry to him, would often result in nothing to eat towards the end of the week, and he would spend a day hungry and self-accusing.

His self-disgust grew when he realised that he had nothing with which to occupy his mind except thoughts of home, and those were tormenting, and this stupid game of word cricket. He had become so bored he'd even tried reading the New Testament but stopped when it began to demand something from him which he was not prepared to give.

The next word was 'disciples'. D. Two runs. Hassett had broken his duck.

The jungle oppressed him. He had been in it for three weeks and already the marks of Ruslan's parang had been covered in fleshy new growth; in the hot, wet air plants grew obscenely fast. The trees around his clearing filtered the light so that it came through pale green. Everywhere was green. He got sick of looking at green, sick of smelling the thick, rotting smell of the jungle, sick of its regular rhythms—five-thirty, dawn; one-thirty, rain so heavy that it looked like iron bars around his hut; two, sun out; five-thirty, nightfall. He didn't need a clock; the jungle ticked away monotonously for him and got on his nerves.

Remembering the lectures at Seletar, he kept himself scrupulously clean and at six every morning the wild life of Java was treated to the sight of a tall Englishman in vest and pants doing press-ups. But as far as intellectual exercise went he was crippled.

The weekly arrival of the kepala became a breathtaking event in his life. When the day came—and he notched them off in sevens on his bamboo wall—he couldn't settle and just sat waiting for the figure with its brightly coloured sarong and thin, brown face to materialise out of the jungle. It always seemed a navigational marvel that the man found him at all. If he didn't turn up until late John's nerves would itch as he realised that his survival depended solely on this man. Nobody else knew where he was. If Ruslan met with an accident he, John Dodd, would be marooned in this sea of vegetation until he too rotted and was covered up.

Every week the man brought a letter from Marquita and another from Phiphine, and took back a pile of scrap paper on which John had written his thoughts, his love for Phiphine and his warnings to take care.

The second letter Marquita sent him explained that she and Phiphine had settled in on another plantation belonging to a Dutchman named Martin. 'He is a hard man, but just,' wrote Marquita, 'known to the natives as the Slave Driver. He is a Fascist, but you know I have never cared about a man's political beliefs, only what he is himself, and Martin has been kind to us. We are living in a native hut on the plantation. I think it would be safe for you to come here. You could hide in our hut by day. Martin, who knows nothing, would never guess.'

John had been tempted, but rejected the idea. Kind Martin might be, but if he suspected his guests of hiding a British airman he would, for his own protection, have to turn the lot of them over to the Japs.

'Am having lovely time here,' he wrote back. 'A troupe of dancing girls comes out of the jungle to me every night.' It became a standing joke. Marquita would urge him to rejoin them, and Phiphine would plead, but John invariably sent back: 'Dancing girls would miss me.'

Yet all the time the jungle became more oppressive while boredom grew into an almost physical enemy.

Wearily he turned back to his game, deciding to switch from Matthew to Luke. Flicking through the pages of the testament he came to Chapter Four ... 'And Jesus, being full of the Holy Ghost returned from Jordan, and was led by the Spirit into the wilderness.' Obstinately rejecting the meaning of the word he concentrated on the first letter. A. One run. Hassett three, W. A. Brown ten. Australia was thirty-eight for two.

His mind jerked back to a similar situation at Old Trafford which had been not far from his home where he had spent his summer weekends watching heroes greater to him than historical figures—Bradman, Hobbs, Sutcliffe, Larwood and Constantine—play out great Tests. Those days spent in that most civilised of atmospheres were his only escape from this most primitive of situations. He remembered them with particular affection because they included the few really happy days he had ever spent with his father.

Mr. Dodd was a remote, taciturn man who blossomed only when watching sport or listening to classical music. The rest of the time he was withdrawn, particularly from his sons. On his honeymoon he had been involved in a farm accident which left him partially disabled for the rest of his life, leaving the onus of bread-winning on the shoulders of his wife.

She had been a trained nurse who served with the Red Cross during the 1914–18 war. Between them they started a maternity home which Mrs. Dodd ran while Mr. Dodd helped out doing repairs and odd jobs. It seemed to John and Terry that whenever a family outing was planned, some vastly pregnant woman would come waddling into the nursing home to monopolise their mother's attention. Terry, the smaller and more withdrawn of the two, was nearer to his father. John was always closer to his mother and perhaps because of her had always liked women, feeling comfortable in their company and conversation. He wished, desperately, he was in their company now.

The quality of light changed abruptly. It was five-thirty and therefore the sun was going down. Having no light, there was nothing to do but go to bed on the hard bamboo shelf and listen to the howls of the jungle where tigers and wild boar still hunted.

Inevitably his thoughts turned to girls, but even that depressed him. It seemed to him that there, too, he had been a failure. There had been Barbara, for instance, who had gone out with him because he was tall and made her laugh. But he hadn't been able to compete with the fact that she came from a wealthy family and mixed in circles where boy-friends had racing cars and yachts, the sort of thing that his income of twelve and sixpence a week as an articled pupil with an estate agent didn't exactly run to.

Then there'd been Pat. He'd been very fond of Pat, but she had a dominating mother and it had come to the point where she had to make a choice—John or her mother. Pat had chosen her mother.

After that he'd given up being serious about girls and had

gone through a long succession of flirtations and love-and-leave-'ems with no real relationship behind them. Now there was Phiphine. John's thoughts shied uneasily away from Phiphine. He was very fond of her; he would be happy to marry her after the war. But from the odd careless remark he was beginning to get the idea that she was considerably younger than she had allowed him to believe. The first thing he'd do when and if he got out of this jungle would be to ask her how old she really was.

Eventually he fell asleep. In his dreams there were no women, instead he slipped into an old, friendly school dream of his in which he scored the winning try at Twickenham before a delighted crowd of seventy thousand.

But even in his sleep he was aware with part of his mind that this was a sadly adolescent thing for a twenty-five year old man alone in the jungle to be dreaming.

By the end of six weeks he'd had enough. He had become depressed to a point where he didn't recognise himself. His exercises and washing were allowed to lapse. He became disorientated and made mistakes notching up his days, no longer able to remember whether he'd marked his bamboo calendar already that morning or not. Tiny decisions, like when and what to eat, became distorted into matters of importance and drove him to distraction. He became reluctant to leave his hut even to go to the latrine he had dug in the jungle, and would put off doing so for as long as possible.

Eventually he woke up one morning and realised that he didn't want to leave the hut at all. The outside world was full of problems he didn't want to cope with—Japs, the question of Phiphine's age, his duty to escape. If he just stayed here long enough perhaps they would all go away.

But even six weeks of solitary confinement such as this couldn't turn John Dodd into a neurotic. The discovery of what he was feeling shocked him to the core. It was un-British.

When, for the sixth time, the headman came bearing another note from Marquita and Phiphine begging him to rejoin them, he found John with his small belongings already packed, waiting to go.

The Martin plantation was deeper in the interior of western Java than any place they'd yet visited and more closely surrounded by jungle. It was the jungle, in fact, that Martin regarded as his main enemy: the Japs were a minor irritation. His house was more stark and ill-furnished than the average planter's—more of a campaign H.Q. than a home. Luxury was relegated to another house in Bandoeng where his wife and sons spent most of their time. Food was short but he had greeted Phiphine and Marquita with courtesy and allowed them to set up home in an estate hut only one hundred yards from the main house. Luckily Marquita and Phiphine had been able to pay their way in the matter of provisions since Fatmawati had transferred her allegiance from Kolmes to them and had joined them at Martin's in Salih's taxi, bringing with her enough food to keep them for weeks, having apparently ransacked Kolmes's place of every moveable, eatable thing in it. Then, in the easy way of the Sundanese, she had joined the servants of the Martin household to make herself useful as assistant cook-cum-laundry maid.

Not the least of her duties was to smuggle food to John, hiding it in the big basket of washing that she delivered to the hut where he lay concealed all day. 'You be nice to her,' Marquita had commanded, 'she is important. Flirt with her if necessary.'

John did his best, tickling the delicate little thing and addressing her as 'Fatty', to which she responded with giggles and sultry looks from her great brown eyes.

The first opportunity he had of being alone with Phiphine, John asked her point blank to tell him how old she was. At first she insisted that she was seventeen, but John had done a lot of thinking and figuring and he persisted.

Eventually she broke down and told him she was fourteen. 'Nearly fifteen,' she added.

John had never been so shocked. 'Do you realise,' he shouted at her, 'that back home girls of your age are still playing with skipping ropes?' Phiphine cried and John raved and Marquita came in to be berated for having helped to conceal her daughter's age. There was a scene, made all the more distressing because they had never quarrelled before.

Marquita kept saying: 'What difference does it make? She loves you. I welcome you as a son-in-law. Here in Java things are different.' It was impossible to make them see why he was so hurt and angry, or why he felt such a fool. John said finally: 'Well that does it. I'm going to find a boat if it kills me.'

There was no time to find a boat. The next day Marquita and Phiphine were sitting on Martin's verandah waiting for the arrival of Salih. When a car suddenly roared up the track they thought it was his. Then the door opened, and out stepped Kolmes.

It was like seeing a stalking tiger come out of the bush. They felt sick, trapped and revolted. Since they had seen him last this man had betrayed them to the Japanese—they were sure of it. Now, with John sitting in a hut only a few hundred yards away, he was walking towards them smiling and waving.

Marquita, as she said later, had a great desire to spit in his eye, but she got up and shouted a gay 'Hello'—there was no point in letting the man see their suspicion.

Martin was out, but coffee was ordered and Kolmes sat with them courteously making pleasant small talk until they took the first sip. The indigenous politeness of Java holds in the most macabre circumstances.

'I was wondering,' said Kolmes, after the preliminaries, 'if by mistake you took with you when you left a pair of my trousers. I don't seem to be able to find them and I know how easy it is in the haste of packing to overlook an extra item.'

They knew instantly what he was talking about. While they were at his house and in his absence, Phiphine had insisted that John change out of his travel-stained boiler suit so she could wash it for him. With typical largesse, Marquita had suggested he rifle Kolmes's wardrobe. Not without a few qualms John had done so, choosing for himself a natty pair of white slacks and a silk shirt. They had been very nice trousers, better than he had been able to wear even in civvy street. He'd enjoyed wearing them, particularly when Marquita had pointed out they probably didn't belong to Kolmes either.

Kolmes knew perfectly well who had taken the trousers: what he really wanted to know was if John was still around.

Kicking her daughter sharply on the ankle, Marquita said:

'Phiphine, go and see if among our luggage we have Meinheer Kolmes's trousers.' Phiphine got up and began to walk smartly off to warn John.

Abandoning politeness, Kolmes got up too and followed her. Phiphine lost her head and began to run. Kolmes broke into a gallop. Together they raced towards the hut—Phiphine a length ahead and hoping to hold the door against him.

But Kolmes was too fast for her. Elbowing her out of the way he rushed up the steps and peered into the hut where John Dodd, sitting on the lower bunk, looked up in amazement.

Nobody said anything. Kolmes turned round and walked back to Marquita. 'I want that brooch,' he said.

'What brooch?'

'The brooch you were wearing when I first saw you in Pala-boehan.'

At first Marquita didn't believe what was happening; blackmail was something outside her understanding.

'I haven't got the brooch,' she said, which was true. John had given it back to her and she had transferred it to Martin's safe.

'You haven't sold it or I'd have heard,' said Kolmes. 'I know everything that happens round here. If you don't give it to me, I'll tell the Japs about him,' the man nodded his head in the direction of the hut.

If she'd thought it would save John she would have handed over the brooch, although it was fast becoming her only realisable asset. But she knew, quite surely, that once he'd got his hands on it Kolmes would go to the Japs anyway and claim the reward on John. Her only chance was to keep it and play for time. It was unlikely Kolmes would act while there was still a chance of getting the brooch. In good round Dutch she told Kolmes what she thought of him and walked away.

Kolmes drove off.

When they told John of Kolmes's blackmail he was furious, mainly with himself. He should never have come back.

Marquita and Phiphine watched in amazement as he started searching through the luggage, flinging out clothes and shoes and muttering: 'I'll shoot the bastard.'

'What have you done with my gun?' he demanded.

'I got rid of it.'

John directed his accumulated anger at Marquita. 'What did you do that for?'

Marquita sighed. For weeks she had carried with her through occupied territory a flag and a watch which, if the Japs had found them, could have meant instant execution. She had finally baulked at the gun, not because it was more difficult to hide, but because it leaked oil all over her packed underwear.

She sighed again.

John left for the jungle the next morning.

He had never loathed the thought of anything more. He was more afraid of solitude, having tasted it, than of the Japs. In fact, it would have been a deal more sensible to have given himself up and become a prisoner of war, but the idea never even crossed his mind: surrender was not in his nature and keeping one jump ahead of the enemy had become his mode of life.

He went, insisted on going, because he had become too great a threat to Marquita and Phiphine.

It was the procedure as before; six hours of marching with his eyes fixed on the brown legs and bright skirt of the faithful Ruslan. Only this time, owing to the situation of Martin's plantation, they seemed to penetrate the jungle even more deeply than before. John noticed that the vegetation was thicker, more obscenely alive yet decaying even faster than he remembered.

Again they stopped in a small clearing and again the headman performed the miracle of hut-building and again, when he had finished, bowed and left—leaving John in a shelter and surroundings so like the previous ones that the nausea of boredom he associated with it came back and he nearly heaved.

Automatically, he spread out his belongings in exactly the same order, got out a paper, a pencil, the Moffat Testament and started playing word cricket.

He was terrified of the time that stretched before him. It all came back—his dissatisfaction with himself, his tormenting immaturity and indiscipline and the constant reminders of the failures in his past. Once again he was looking into the state of his soul and disliking what he found there.

Then Nature, seeming to abhor an intolerable situation as much as a vacuum, stepped in. After the first week she brought on the monkeys.

He was sitting at the entrance of his hut, legs dangling, listlessly playing the cricket game when he became aware that the encircling edge of the jungle had changed in content. He had been aware of no movement, no sound, but something had materialised that was not there before.

At first he couldn't see them because they had chosen deep patches of shade. Then he did. In the arc of the jungle in front of his hut were dotted ten or twelve black-haired, long-tailed monkeys.

He thought he had never seen anything so beautiful and sat motionless, afraid they would go away. The monkeys sat equally still and stared back.

Then he made a mistake. After the stillness had lasted about ten minutes he laid down his pencil slowly and got to his feet. Backing carefully into his hut he grabbed some fruit from his food store and crept cautiously outside. It seemed vital to him to make contact.

The monkeys watched uneasily as he edged towards them. But when he stepped over some invisible line, predetermined by them as their margin of safety—about fifteen feet away—they all turned and leaped into invisibility among the trees, leaving his part of the jungle silent and venomously green.

He could have cried with disappointment. The depression returned worse than ever.

The next morning, however, at almost exactly the same time they were there again. This time he stayed where he was, moving carefully and only occasionally and not attempting to go towards them.

They watched him for half an hour and then, at some soundless signal, disappeared again.

From then on they came every day, always at the same time, and for slightly lengthening periods.

Their visit was the most important part of his day and he was as thrilled with it as if Marlene Dietrich and Greta Garbo had been perching in the branches.

Desperately he wanted to get involved with them, to be accepted by them.

They taught him patience, those monkeys. Time and again, having strewn fruit on the ground near the edge of his clearing, he thought he was on the point of a breakthrough. Time and again they just sat in their trees, refusing to touch it.

The day the biggest of them, the one he called Groucho, scrambled down, snatched a banana and raced up the tree again with it, was a landmark in John Dodd's life. Within another fortnight they would sit in the clearing in groups.

He got to talking to them, not merely to soothe them but because he had to talk to someone. 'I'm not going to hurt you,' he would tell them over and over. 'Let's be friends.' But gradually he settled his mind to the fact that it would take months before they would trust him.

They assumed personalities; although their numbers varied from fifteen to eight, they always included the same 'regulars'. Groucho turned out to be a female who had more daring than the rest put together. Then there was Harpo, a big male, who seemed to be in charge and took no chances, only reluctantly allowing his tribe to follow Groucho's example and descend to eat John's fruit. John's favourite was Astor, a perky young female with a terrified-looking baby clasped permanently to her chest.

He began to see a future for himself in the jungle working to become friends with the monkeys. It seemed one of the most worthwhile and creative jobs he'd ever been faced with. For the first time in his life he set himself to do something that would take months, possibly years, involving set-back and disappointment.

Slowly he was reaching maturity.

Ironically, just as the jungle reconciled John to its life, it became impossible to go on living in it. By the third week he had developed a fever. He woke up one morning feeling light-headed and hot. By the end of the day he was exhausted. When the third visit of the headman, Ruslan, came round the Javanese looked closely at John's face and asked something which obviously meant: 'Are you sick?' John shook his head. He was determined to stay where he was.

The letters from Phiphine and Marquita told him that nothing had been heard from Kolmes and that no Japs had come; they thought it was safe for him to return. He sent back the usual: 'Can't leave the dancing girls.'

During the next week he deteriorated badly, even washing

tired him and he couldn't manage the physical jerks. He would rouse himself for the visit of the monkeys with whom he was making progress—Groucho had ventured within three feet of him. But the rest of the time he spent lying on his bunk. There was no question of boredom now, he was fighting to keep his mind from wandering off into the distorted dreams of fever.

He became disorientated in time again. For one short period he became convinced that the Japanese had cut down all the jungle except the little circle round his hut and were spying on him. At other times he began to wonder whether the past was just a complicated structure he had built up in his imagination which didn't really exist at all; then his mind would switch over and the past seemed the only reality there was and the jungle life was merely a nightmare.

One morning—he can't remember which it was—he dragged himself out into the clearing and scattered fruit: he wasn't eating it.

And this time, five of them, including Groucho, Harpo and Astor, grabbed it and instead of scampering off among the trees to eat it they started to strip the bananas right there down in the clearing. He was so grateful to them for doing that, and so weak, that tears came into his eyes.

By the time Ruslan came again, two days early, John was barely conscious. The Javanese took one look at him and started to gather up his belongings, speaking the first English words John ever heard him say. 'We go,' he said.

Too weak and befuddled to do anything but what he was told, John went—and left the jungle for the last time.

All the marches to and from the jungle had been tough, but the last one back to the Martin plantation was in a category of its own. At times John could see three kepalas all dressed alike bouncing along ahead of him. At other times he couldn't see him at all and would stumble into a run, in terror at being left behind. By the time they got to Marquita's hut it was dark and John was reaching a dangerous point of exhaustion. Ruslan helped him in and then went away, and John never saw him again.

He remembers the next four days as a return to babyhood, with the two women dosing him and caring for him as if he were a sick child. It seemed to him that it was a time of weakness, complete dependence and defeat.

Marquita and Phiphine were to remember it differently: 'He was so brave. He looked like death but he kept us in fits of laughter.'

Every evening they left him to go and dine with Martin, who was still unaware of his uninvited guest. There they would listen to the B.B.C. because Martin, despite his Fascism, was prepared to risk execution to get the facts rather than depend on Jap-inspired Javanese broadcasts. Marquita and Phiphine would store up the news and tell John on their return; the Japanese were invading anything invadeable, the Germans were advancing into Russia and—the last bit of news they gave him —Tobruk had fallen.

Having witnessed the fall of Singapore, the worst bit of inefficiency of the war, it seemed almost impossible to John that the Axis powers should suffer a defeat. In actual fact such a reversal was only about a month away, but John wasn't to hear about it for a long, long time.

On the evening of the fourth day Marquita and Phiphine went to dinner at Martin's house as usual. John lay on the bottom bunk in the darkness, ready to clamber up to the top shelf that ran around the hut if anyone came. His fever was better; all he needed now was rest.

Suddenly he realised that there were people outside the hut: there was no noise, only an almost imperceptible disturbance of the heavy air. Then he heard the scrape of a boot, and he knew. He just had time to think: 'This is it,' and to feel a strange relief that it was all over.

Then the door crashed open and a torch shone into his eyes and a bayonet pressed against his stomach.

Up at the house they had just finished dinner and were listening to the B.B.C. news. There were four of them, Marquita, Phiphine, Martin and his wife, a greedy and complaining Eurasian who Marquita couldn't stand. The french windows leading out on to the verandah were open and they had a few seconds' warning from the sound of boots crunching outside on the gravel of the drive.

With perfect presence of mind, Martin leaned over to the sideboard and flicked the tuning knob of the wireless neatly off the B.B.C. wavelength and on to a Javanese music station. Then he leaned back in his chair.

John Dodd was shoved through the open windows and behind him came a sergeant with a fixed bayonet, followed by a Japanese officer with a revolver. They could hear other soldiers outside. There came a small sound from Phiphine and then silence, except for the jangle of the wireless.

They were made to line their chairs against the wall at one end of the room while John was shoved roughly into an old rattan armchair at the other. Like any other man John had always wondered how he would react when face to face with the enemy. He was surprised at his calmness: his fear was reserved entirely for what might happen to Marquita and Phiphine. He prayed to a neglected God that Marquita would remember and stick to the story they had pre-arranged.

The officer levelled his gun at Martin: 'You know this man?' he asked in good English.

Martin replied with perfect honesty that he'd never seen John before. His wife's transparent shock spoke her ignorance.

'He was in the hut out there.'

'It belongs to these ladies.'

The gun swivelled round to Marquita and Phiphine. Phiphine was nearly fainting and Marquita remembers being almost out of her mind with fear. There was nothing now she could do to save Johnny; she must concentrate on saving her daughter and herself. Superbly, she set about doing it.

'I do not know him,' she said, with her hand clamping Phiphine's arm to her side.

In his armchair John expired with relief.

Acting the weak and foolish woman Marquita explained that this stranger had staggered out of the jungle that very evening and asked for shelter.

'What could I do?' she asked, 'I am a Christian. I let him stay. Tomorrow, as soon as it was light, I was going to inform the authorities, of course.'

And all the time she thought of John's belongings scattered in the hut and among her own luggage, like those of a man entrenched in a home.

She got up and went close to the Japanese officer, extending every ounce of her considerable charm. 'Do you know,' she said, 'that you remind me so much of my husband? Let me go and get his picture and I will show you.'

Without waiting for permission she walked out of the room, down the verandah steps and raced to her hut.

Why he ever let her go and why he allowed her two minutes' grace before sending the sergeant after her, nobody but that officer will ever know. Perhaps she had charmed him, or perhaps he was an idiot not to see through the flimsy story, or perhaps he didn't think it part of his job to wage war on young women.

To Marquita it was nothing less than a timely miracle. Those two minutes enabled her to whirl round the dark hut like a madwoman, picking up shaving tackle, emptying her suitcase of pants, ties, etc. and pushing them all down a crevice between the bamboo flooring under her bunk. The white duck trousers had been burnt some time before. As she worked she tried to think what a man on the run in the jungle might be expected to have with him, and chucked those things on the bed for the Japs to find.

She heard the sound of the sergeant coming up the steps of the hut and remembered that the flag from Seletar was still tucked among her underclothes. It was too late to retrieve it now; she could only pray they wouldn't see it in the darkness. The sergeant motioned her back to the house with his bayonet and she went, realising as she did so that she was holding Smudge's Air Force issue watch in her hand. She had picked it up and, in the rush, forgotten to hide it.

She could probably have explained it away, somehow, but at the time it seemed as dangerous as holding a live grenade.

She returned to the house by the front door instead of going straight into the dining-room by the french windows. It gave her a few seconds to think. Inside a badly lit corridor leading to the dining-room squatted an elderly Javanese woman servant, an integral part of Dutch colonial furniture.

As Marquita went past the old woman she opened her hand and let the watch fall out of it and into the servant's lap. The woman never moved.

No bayonet went into her back; the sergeant hadn't noticed. They went into the dining-room.

'Have you got the photograph?' the officer asked.

Marquita had forgotten about her excuse. She explained she hadn't been able to find it in the dark.

'We will look for it later,' said the officer, courteously.

They sat in that room all night.

It wasn't a place to linger in at the best of times. The walls were drab, a harsh light was topped only by a cheap white shade against which a score of moths were wearily hitting themselves, while the big fan in the centre of the ceiling squeaked as it revolved.

The officer went in and out of the room. When he was outside they could hear him ordering the search of the grounds; when he was inside he questioned them all over and over again.

Seven or eight times John told the man his name, rank and number and explained that he had been hiding in the jungle continually since the fall of Java, occasionally stealing from unknown villages.

He was not believed. 'No man,' pointed out the officer, 'can survive in the jungle without help.'

Nobody knew this better than John and his story sounded thin even to his own ears. He couldn't understand why the Jap was even bothering to question him. Since they had gone straight to his hut their information had obviously been given to them by Kolmes, and Kolmes knew that he was R.A.F. and that Marquita and Phiphine had been concealing him for months. Every minute he expected the Japs to produce the big Eurasian to accuse them all, after which, he assumed, they would be shot.

As the questioning and the night wore on and no Kolmes appeared John's hopes grew. There had been a foul-up somewhere. Perhaps Kolmes, still lusting after the brooch, had not told everything he knew. Either that, or the Japs were being damned inefficient.

Nerve-wracking as the questioning was, they began to dread the officer's absence more than his presence, for whenever he left the room the sergeant took charge: and the sergeant was a brutal man. He would make lunges at the four civilians with his bayonet, deflecting it at the last moment and laughing as they flinched. If John so much as shifted in his chair he was hit a crashing blow on the side of his head with a rifle butt and had his bare feet stamped on by the sergeant's boots. They learned to remain silent as any attempt to talk to each other brought screams of rage and more blows for John. It was like being left in the room with a wild animal. So they sat all night long in perfect quiet, except when the officer returned, their nerves screaming at the squeak of the fan and the enormous moths that hit and hit against the light.

John knew that he was very near death. The Geneva Convention meant nothing to the Japanese who had already murdered hundreds of prisoners of war; they would have no mercy on one who had managed to fool them all this time. Soon he would be taken out of this room and executed. He was sure of it. All he wanted from what little life remaining to him was that it should not happen to Marquita and Phiphine as well.

Despite this, and despite the pain in his head and the blood that dripped from his scalp on to his collar, he remained in the grip of amazing calm. He just felt sad at all that he had left undone. He gazed at Marquita and Phiphine, imprinting their image on his memory and recalled with sorrow the quarrel they'd had about Phiphine's age. He looked at her small pale face. Marquita was right; what did her age matter?

'They're strangers,' he kept telling the officer in response to questioning. 'I just wandered into the first hut I saw.' And all the time Phiphine's agonised expression told anyone who cared to look at it that they were not strangers.

Somehow the night ended and the abrupt dawn came. The sergeant was gesturing to John with his bayonet to tell him to get up. Swiftly he was marched out of the house and, with his hands tied behind his back, was put in the middle of a file of soldiers.

The officer told the remaining four that they were not to leave the plantation, then turned to Marquita: 'You are a very brave woman,' he told her, bowing, and went outside.

They watched as he gave the order to march and the procession, with John in the centre, looking like a giraffe surrounded by a pack of hyenas, moved away.

Immediately Martin's wife began a tirade against Marquita and the sobbing Phiphine for risking all their lives, but Martin stopped her. He looked at the two women with compassion. 'I'm sorry,' he said, 'I am afraid they will shoot him.'

PART TWO

THE YELLOW MONKEY

CHAPTER SEVEN

THE FIRE

John was sure they were going to shoot him.

His mind kept clear, calculating the chances of a dash into the jungle on either side of the path, but his body became hideously afraid, making his lungs expand and deflate with furious energy. His skin kept flinching at every bend in the track or hesitation in the officer's step, waiting for the blow at the back of the knees which would bring him down and then the pause before the piece of metal entered his flesh.

But the officer didn't stop and the boots of the soldiers kept a steady rhythm; every so often one of them would prick him in the back with a bayonet to remind him that an escape attempt was suicide.

The walk went on for three hours. After the first hour John's body relaxed but his mind became disturbed. It seemed unlikely that the Japs would do the decent thing and put him, without further ado, into a p.o.w. camp. So if they weren't going to do that, and they weren't going to execute him it could only mean that he was to face further questioning—and the Japanese method of 'questioning' had become notorious. He became even more alarmed as the march went on and on and he realised how much trouble they had gone to in order to capture him. They had gone to the lengths of leaving their transport miles away from the Martin plantation and creeping for hours along terrible paths in order to take him by surprise. Twisting his neck round, John counted the number of his escort: it consisted in all of ten men—rather a large number to take prisoner an insignificant R.A.F. corporal on the run.

John's uneasiness grew.

After three hours they reached a road where a car, flying the rising sun pennant, and a lorry were waiting. John was pushed into the back of the car next to the officer, who kept his gun on his knees, pointing at John, during the long drive that followed.

They drove to a barracks where John was merely put into a room, locked in and left without food or water for the night.

The next morning, thirsty and with cramps in his stomach through lack of food, he was hauled out, cracked on the side of his head by the sergeant's rifle butt, put into another car and driven through the fragrant Javanese countryside to a large, brick-built school which stood on a hill overlooking a sizeable kampong and a fine view. The place was alive with Japanese soldiers, who had obviously requisitioned the school.

John's guards took him along corridors smelling like schools anywhere of chalk and ink and varnished wood. It could have been the William Hulme Grammar School and he a small boy again going to the headmaster for a beating. In fact he was shoved into a room which reminded him vividly of his old headmaster's study where he had spent so much time as a boy bent double listening to the swish of the cane as it descended and stung his backside. It was small, dark and overlooked a playground; the shelves were empty of books but a cheap globe stood on the windowsill.

Behind a worn desk sat a youngish Japanese dressed in the uniform of the Kempei Tai, the Jap equivalent of the Gestapo. With much heel-clicking and harsh speech John was officially handed over and then his escort left, leaving a vacant-looking guard with a rifle standing near the door.

There was silence in which the officer took no notice of his prisoner and went on studying the papers he'd been reading when John came in. John recognised the technique from past Sidney Greenstreet films and waited in patience for the man to look up slowly and stare at him out of hooded eyes which, after about five minutes, is exactly what the officer did.

'We have pick' up your messages,' he said in mangled English.

John wondered what he was talking about and stood in silence.

'We know for long time you radio news to Australia. We know.'

In one terrible moment John realised why they had taken so much trouble over his capture, why they hadn't shot him out of hand, why he was having the dubious honour of being interrogated by the Kempei Tai.

They thought he was a secret agent.

It would be better if they had shot him. They were going to torture him for information he did not have and he was not going to be able to prove that he was simply an R.A.F. type on the run because doing so would involve Marquita and Phiphine and all his Javanese friends in the capital offence of hiding an Allied serviceman.

With a change of tempo straight out of the brainwasher's manual, the officer leaned forward and screamed the accusation: 'You spy.'

'Look,' said John, 'I'm an R.A.F. corporal. I was in Batavia when your blokes landed and tried to get to Tjilatjap. I didn't make it and I've been on the run ever since. That's all.'

The Kempei Tai officer relapsed into his Sidney Greenstreet pose and picked up a ruler which he tapped against his hand. John wondered if they'd both seen the same film.

'Only one,' said Sidney Greenstreet. 'All British, Australian, Dutch people prisoner or dead. Only you not.'

Which was how John Dodd learned that he was the last Allied serviceman to be captured in Java. Just for a second it made him feel proud but rather lonely.

'Why you lie?' went on the officer reasonably. 'We know about you. You radio news back to Australia. You tell us. Not lie.'

'I'm not lying. I'm a corporal—not even a flyer.' He gave his name, rank and number to which the officer listened with disinterest.

'Where your transmitter?'

'I never had one.'

'Who help you?'

'Nobody. I've been living in the jungle.'

'Where you get food?'

'I stole it from various kampongs.'

'Where?'

'I don't know their names.'

Sidney Greenstreet crashed the ruler against the desk.

'You bloody liar,' he shrieked. 'You spy. I know plenty English. All bloody liars. You have women friends. They help you spy. You parachute into Java. We know. Nippon intelligence number one in world.'

Privately John thought Nippon intelligence had proved just about bottom in his case. He couldn't understand, although he was thankful it was so, why—if they knew about Marquita and Phiphine—they had not brought the two women along for questioning too.

Then they were off on a different tack. 'Okay,' said Greenstreet. 'If you prisoner of war, where you go from Tjilatjap?'

'I don't remember the names of the places.' John had heard of reprisals in which the entire population of villages were shot for sheltering an enemy of the Japs. He was determined not to mention names.

'Who hide you?'

'Nobody.'

'Who feed you?'

'Nobody. I stole food.'

'Women hide you.'

'No. I don't like women.'

'You like these women.' The man made an obscene gesture.

'No.'

'You radio to Australia.'

'No.'

'You bloody liar. All English bloody liars.'

The officer was getting tired of questioning. He gave a signal to the guard standing behind John and the next second a rifle butt came thudding down on his shoulder with such force that he fell to the ground where he was kicked by the guard's boots several times before being allowed to stagger to his feet, to go through the whole rigmarole once more.

'You radio to Australia.'

'No.'

'Who hide you?'

'Nobody.'

'You bloody liar. All English bloody liars.'

The guard's rifle came crashing down and again John fell on the floor and was kicked as he lay there.

It happened time and again until he lost count; the questions, then the rifle, then the kicking.

That morning he learned the first principle of survival in Japanese hands, a lesson that thousands of his countrymen had digested five months before; if you stand to attention the Nips don't hit you as hard or as often as they do if you try to protect your head. When the rifle butt came down he would try to avoid falling by hanging on to the edge of the desk; he always got another blow, but at least it avoided the kicking.

After about the seventh bout of questioning and bludgeoning he was semi-conscious and realised only vaguely that he was surrounded by four or five Japanese soldiers who were dragging him out to the playground.

They stood him in the centre of what looked like a netball pitch marked out on the asphalt. The sun burned down straight on his head, telling him it was about midday and increasing his thirst so that he almost forgot the vibrating pain in his shoulder and back. He could see the face of the interrogator watching from the window of the headmaster's study.

The heat made the asphalt spongy and caused the mountains in the distance to quiver.

Then, at some signal he didn't see, the soldiers surrounding him started in. They beat him all afternoon.

They took it in shifts. Sometimes it was two of them using fists and boots. Sometimes it was the guard with the rifle, using the butt against his legs and stabbing it into his groin. When those two were tired a Jap with a multi-thonged stockwhip would take over, standing back and slashing at John's face and body.

After a while the faces of the soldiers receded into a mist and the different pains formed the only real shapes; the fists were knobbly rocks, the whip strokes were long, thin and brilliant and the butt of the rifle was a slab of concrete, which was to be feared most of all. He kept losing consciousness, which was beautiful, but they kept bringing him round by pouring water on his face and kicking him in the ribs.

And all the time, despite the pain, it was as if it was happening to somebody else and the real John Dodd was standing aside, stonily watching.

When he came round from the final bout of unconsciousness, he thought they were still beating him because pain was stabbing him all over his body. But they had stopped. It was evening and they were dragging him back to the headmaster's study.

Sidney Greenstreet was still there and still wanting answers to his questions. 'Where you hide your radio?'

It seemed like some boring and stupid game they had played together a long time ago. He couldn't believe the man wanted to go on playing it, so he said nothing.

'Who hide you?'

John opened his swollen lips and said the only thing that mattered: 'I'm thirsty.'

The next thing he knew he was in a small dark room into which the moonlight filtered from a high barred window. There was nothing in the room to sit or lie down on except the floor. But in a corner by the door was a jug of water and a small bowl of rice.

He drank the jugful in gulps. Once his thirst was slaked the pain that made his whole body throb took over, but while he was still moaning he fell asleep.

The next morning it all happened as before, but in reverse.

They came for him in the dawn, dragged him to the playground and beat him up in shifts until the afternoon when he was taken to the headmaster's study for questioning.

Again, although the pain of the fists, the rifle butts and the whip belting down on the one big bruise that was his body was immense, he was saved by that strange sense of remoteness. It was as if something that didn't want him to suffer any more than he could stand had dissociated his mind from his body. In a way he was less afraid of the pain than of the Japs themselves. He found them alien and horrifying with their grunting speech and their sudden outbursts of screaming and capering. Almost more hideous than anything was the way that the one with the stockwhip would, after a period of lashing at John until he grew tired, gently hold a cigarette to John's puffed-up lips so that he could take a couple of drags.

At one point during a lull in the beating-up he looked down and saw his own blood dripping on to the netball pitch markings. He felt great pity that he and the Japs were fouling a place that should have no knowledge of obscenities like torture. He hoped that the children who played here would never know what had gone on.

When he got to the headmaster's study for the questioning, he found that he couldn't see. With a great effort he could open his left eye enough to let in a crack of vision, but his right eye

On honeymoon with Alyson
at Scarborough, 1951

Marquita

After the programme

JAPANESE KEMPI (GESTAPO) LANCE-CORPORAL, TYPICAL OF THE PRISON GUARDS.

(See page 204.)

(The original of this drawing is now in the possession of Earl Mountbatten of Burma, K.G.,
P.C., G.C.S.I., G.C.I.E., G.C.V.O., D.S.O.)

Japanese guard

Elderfield, Otterbourne

HRH Princess Alexandra visits Forncett Grange

John and Alyson today

Residents at work, Langley House, Wing Grange Community, Rutland

was just blackness.

He put up his hand to it and touched flesh before he expected to; the rifle-butt soldier had been concentrating on it that day and it had swollen into a puff-ball. His hand was twice its usual size too. By squinting hard he got a glimpse of his legs and saw that they filled his trouser legs so that the material was stretched tight over them with purple, bleeding flesh bulging through torn patches. He couldn't focus as far as his feet but a hot, thick wetness told him they were bleeding.

This time Sidney Greenstreet allowed him to sit down. 'We are merciful people,' he said, looking sorrowfully across the desk at the battered mess that was John Dodd. 'You tell us about radio and you go to nice camp. Plenty food. Plenty women. All nice.'

John hardly heard him. The pain that burned up his entire body seemed to make noises so that he was almost deaf.

'Where is the radio?'

John peered at the man whose questions demanded an attention it hurt him to give. The effort required to withstand such beatings is so great that anything that has happened before recedes into an almost prehistoric past. He had forgotten they thought he was a spy. Through his waves of agony he was aware of only one thing: that this silly little man wanted him to betray Marquita and Phiphine and that he wasn't near being even tempted to do so. With a heroic effort John forced words out:

'I wouldn't . . . tell you . . . about my Aunt Fanny.'

It was the wrong answer and to prove it the guard brought down his rifle butt, throwing John off the chair on to the floor to get another kick in his kidneys. He blacked out for the last time that day.

On the third day when they dragged him into the headmaster's study, the boundaries between consciousness and unconsciousness had become undefined and pain kept jerking him back and forth until he didn't know which was real. A lot of the time he heard voices from the past.

'Who hide you?'

'Where is your radio?'

'You're a very naughty boy, John Dodd. Until you can learn to be a little gentleman, we'll tie you to your chair.' That was the elder Miss Mellor speaking. She and her sister had taken him into their nursery school as a favour to his mother; their main requirement of four-year-olds was that they should sit still and be quiet. John earned the distinction of being the only child they ever expelled ...

Miss Mellor's face became squat and liverish and turned into that of the guard with the stockwhip. They had tied his hands again and he was out in the Javanese children's playground. He was in for another beating.

'You're a very naughty boy. Can't you even go to Sunday School without getting into a fight? You've got blood all over your lovely little sailor suit.'

There wasn't a muscle in his body that wasn't wrenched and shrieking nor an inch of skin without contusion. He was sobbing at having made his mother so angry.

The noise in the classroom was terrible. He wished it would stop except that he was making it, leading the others in a scrimmage over the desks. The pounding grew louder into the steps of the dreaded English master and louder again as they rushed back to their places.

The master came in, swishing a cane, walked to his dais and looked them over. 'All right, come out the Lilywhites.' John stepped out into the aisle and led the procession to be beaten. And beaten. And beaten. The man was flogging the life out of him.

'We merciful people. You tell us. Who hide you? You bloody liar. All English bloody liars.'

He and Henry Barr were coming home from a night out, kicking John's bowler hat along a deserted Lord Street in Southport. He could see and hear them quite clearly: two irresponsible young men, worlds away from him. 'We'll go to London, John.' Kick. 'And we'll make some real money.' Kick. 'That's what we'll do.' Kick. He could see they were heading for trouble. He had to prevent it. But before he did anything he had to stop them kicking the bowler hat because it was his head.

The incident remained in his mind as a confused worry for a long time after they threw him into the bare, dark room for the night. Then the mists and pains receded a little and he remembered that the war had intervened and they'd never got to London and trouble. He'd gone to Singapore and trouble instead.

The next morning three Japanese guards with a lorry took away the walking gargoyle that was John Dodd, throwing it on the floor of the lorry so that it bumped about and rolled against their boots.

After some miles they stopped the vehicle on a deserted stretch of road and threw it out into the dust. Then two of them got down, tied the swollen, bruised hands together with a long piece of cord which they attached to the tailboard. Finally they climbed back into the lorry, started it up and laughed as they watched the figure behind try to run to keep up, fail and slide through the dirt.

The next time he was aware of anything much he was in the primitive home-made hospital of a smallish p.o.w. camp in western Java where Dutch doctors did their best for him, stitching up his legs, his head and the gaping wound near his right eye. Being young and healthy he recovered surprisingly quickly, although he suffered from double vision in his right eye for months afterwards; and pain in the small of his back and in his bladder became a constant factor in his life for the next three years. His mental recovery was even more amazing. He heartily disliked the Japs and his stomach would turn over when one of them hove into view, but only as a man might feel uncomfortable when a tarantula crawled into his vicinity—not knowing what it might do. There was no lasting bitterness such as consumed some men who suffered under the Japs. How much of this was mental self-preservation and how much due to the fact that his C.O. in the camp was Colonel Laurens Van Der Post, a man who, while resisting the Japs with all his might, understood their code of Bushido which made all prisoners dishonourable, it is impossible to say.

Whatever it was, John's spirit remained obstinately unbroken and even in the hospital he began planning a way of escape. To this end he began cultivating the Dutch and Ambonese prisoners who, knowing that they would find support from friends and families outside the wire, were full of bids to break out. He had a plan set up when the order came to move out.

They were taken to the rail sidings at Bandoeng and crammed into cattle trucks as even cattle had never been. John, one of the first in, found himself pressed face forwards against the side of the truck with his nose sticking through one of the openings in the slats. It was supremely uncomfortable but it was, he realised as the sweltering journey began, first-class accommodation compared with the inner recesses of the truck where men standing shoulder to shoulder fainted and, because they were wedged so tightly, remained unconscious but upright.

Rumour had it that they were going to Batavia, which John found cheering. All his plans for escape had been for one purpose—to discover what had happened to Marquita and Phiphine. The thought of what might have happened to them was a constant worry to him, riddling him with guilt that, somehow, he had let them down. In Batavia he would escape and make his way by night to Marquita's bungalow to see if, by some miracle, she and Phiphine had got back there. It was just possible that they had; the Japs had obviously lost interest in him, perhaps they had done the same in the case of the two women.

It was as they were drawing into Batavia's dockyard station that he saw the girl. She was standing on tiptoe watching the train with her bicycle leaning against some railings. She was slim and young and, as the train passed, she waved. She was too far away to identify clearly but John felt sure it was Phiphine and rattled the slat of the truck trying to dislodge it, cursing the blurred sight of his right eye. Then he decided it was merely wishful thinking. Nevertheless it had been a lovely thing to see, and every man down the side of that truck scraped his fingers trying to put his hands through the slats and wave back.

They were put into the native gaol in Batavia and the months they spent there, twenty crammed into a cell that had been designed for four, were like the months anywhere for prisoners of war under the Japanese—brutal, starved, filled with the screams of orders and the sound of rifle butts breaking bones. And work.

They were taken in work parties every day to the docks to clear the rubble left by the bombing and to load and unload ships. On a diet of four ounces of polished rice per day per man they worked as did the slaves building the pyramids, staggering under huge weights, lashed with whips and beaten to death if they collapsed.

It took four months for the malnutrition diseases to cause men to die, and then the amazing thing was not the numbers that died but the greater percentage who lived and worked on.

John Dodd didn't die, but he didn't really live either until the particular day when, like every other day, he scrambled into an overcrowded truck to be taken down to the docks. Ever since coming to Batavia he had volunteered for every possible working party in the hope of finding an opportunity to escape. Every morning he and the others were driven in open trucks, each with two armed guards, to the dockside. The drives were an education to John who had found little reason during his stay in Java to admire the colonial Dutch. Now, however, he saw the courage of their women. Each morning on the way to the docks and each evening on their return, the white, Eurasian and Javanese wives, sisters and daughters of his fellow-prisoners would line the route to wave and throw food and cigarettes, despite the inevitable retaliation from the Japs.

It was both warming and terrible to receive the gifts of the cheering women and then watch as they were kicked and punched by angry guards.

On this particular morning the women had turned out as usual but above their welcome came a scream of 'Johnny'. He turned in his seat and there on the side of the road, looking exactly as he had first seen her and in an identical betja, was Marquita.

She for her part saw a barely recognisable scarecrow leap up and wave both arms, shouting and dancing like a madman, only to drop an instant later under a torrent of blows from the guards. Even then, as the truck passed her by, she saw a thin arm waving cheerily until it disappeared from view.

The effect on John was incalculable; the responsibility and worry that had seemed to cripple him ebbed away in the knowledge that the two women had survived.

He was to need every ounce of this boost to his morale. Three days later he and five hundred other men from the gaol were marched to the docks of Batavia and herded up a gangway and aboard what looked like a wreck of a Dutch cargo ship of about six hundred tons, so battered that not even her name was decipherable. The Japanese had been shuttling prisoners around South East Asian waters in hulks like these in such conditions that in December 1942 even the Jap High Command became concerned at a death toll which was decimating this source of labour, and issued an order that those responsible for the transport of prisoners should ensure that they arrived in their destination 'in a condition to perform work'.*

This had so little effect that in 1944 another order had to be issued to all units concerned by the Vice-Minister of War, Tominaga, which made the understatement of the decade in pointing out, 'The average prisoner of war's health condition is hardly satisfactory', and urged that the 1942 order for the transport of prisoners be applied.

In February 1943 when John and the others made their enforced sea voyage they found that the hold of the ship had been fitted with wide shelving up each side, placed in tiers at intervals of three feet. With the usual persuasion of rifle-butts they were made to crawl on to these, take up a cross-legged sitting position and breathe in, until every tier was crammed with men. The effect in the airless dark was suffocating. There were no lavatory facilities, but they were allowed up on deck at regular intervals to use the latrine, which turned out to be an improvised gutter.

They were bound for Singapore, a voyage which would normally take two days. This time it lasted for five days and four nights since the hulk kept running for the cover of Sumatra to avoid Allied air attacks. The ship was unmarked and John, who was fighting claustrophobia anyway, nearly panicked at the sound of planes and the thought of what would happen to them all if she should be hit.

Except for the visits to the latrine they could not stand up, nor could they lie down but slept where they were with their head on the shoulder of the next man. Many of them had been suffering from dysentery when they came aboard and, since the visits to the deck were strictly controlled but dysentery isn't, the excreta of the sufferers dripped through the slatted shelving on to the men packed on the tier below, spreading the disease.

Those who didn't contract the infection like this got it from the rice which was lowered to them in buckets on ropes by the guards, having previously stood cooling for half an hour or so on deck next to the open latrine gutter, to the gratification of the flies which swarmed back and forth between the two.

By the end of the voyage it was difficult to tell the dead from

* *The Knights of Bushido* by Lord Russell of Liverpool.

the living. When they were eventually sorted out it was found that, surprisingly, only four hundred or so of the original five hundred were still alive, of which one was John Dodd.

These survivors, many of them semi-conscious, were then transported to Selarang Barracks, which was part of the huge complex of buildings that—taking its name from the old British gaol—became known throughout the world by the generic term of Changi.

CHAPTER EIGHT

CHANGI

The hospital huts at Selarang among which the survivors from Java were distributed were merely giant versions of John's shelter in the jungle—long low shacks of atap and bamboo in which the patients, one hundred and twenty to a hut, lay on hard wooden bunks with one blanket apiece.

When John came to that first night, almost a year to the day since he was evacuated from Singapore, and found himself lying on such a bunk in such a hut he knew that, for the first time in his life, he was seriously ill. You had to be seriously ill to be there at all: the 'fit' men walking around outside had enough things wrong with them to keep a peacetime hospital busy for a year.

Pellagra, beri-beri, malaria, dysentery, all the vitamin deficiency diseases known to man and some that weren't, all the illnesses caused by bad food, bad water, bad sanitary arrangements were here and every single one of them raging away without benefit of medicines. There was no quinine for the malaria victims, although the Japs had now conquered the countries which, between them, produced ninety per cent of the world's supply. The minute stocks of M. and B. were reserved to pull back pneumonia cases from the brink of death. For those with dysentery there were only pinches of Epsom salts and a foul drink concocted from extract of lalang grass which the British doctors, desperately experimenting to keep down the death toll, had compounded themselves.

John had acute bacillary dysentery. Ill as he was he conformed to the unwritten law of p.o.w. hospitals that, if you could walk, you dragged yourself outside to the latrine to relieve your griping bowels. If the overworked medical orderly told you not to bother and handed you the bedpan—a boat-shaped slice of bamboo—you knew you were dying. Painfully he clambered off his bunk and made the archway leading to the night air and the latrine at a staggering run. He was squatting down over the pit in the semi-darkness, holding his breath against the stench, when he felt a movement round his thighs. Standing up he saw from the dim light that the latrine was squirming and heaving with a million fat white maggots and that his own backside and legs were crawling with them. Howling, he brushed them off and then vomited. It seemed the lowest point of all. This was him, John Dodd. This was Changi.

During the next twenty-four hours, dysentery being what it is, he was forced to go to that pit some sixty times, returning to the bare wood of his bunk utterly exhausted.

But this too was Changi; that humour never quite flickered out. Lying adjacent to him in the next bunk was an Australian called Ned who had somehow got hold of a 1918 Black's Medical Dictionary and kept reading out some of the more enlivening extracts:

'Listen to this, cobber: "The Bacillus Dysenteriae is sometimes known after its Japanese discoverer as Shiga's bacillus." I tell you, the bloody Nips invented it.'

Then after a pause: 'Christ, it says here: "Persons liable to this bowel complaint should practise the severest temperance in eating and drinking." '

John, now down to eight stone from his original thirteen, led a chorus of cheers.

Finally: 'Listen to this: "A change to cooler climate, such as a year's furlough in England for persons employed in the Far East, will sometimes banish the disease when other means fail." '

Collapse into laughter of thin parties.

When a British Medical Officer informed the men of Changi that their diet of three cupfuls of rice per day—later to be reduced and continually to be shared with the sick who got no official rations—was sufficient to maintain life only if they lay down and did nothing more strenuous than breathe, they found it very funny. On those three cupfuls for three and a half years they were forced to build bridges and railways, cut down trees, level airstrips, load and unload ships.

They even laughed when another M.O. told them solemnly that, owing to the diet, they would probably be permanently sterile. (It is said that this M.O. was bombarded with telegrams after liberation telling him he was wrong.)

They nicknamed Happy Feet the disease which caused searing pain in the sole of the foot and kept half the Changi population walking restlessly round the camp at night. To the other result of avitaminosis from which they *all* suffered, which peeled away the skin from the scrotum leaving it raw and suppurating, they gave the name of Rice Balls.

This perverse humour or the inner strength that produced it was often the factor that decided which man died and which, equally ill, recovered. Those who gave up hope, dwelling too long on thoughts of home and the girls they were missing out on and the service promotions passing them by, were dead men long before they stopped breathing as eventually they did.

John got used to seeing men, fit by Changi standards, carried into hospital, turn their face to the wall and die within an hour or two.

He could understand them.

He had come into Changi believing the British were beaten; worse, he had come in a loner belonging to no unit and sustained by none of the companionship common to men who surrendered together.

But he refused to join them.

On the third night in the hospital hut a voice cut through his nightmarish dozing. 'Thank God, Boy. I thought you were dead,' it said. Only his family called him Boy.

It was Terry.

John stared at him and thought he was a ghost. Terry looked like a ghost, with transparent skin stretched tight over the bones of his face and body. "But I thought *you* were dead," was all John could say. Embarrassed by their emotion the brothers shook hands, and a weight that John had carried for a year went away.

Terry's hospital had been taken over in a fairly orderly manner by the Japanese occupying Singapore and he had been transferred to a prison camp hospital. The operation for peritonitis had not been a success because there had been no good food to build him up afterwards and the result had been severe ventral hernia. After that the boy had contracted malaria and dysentery and his weight had gone down to five stone five pounds. His recovery had not been helped by hearing, falsely, that the *Empire Star* had been sunk. Knowing that John couldn't swim he had faced the fact that his brother was dead. Somehow or another he had pulled through and after eight months had been allowed to leave hospital.

'I'm fine now,' he told John, 'I've got a job in the library—everybody who brought books into Changi has pooled them. Got a bit of trouble with my eyes, but basically I'm fine.'

He was, in fact, going blind from vitamin deficiency, but since John's appearance shocked him as much as his shocked John he didn't add to his brother's problems at that point by telling him so.

From then on John got better. Terry visited him regularly, bringing him books, and acquainted John, who had never until then been one to read much, with a new world of good light literature. A. J. Cronin, C. S. Forester, Somerset Maugham, Howard Spring—John read and enjoyed the lot. But with his returning health came the itch to be up and doing and at the first opportunity he got himself discharged and went out into the world of Changi.

It was a strange world, presenting a different face to every man who lived in it. On the one hand was a complex civilisation that the slaves who populated it had built up, offering plays, concerts, church services for every denomination, welfare organisations and the famous 'University' in which experts on everything from philosophy to basket-weaving squatted in the dust and passed on their knowledge. On the other hand there was the barbarism of the meal queues where men watched the doling out of rice like hungry animals and, like animals, took their share into a corner to eat alone. Some men expanded in the environment, showing incredible heroism and selflessness; others, possibly decent men in nicer times, couldn't take the constant hunger, overcrowding and discomfort and shrivelled mentally into savagery.

Such men formed or condoned the drug racket, stealing medicines from the hospitals and selling them over the wire to the Chinese, or stole their comrades' food. John was aware of the selflessness and courage but found the blacker side of camp life more obtrusive. Like everyone else he glowered in envy at the American sergeant who stayed rosy-cheeked and rich by Changi standards and on whom, it was supposed, James Clavell later based his novel *King Rat*. Like everyone else he seethed under the pettier rules of camp administration, which the Japs left mainly to the p.o.w. top brass and which strictly maintained the distinction between officers and other ranks. One of these ordered that O.R.s give up any good shirt they possessed to the officers, the reason being that decently dressed officers were 'good for morale'. The question, John thought as he watched a particularly resplendent major stride past a crowd of living skeletons in G-strings, was ... 'Whose?'

Rejecting both the culture and barbarity of Changi he formed his own blueprint for survival and self-respect. He would eat everything possible and use all fair means to get more. (Fair means to him included trading over the wire or with the Japs themselves which was strictly forbidden by camp law.) He would think of the past and future as little as possible and, most important, he would steer very clear of the men in his hut.

He had been allocated a bunk in a hut which he shared with half a million bedbugs and up to eighty men, mostly British, who, like himself, were remnants from long-vanished units. Of the two he preferred the bedbugs. His other bunk mates, he decided, were mainly lost souls, embittered and full of a self-pity which could and often did prove fatal. As a matter of self-preservation he must avoid them.

He did this neatly enough by going back to hospital within the week with a bout of amoebic dysentery.

The moans coming from the medical orderly's room were unusual even in hospital where amputations without anaesthetic were an everyday affair. John, waiting in a queue to enter the room himself, turned to the next patient, a depressed-looking Australian who seemed to know the ropes. 'What are they going to do to us?'

'Sigmoidoscopy.'

'What's that?'

'Sticking a periscope up your arse.'

On one of his visits Terry told him about the work parties the Jap commandant had ordered to be made ready to go to Thailand on what was to be—according to the Jap commandant—nothing less than a holiday from care. As a matter of routine nobody believed him, but: 'I think I'll go, Boy,' Terry said, 'It'll make a change.'

'Tell them to put my name down for when I get out of here,' said John.

Neither had as yet become institutionalised, as so many p.o.w.s did, so that they were reluctant to leave their bug-ridden hovels even to cross the camp.

But Terry's C.O. turned down his application, saying he didn't think the trip would be *that* much of a rest cure. And John was released from hospital just one day too late to join the last work party that went up to die on the Burma–Siam railway.

Again, by a hair's breadth, John had missed almost certain destruction.

His nights were spent with the bedbugs and the moaners, but by day he crossed the no man's land that divided Changi and spent his time with the Australians. He had become re-acquainted with his old fellow-patient Ned who had then introduced him to other Aussies like Joe, a wizened little bugler, and Rupe, who was as tall as John himself and who had been a drover in peace-time. Among them he was with kindred spirits.

There is little doubt that the Australians survived p.o.w. life better than any other nationality. Perhaps they were more used to roughing it and withstanding the heat. Perhaps they suffered less bull than the British officers inflicted on their other ranks. But undeniably they had, as a race, a mental stamina that enabled them to take each sufficiently evil day without hankering for the past or worrying too much about the future. They were not necessarily conspicuous as students at the 'University', although they made great contributions to the arts and entertainment. Their most admired accomplishments lay in trading and theft. They stole. And how they stole. They stole from the Japanese 'like', as someone said, 'there was going to be a tax on it'. Food from the ships they loaded and unloaded, boots from a resting guard's feet, the Jap commandant's pet monkey—nothing was safe from the Aussies. And when they weren't stealing from the Japs they were trading with them.

In this last industry they found a welcome and enthusiastic ally in John Dodd.

Transactions with the Changi guards were complex affairs,

usually involving a whole chain of prisoners, stretching from the original owner who would not or could not sell the object himself down to the end-salesman, passing through several percentage-taking hands on the way. John, Ned and Rupe considered the camp law against such trading ridiculous and ignored it, but the M.P.s, who patrolled Changi and enforced the law, complicated a business which was risky enough anyway, since the unpredictable Japanese were likely to beat up anyone who sold them false goods. The trouble was often that there were only false goods to sell. The value of advertising was apparent in the Japs' willingness to buy only what they had heard about; a lighter must be a Ronson or a Colibri, a watch an Omega or Rolex, a camera a Leica— nothing else would do. But the p.o.w.s had a limited and fast-dwindling supply of such luxury goods, most of them having been searched before entering camp. So an enterprising prisoner who had been an engraver pre-war set up shop as a forger to make any Consumer Association blanch. Under his skilled hand humble pens which had started life on a Woolworth's counter became resplendent with the name of Parker and were sold accordingly. If the guard then re-sold it to a Chinese trader in Singapore for three hundred per cent profit all was well: if the deception was discovered before then his source of supply was lucky if he escaped with a severe beating up.

John's natural genius quickly promoted him to the honoured but risky position of end-salesman and his most frequent customer was a guard whose unpronounceable name was shortened by the Aussies to 'Toots'. Toots was, in fact, a Korean, a paddy-field wallah, an ignorant and rapacious peasant and a handy man with a rifle butt when angered who could, according to John, be sold anything when in the right mood.

Judging the mood could take days. Given something to sell by Ned or Rupe, John would haunt Toots's footsteps, keeping out of sight, but watching him closely. At the end of an hour or so during which Toots had usually bashed some recalcitrant Changi-ite, John would return saying: 'Today is not the day.' If, however, during that time Toots did nothing more offensive than spit, John would approach him, bow low and address him as though he were a credulous suburban housewife.

'Madam,' he would insist, 'a friend of mine, having fallen on

bad times, has an object of inestimable worth which he is forced
to give away . . .'

Toots, uncomprehending but gratified, would listen to the
spiel at the end of which they would revert to pidgin English.

'Me got lighter,' John might say, flicking his thumb in pan-
tomime, 'Ronson. You changy-changy?'

'Ronson-ka. Okay?'

'Certainly ka. Number One Ronson.'

The next day would allow Toots a sight of the lighter or
whatever it was while Ned and Rupe stood guard on the look-
out for camp police, and the next was spent in arguing price. If
all went well the transfer would take place, in great secrecy, on
the fourth day.

Profits from such transactions were invariably spent on food
or, an equally high priority, tobacco, which he then shared between Terry and his Australian friends.

Luxuries like eggs or cigarettes were most easily obtained on
the work parties. By this time the Japanese, strictly against the
Geneva convention, like everything else they did, were using the
men in Changi to build an airfield. Every day large numbers of
skeletons would troop out under guard to fell trees, or dig, or
load trucks with soil and then manhandle them along the railway tracks into cuttings in the hillside for emptying.

The aim of the skeletons was to slow down the Japanese war
effort by working as little as possible, thus indulging a natural
inclination considering the heat and their condition; the Japs
contested this view with the usual rifle-butt argument, insisting
on 'speedo, speedo'. Human nature being what it is, however,
the guards would get tired and take a nap. This was the signal
for the trade-minded of the prisoners to leap like jack-rabbits
for the scrub surrounding the work area and wriggle on their
bellies through its long, green tunnels where, at the end of each,
an affable Chinese would be waiting with goodies to sell. If the
guard woke before they got back they were beaten up, but an
even more serious risk lay in getting a scratch from prickly
bamboo or saw-edged blade of grass; their skins had become so
thin and poor that the smallest nick developed quickly into a
jungle ulcer. John's legs had never healed properly from the
attention they got on the playground in Java, now they became
a mass of deep-rooted sores which were cauterised daily by the

medical orderlies with a solution of copper sulphate.

He kept going on the work parties, however. His concern now was to obtain either a tin of Marmite or some vitamin B tablets for Terry whose sight had deteriorated so much that he had become useless to the library and was working as batman and laundrymaid to a brigadier. Just one spoonful of Marmite or one tablet of Vitamin B a day would have been enough to stop Terry's descent into total blindness, but the Japs kept for themselves the Red Cross parcels containing such things and even the ubiquitous Chinese traders couldn't come up with any. (Near the end of 1943 the Japs allowed a consignment of Red Cross parcels through and one of them, containing a tin of Marmite, saved Terry's sight in the nick of time.)

When John's legs and a recurrence of dysentery became too bad for him to continue work on the airstrip he was transferred to tilling the camp gardens—a smelly job, since the lack of proper fertilisers forced the p.o.w. gardening experts into using urine, which was brought in large buckets from the latrines every morning and sprinkled over the dry earth. Sometimes the middleman was cut out and it wasn't uncommon to see a prisoner piddling helpfully on to the vegetables.

Deriving little joy or interest from his work, John devoted his greatest energy to trading. There was a big deal in the offing. Ned had been given an ancient Marks and Spencers watch to sell which was now at the engraver's being transformed into a Rolex. John was nervous about it; even polished up and inscribed the watch remained stubbornly un-Rolex-looking. When, after the usual preliminary scouting, the day came to show it to Toots, he was even more nervous. The watch had a distressing tendency to stop unless shaken vigorously.

'Rolex-ka?' asked Toots, incredulously, looking at it in John's palm.

'Rolex Number One,' said John firmly, waving his hand energetically up and down to keep the thing ticking.

Somehow he wheedled five hundred dollars out of Toots and from that moment on began growing a beard and adopted a large coolie hat, hoping to make himself unrecognisable should Toots discover the truth about the watch. Ned and Rupe kept look-out for him.

On the second day after the deal had gone through there

came a warning cry from Rupe and seconds later a berserk-looking Korean came screaming into the area, swiping at any tall prisoners in his path and peering madly into their faces. He even rushed through the hospital huts like a hurricane, tearing the blankets off patients and jerking those he couldn't see on to their back with his rifle butt.

The next fortnight was wearing, with Toots spending every moment of his guard duty ransacking the camp for John. The yell of 'Toots coming' would galvanise John into action and send him scooting off in an opposite direction. By the end of that time, his beard being long and Toots's memory short, the worst of the danger was over, although John still had a tendency to sweat when Toots was on roll-call duty and passed within inches of him during the count.

But it was the end of his career as end-salesman. He would be a marked man with all the guards from now on. The fun was over.

Immediately he branched out on a new career—duck farming. Ducks, he decided, were the coming thing. Buy a dozen ducklings, nurture them, let them breed, more nurturing, more breeding and—bingo—he and Terry would be selling roast duck and giving eggs to the sick with the largesse of rich men.

It didn't work out like that. For one thing, raising the money necessary to buy such a consignment meant forming a syndicate of twenty-five men. For another, the ducklings when eventually smuggled into camp were not the golden balls of fluff he'd imagined but scrawny, listless creatures with every appearance of being marked down for an early grave.

Undeterred by this, or the fact that camp rules allowed only officers to keep poultry, John put his brood in a fenced-off area near his hut and tended them like a mother duck. He and the syndicate, which included Terry, would sit for hours gazing at their bedraggled investment until they could distinguish one from another and discuss the progress of each with the expertise of veterinary surgeons. Each duckling was given a pet name and lavished with rice and chopped worms prepared by the thin hands of its foster-fathers.

Ducks, however, give up more easily than men. Three died, one after another, within the first week and were stewed with full military honours. The others looked even more miserable and obstinately refused to grow. The nerves of the syndicate became strained and some men demanded their money back. Using the last of his savings, John bought them out. There were more fatalities. After a quarrel other members formed a split and bore off their share of the ducklings to newer pastures.

By the end of three weeks the syndicate had dwindled down to five and the number of ducks to one. His name was Donald and he was the original Ugly Duckling, quacking sadly for his missing brothers and sisters. Despite his isolation, however, he kept on living ... and won John's heart, stirred as it was with fellow feeling.

The Dodd brothers would pass their evenings looking at Donald, forcing each other to believe he was improving. 'He's fatter than yesterday, I think.' 'Definitely, he's fatter.'

They forgot their commercial plans in the emotion of watching growth.

Since the other three were out on work parties and Terry was usually exhausted after a day's fetching and carrying for his brigadier, the main task of looking after Donald was left to John.

On this particular evening he was out in the duck-run, energetically bashing away at the hard earth with a changkol and shouting to Donald, now a fleshless adolescent, to come and peck the exposed worms.

Suddenly the duckling had one of his rare flashes of activity and ran between John's legs just as he brought the changkol crashing down. The blade bit through the neck, severing it. The small body twitched once and then lay still.

Terry was lying on his bed when John came bursting into the hut, carrying the pathetic remains in his outstretched hands.

'Terry,' he said, 'Terry, I've killed Donald.' Then he sat down and burst into tears.

Terry stared at his brother. It was a major catastrophe. Donald had been their only stake in the future, and a great deal of time, risk, money and affection had gone for nothing.

When the other three members of the syndicate came back, tired and irritable, from their day on the airstrip John still couldn't speak and Terry had to tell them.

There was a long, long silence.

'Where is he?' demanded one.

'We buried him.'

'Go and dig the bugger up.'

That night five silent men fed on watery stew faintly flav-
oured with duckling. John nearly choked on it.

With the death of Donald some of John's energy evaporated.
Time began to hang heavy on him—and it never hung heavier
than it did in Changi.

It was 1943 for ever. Then some thin, wild yelling from the
Argylls' huts denoted that somehow the year had dragged itself
into 1944.

Nineteen forty-four was eternity.

He spent as much of it as possible with the Australians, gambling. Interminable nights were passed with Ned and Rupe playing poker or two-up, a desperate and forbidden game, that involved comparatively huge sums of money on the fall of a coin.
Daytime non-working hours were passed scrambling in the dust
betting on and yelling encouragement to a line-up of bedbugs
that had been persuaded to race for a drop of blood that one of
the men had enticed from his fingertip.

It wasn't a way to expand their souls exactly, and they got
cold looks from officers who muttered about morale. But what
was good for their morale was to pass an hour without thinking
about the next meal or the next smoke or the continual pain
from the Rice Balls and the bedsores caused by their hipbones
and shoulder-bones chafing their papery skin. They gambled
on.

Hunger was a torture and a man, unless he had something to
occupy his mind, could literally writhe in the agony of waiting
to queue for the next meal. The prisoners spent hours discussing
and arguing the best method to use the flattened teaspoonful of
sugar they were allowed daily; some ate it from the spoon, some
spread it on their rice pap, while others put it in a jam jar and
saved it for a celebration.

There wasn't much to celebrate. The news transmitted by one
or other of the camp's secret radios was passed in whispers and,
by the time it reached the lower ranks, had often become merely
a garbled rumour. The men called it 'borehole' since they got to
hear it mostly while squatting over the deep borehole pits which
served as lavatories and social centre. By 1944 the news had

improved so much that it was difficult to believe. Could the Reds really be driving back the Germans? Had the Yanks really landed on the Marshall Islands? Over this last piece of borehole there hung a heavy, black question mark. What would the Japs do to them, the living evidence of Nipponese inhumanity, if the Allies ever did get within striking distance? Borehole made them nervous. For the most part they had become so institutionalised that they regarded the outside world as a sort of dream and Changi as the only reality.

Even John Dodd, the loner, was being affected. He felt the pull of the camp if ever he had to go outside it and the slight unease when he was not in the company of Terry or his Aussie mates. His thoughts became dominated by events like the cat that Ned had caught and skinned for the pot, or his own contribution to the frying pan—a snake—or his chances of using his pay for a fortnight's labour to buy an ounce of red Java tobacco, and whether he could get a page from the Bible for cigarette papers or would have to use the *Nippon Times* again. The Bible page was better, being thinner and of better quality, but either way the resultant smoke was awful, nearly knocking a man's tonsils through the back of his neck. Its virtue was that it made him forget he was hungry for ten minutes.

It was only with Terry that John occasionally relaxed his rule against remembering the past and its food. Even then they didn't hark back to exotic meals but to an even remoter time when they were small boys in their mother's maternity home and had been sent to bed each evening with a night-cap of whatever baby food she had been feeding to the newly-born at the time.

The two of them would squat in the dust of Changi and fill the heavy evening air with the familiar trade names:

'Bengers.'

'Farex.'

'Cow and Gate.'

'She always said it would make us grow into big strong men.'

'As we're surviving this lot, I reckon she was right.'

But when John looked at Terry he knew it wasn't physical strength that was keeping him alive but some spirit that refused to give in. His respect for his brother and the men like him went up with every day that passed.

About his own survival he was becoming less sure. As 1944 crawled to an end his mental and physical condition deteriorated. His boredom had become overpowering and a new pain had sprung up in the small of his back dominating even the continual discomfort of the septic scabies and ulcerated legs.

Then, soon after Christmas, when he was working on the gardens the pain shifted suddenly, searing down towards his groin and making him double up in agony. He thought perhaps it was an intensification of his usual dysentery, caused by the Christmas issue of palm oil and, when the attack had passed, he worked on. Then it happened again and he passed out.

The M.O. said the pain was renal colic, that one of his kidneys had been damaged, probably during the beating-up in Java, that stones were forming owing to the rice diet and that he would need an immediate operation to drain off the suppurating matter that was poisoning him.

John didn't like the M.O., a major, a cold fish who, like the other doctors in Changi, had seen too much unnecessary death and who, unlike most of the other doctors, reacted by becoming detached. All John's considerable individuality rebelled against the man's purely clinical attitude. But his dislike saved his life.

After the operation—and the camp hospitals now had anaesthetics—John became very seriously ill. While in Europe the Allies moved forward at speed, while the Germans retreated from Holland, while the Japanese suffered heavy losses of shipping, John lay in a coma, shaken by fever and rigors. His weight went down to six stone. Underneath the layers of unconsciousness he was aware of the pain in his loins and that he was losing a battle.

One night the medical orderly, Monty, called for the M.O.

'I wish you'd have a look at Dodd, sir. He's very bad.'

'I cannot understand,' said the major, 'why he's alive at all.'

Something stirred deep down behind the eyes of their patient and his lips moved.

'What did he say, Monty?'

'I think, sir, he said: "I'll show you, you bastard." '

He did. By June all of the fever and some of the pain had left him and his weight improved to six and a half stone.

Those last months of the war were nerve-racking for prisoners of the Japs. Outside their walls momentous things were happening and all they could do was to wait like sitting ducks for something, probably nasty, to happen to them.

John Dodd spent them being drawn by the cartoonist Ronald Searle, who had the next bed to his, and watching the Ambonese on the other side of the hut fight for his life.

Later to be famous, Searle was at that point merely an art student who considered the war as somebody's thoughtless way of holding up his career. He had survived a year on the Burma–Siam railway with one ambition: to hold a pencil in his hand again. Despite his emaciated condition and his legs which were so badly ulcerated that for a time it was thought they might have to be amputated, he drew ceaselessly, using as models John and the cats that spent their time wandering in and out of the huts before being popped into a stewpot. He was obviously unstoppable and made John conscious of his own lack of purpose.

The Ambonese was young, a member of the Dutch native forces, who seemed to have been sucked into the war without knowing why. His only aim was to get back to his wife and children whose photographs he would hold up for the other men to see. He had gangrene in both legs and it had spread too far for amputation to be useful. The stench of rotting flesh that emanated from his bed was appalling, but he had won the hearts of his fellow-patients by remaining alive long after the M.O. had said he possibly could. To them his struggle to stay alive became a symbol that mystically represented the fight going on in the outside world and it became important to them that he should see liberation. 'Hang on, Dutch. The war's nearly over,' became almost a catch-phrase. But on the day that the Japanese commandant surrendered to their own C.O., Dutch's bed was occupied by someone else. He had died in the night.

Liberation was a surprisingly painful business. Their liberators, men in smart clean uniforms, seemed so full of health, energy and confidence and bore—on the p.o.w.s' behalf—such a hatred of the Japanese that it seemed like an intrusion by an outsider on a family quarrel. Under their pitying scrutiny the men of Changi realised fully what wrecks they were and how badly fitted to cope with the lusty, transformed world that awaited them. John didn't mind the men so much, but his first sight of a

woman, a New Zealand war correspondent who came marching
sturdily into the hospital hut, sent him hiding under the blankets.

Then there were the terrible goodbyes to Ned, Joe and Rupe
who were being shipped off to Australia, and to Terry. Terry
had been judged fit enough to go straight back to England on a
hospital ship but John, whose weight had remained obstinately
at six stone seven, was to be carried on a stretcher by ship and
then by specially fitted hospital train for treatment at Bangalore.

They parted with a sense of finality. In Changi they had
become closer than ever before in their lives and they were never
to be quite so close again.

Laurens Van Der Post was to say that those who survived
places like Changi did so without spiritual or mental scars. It is
a statement that only a true aesthete could make.

Nevertheless there is something in it. If you survived Changi—
and it was a big if—you had known a purpose in life, even if
that purpose was survival itself. Among the 20,000 or so men
who were imprisoned there at one time or another there had
been very little mental illness and only three known suicides. If
you survived Changi you had seen human nature at its worst
but also at its very finest—an experience that can have far-
reaching effect.

The effect on John Dodd and, through him, on thousands of
other men was to be far-reaching indeed. But as he left Singapore once more he was aware of none of it.

He thought only that for over three years he had been bored,
very nearly to death.

CHAPTER NINE

TIME TO GO HOME

The R.A.F. intelligence officer going round the ward at the Bangalore hospital was a pleasant young man and only doing his job, which was to collect evidence of Japanese brutality for the War Crimes Trials about to start in Singapore, but he wasn't getting anywhere.

The physical evidence was all about him; on the bodies of the men in each bed; in the way they nestled luxuriously into the pillows and fingered the clean sheets as if still unable to believe in them, in the way their skin expanded visibly with every vitamin-packed meal, in the way they battened emotionally on the nurses, hardly allowing them out of their sight.

But the intelligence officer's notebook was empty. The men in the ward wanted one thing only—to go home. Anything likely to hold that up, even by a day, was anathema. Already it had taken too long. Already R.A.P.W.I. (Rehabilitation of Allied Prisoners of War and Internees) had been renamed Retain All Prisoners of War Indefinitely. Yes, they'd been starved continually, beaten up occasionally, and the Japs hadn't been much fun, but they weren't giving evidence about it if he didn't mind, they just wanted to go home.

It wasn't until he came to the bed of a Corporal J. S. Dodd that the intelligence officer struck oil and even then it wasn't exactly a gusher.

Like all the others, John felt he was in a heaven of comfort. Gradually all the pains he had taken for granted for so long were ebbing away, although the doctors warned him he would have to face an operation on his kidney when he got back to England. The cleanliness of the hospital was an almost sensual delight, and his eyes kept returning to the glass of ice-cold tomato juice and the bowl of fruit on the table by his bed as to a beautiful sculpture.

On his first venture with a walking stick into the hospital

grounds he had, by a delightful coincidence, bumped into Irene Symons recovering from her own internment. She was able to tell him that although the family had been split up, they had survived the war and were now gathering in Singapore.

In his pocket was a letter from his parents—who had now moved to the Isle of Wight—thanking God for his delivery. They had suffered awful anxiety. The Singapore holocaust had swallowed up both their boys who were posted as 'missing'. After a year they heard that Terry was a prisoner, but news of John's survival didn't come through until late 1943. That had been followed so closely by Anthony Eden's statement in the House of Commons about conditions for p.o.w.s under the Japanese saying: 'Our information is that their health is rapidly deteriorating and that a high percentage are seriously ill, and that there have been some thousands of deaths,' that their worry about their sons continued until they received their letters after the liberation.

John wanted to get back to England as much as anybody, but he couldn't. Amid this welter of good news there had been none of Marquita and Phiphine, and he knew that he would never rest until he could find out what had happened to them.

The Red Cross had done their best to locate them for him, but conditions in Java were against it. The revolutionary Republic of Indonesia had been proclaimed and saw the end of the war as its opportunity to throw off Dutch rule for good. British and Australian troops in Java not only had to disarm the Japs and return them to Japan, they also apparently had to deal with the nationalists until the Dutch, still recovering from German occupation, could return and take over. Fighting had broken out between the British and the Indonesians and the mad situation had developed in which the British were using the Japanese army to recapture towns like Bandoeng held by the nationalists.

John had spent most of his convalescence making enquiries as to how he could stay on in South-East Asia and get to Java to find the two women to whom he owed so much. He had been told it was impossible, but now the advent of the young intelligence officer gave him an idea.

'Do you mean to say,' John asked him, 'that if I give you something on the Japs I have to stay on and don't go home?'

The officer had heard this question a hundred times before. It

usually presaged a refusal to give evidence. He had also got used
to the apparent inability of these strange men to address him as
'sir'.

He said wearily: 'Well, Corporal, it might.'

'My bit of trouble happened in Java. Could I get back to
Java?'

The intelligence officer was prepared to fly him to the moon
if it meant getting some solid facts.

'I should think so,' he said, 'what happened?'

Basically, John was unwilling to tell him. He had no wish to
get back on the Japs. All that blood and terror had been pushed
to the back of his mind and he didn't want to resurrect it. But
he did want to get to Java.

'Well,' he said, reluctantly, 'some Japs there beat me up a bit
in 1942.'

Bit by bit, like pulling teeth, the intelligence officer got the
story out of him and became excited about it. 'You'll have to
come to Singapore, Corporal,' he said. 'When will you be fit to
travel?'

'Now,' said John.

The doctors were unwilling to let him go but John persisted
and eventually they gave way on condition that a medical
orderly travelled with him.

John was given priority V.I.P. treatment on the many-staged
journey and enjoyed it hugely, especially when high-ranking
officers had to give up their places to him and his medical
orderly.

In Singapore he was put into hospital immediately and allowed out for short spells which he divided between signing
affidavits of his evidence for the trials, visiting the camps in
which many of the women internees from Java were awaiting
rehabilitation, and pestering people at R.A.F. headquarters to
send him to Java.

The female camps were a revelation to him. It was a slim
hope that Marquita or Phiphine would be in any of them, but
he went nevertheless in the hope of finding someone who had
news of them. They contained thin, hopeless women and children of all nationalities who, having been separated from and
having no knowledge of husband, father and family for three
and a half years, had still not been reunited with them and now

probably never would be. John had a sharp pang of pity and identification with them when he saw that each one clutched a tattered box containing sometimes a needle and thread or rusty scissors or a bandage, things that had been of vital importance during the years under the Japs and which they still could not bear to let go. He'd had a similar box of such pathetic items himself and it had been a wrench to leave it behind in Bangalore. They would stare at him vaguely as he described Marquita and Phiphine over and over again and then shake their heads.

Despite his persistence he had no more luck at H.Q. The powers there were adamant in refusing to let him go to Java and every string he pulled, every persuasion he tried, couldn't shift them. Things were very bad in Java, they said, with Europeans being slaughtered by the hundred. They could not allow a recently released prisoner of war to go off and get himself killed straight away. There would be too much fuss in the newspapers back home. 'It would not,' they said, 'be good for morale.'

John knew the voice of doom when he heard it. That phrase had stifled at birth too many enterprises in Changi for him not to recognise it now.

Helpless and bitter, he realised he was doing no good.

It was time to go home.

PART THREE

WHAT A LIBERTY

CHAPTER TEN

ON THE RUN

Terry was the first of the family to greet John in England and he escorted his brother to their parents' house at Wootton Bridge on the Isle of Wight.

The Island was very nearly the same size and shape as Singapore, but on that cold January day it looked, in contrast, very white and grey.

The Dodds got off the bus and Terry pointed out the green-roofed bungalow that was now their home, then tactfully he turned and went for a walk while John went to greet his parents. Mrs. Dodd remembered that moment with emotion for the rest of her life. But it was to be one of the last completely happy days she had with her son for some time . . .

The p.o.w.s under the Japanese probably had a tougher war than anybody other than those in Nazi concentration camps. They had been bullied, starved and made to feel shame. Those who died had done so without even the small comfort belonging to soldiers in action that they were contributing to the cause of freedom.

The war had been very tough, but in many ways the peace was tougher.

They came home expecting, like released prisoners everywhere, that people and places would be the same: exactly as they had dreamed of them during those isolated years. Instead they found a new government, bomb devastation, American camps. Old girl friends had got married, some wives had been unfaithful, drinking companions had become respectable commuters. There was the constant irritation of people complaining about food rationing, queues and empty shop windows in what was, to the prisoners of war, a land flowing with milk and honey.

The few good things they had brought back from their suffering, the companionship and sense of knowing what was important in life and what wasn't, seemed to waste away in the general disillusion. Adapting to it all meant considerable mental acrobatics.

Some managed it better than others. Terry, for instance, came back at the time when the country was still aflame with what the Japs had done to 'our poor boys'. Cheering, weeping crowds crammed the dockside to welcome his ship. Distinguishable, as all of them were, by the yellow of his skin from the anti-malarial doses of mepacrine, enthusiasm followed him everywhere. People gave up their seats on buses, porters carried his luggage and refused the tip. He went to a rehabilitation centre—all this helped to lubricate his way into civilian life and within a comparatively short space of time he had married a very nice girl and settled down.

But for John, a more turbulent character, those two years after his return to England were dreadful.

In the first place he came back too late. His yellow colour had had time to fade and his weight to return in Singapore and anyway the first wave of enthusiasm had gone. The British were beginning to turn their backs on the war and face the long haul to win the peace.

He felt the natural but unreasonable resentment that his parents had moved from Southport which he knew and where he had friends, to the alien, unwelcoming hills of the Isle of Wight. He felt a bitterness, too, at the result of the General Election which had been held before he and the others had been released. Winston Churchill had been a name that brightened the worst 'borehole' and John felt that there had been ingratitude to the man who had helped to keep hope alive in places like Changi.

Mrs. Dodd found her son 'coarsened'. Considering everything it's difficult to know what else she could have expected. Nevertheless her son's new restlessness and perverse sense of humour came as a shock. In Wootton Bridge society he stood out with the impact of a Heathcliff in a Jane Austen drawing-room. They were worlds apart, these people who found clothes rationing irksome, and the man who had spent three years in a G-string. He was impatient of their gossip and incapable, it seemed, of sharing their proper grief when one of their number died full of years and in bed. He appeared over-fond of gambling.

Neither could they understand his humour. He was actually seen in Ryde (hanging on to a lamp-post and shouting with laughter at a Blood Transfusion Service van. Painted on its side was the slogan: 'It's Your Blood We're After.' He couldn't explain that suddenly the neat, grey shops had disappeared, and he was back near the latrines of Changi, out of sight of the perimeter guards, swinging his arm in wild circles to induce enough blood to his finger so that when he pricked it some drops would fall to the ground—the signal for his fellow punters, Australians of course, to loose the racing bugs. 'It's Your Blood We're After'—the humour and a little of the pity of it had burst loose and he had laughed until he sobbed.

Over everything hung his worry for Marquita and Phiphine. He wrote letter after letter to them through the Red Cross and pestered that valuable organisation time and again to try and discover their address. The silence seemed ominous and drove him distracted.

Then, in March 1946, a parcel arrived for him containing the R.A.F. flag from Seletar, Smudge's watch and a letter from Marquita. She had, she said, received one of his letters through the Red Cross and nearly dropped dead with shock. They thought he had been killed. An officer in the Japanese Kempei Tai had told them so, and when he didn't turn up immediately after liberation they had become sure of it. Five months later Phiphine had married. She herself was returning to France to try to find her husband. They were in good health and he wasn't to worry.

So that was the end of it. Carefully John put away the letter, the flag and the watch and set the war behind him, determined not to think of it again. It had meant five lost years and that was all.

In April he went into the R.A.F. Hospital at Cosford to have a stone 'as big as a golf ball', so the surgeon described it, taken from his kidney. He was told that he could regard himself as partially disabled, would receive a small pension accordingly, and would need further treatment and continual check-ups, probably for the rest of his life.

Just over a week later he clambered carefully out of bed, dressed himself and crept out of the ward. He managed to limp to the main road and get himself a lift to Chester racecourse. He was so tired that he had to sit on the grass to watch the races, in which not a single horse he'd backed won. Somehow he staggered back to the hospital with a high temperature to face the fury of the ward sister. He was unrepentant. 'Sister,' he said, 'I've missed too many spring days.'

This impatience to get back lost time coloured everything he did. One day, recuperating in the Isle of Wight, he heard a phrase that expressed it perfectly. His mother, a devout Methodist, had persuaded him to accompany her to church, hoping that God would grant him—and herself—some peace. She didn't repeat the invitation. Tied to a pew during a sermon that bored him, John dropped his hymn book, kicked his feet, coughed and pervaded restlessness through the entire congregation. But he carried away with him a quotation from the Book of Joel: 'I will restore to you the years that the locust hath eaten.'

'The years the locust hath eaten...' The words summed up his war, his useless, wasted war, with a fearful aptness, and drummed through his mind.

On the morning of Sunday, October 13, 1946, the wireless was on in the Dodd household where John, having refused to accompany his parents to church, was alone half-listening to a programme of music. Its end heralded the usual Sunday morning religious hour and John was about to switch off when the announcer declared that there would now be a talk by the Right Reverend Leonard Wilson, Bishop of Singapore.

Immediately John was interested. As he knew, the Bishop had been interned in the civilian section of Changi with three thousand men, women and children. Then, for no apparent reason, the Japanese had taken him and sixty other internees out of Changi and put them into Outram Road Gaol, Kempei Tai headquarters, for questioning.

To everyone in Changi the words 'Outram Road' had meant the ultimate in terror. Any p.o.w. who attracted the Japanese' particular disfavour, owning a secret radio for instance, was marched off there. Few returned. Those who did were never quite the same again, and it was gathered from their condition that, compared to Outram Road, Changi was a bed of luxury.

Intrigued, John waited to hear what a survivor of Outram Road would have to say.

The Bishop didn't dwell on the torture, or the hunger, or his tormentors who had tried to make him deny his faith. He had looked on the Japs as children, and would not hate them. His theme was God . . . 'I remember Archbishop Temple in one of his books, writing that if we pray for any particular virtue, whether it be patience, or courage, or love, one of the answers that God gives us is an opportunity for exercising that virtue. After my first beating I was almost afraid to pray for courage lest I should have another opportunity of exercising it; but my unspoken prayer was there, and without God's help I doubt whether I would have come through . . .'

The ordeal had enhanced the Bishop's belief. He had, he said, seen God in the red flame tree outside the tiny window at the back of the overcrowded cell and in one of his fellow-prisoners, a Chinese, who had asked to be baptised . . . 'and I baptised him in the only water available, a lavatory basin at the back of the cell.'

The Bishop's next words came over to John with an especial clarity. 'I know what I say is true, not just because the Bible says so, or because the Church has told us, but because I have experienced it myself; I know that whether you are despondent or in joy, whether you are apathetic or full of enthusiasm, there is available for you, at this moment, the whole life of God with its victory over sin and pain and death.'

Even the words of the final blessing, 'The peace of God which passeth all understanding . . .' which John had heard a hundred times before without really listening to them, came over with a new freshness and did indeed remain with him for a long time after that.

But the immediate impact on him was uncomfortable. He could identify with an experience under the Japanese that had been not unlike his own; what impressed him was the Bishop's total lack of bitterness, and his emergence from the war with something that he, John, didn't have. Just as when he'd tried reading the New Testament in the jungle, he was aware of something being demanded of him that he was not prepared to give. Now, as then, he pushed it to the back of his mind, where it remained like an irritant, increasing his dissatisfaction and impatience.

Like a man on the run, he went through a succession of cars which he drove fast.

One of the few people he got on well with in Wootton Bridge at that time was a teenager, John Wadham, whose grandmother was one of Mrs. Dodd's fellow-members of the Methodist Women's Bright Hour—a title that made John snort when he heard it. John Wadham was a quiet boy and a keen Christian, and his parents looked askance at his admiration for John Dodd. But to the younger John the elder brought a breath of fresh air into the rather enclosed community—even if that breath occasionally had the force of a hurricane. Their relationship at that time rested almost entirely on cars.

Young John watched fascinated, as John Dodd bought car after second-hand car, extolling the virtues of each and then, when its defects became apparent, selling it and getting another. Through the ice and fog of that winter he drove them all at breakneck speed. Nothing was allowed to hold him up. One night, racing back to the Isle of Wight through the New Forest, his latest car skidded on a patch of ice and overturned. Hanging upside down, John tutted impatiently: 'We'll never get the last ferry at this rate,' scrambled out, pushed the car right way up, got in and drove off again.

His attitude to girls was rather like his attitude to engines, and he changed them just as fast. Like other returned war prisoners he'd had the feeling in captivity that the entire female population of England was being monopolised by other men, and that now it was his turn to catch up. He felt a need to be in their company, to command their attention, explain himself to them. Mrs. Dodd found a series of strange, bewildered young women in her sitting-room who told her that her son had virtually pounced on them, saying: 'For God's sake, let me talk to you,' and had then added to their surprise by doing just that.

But, like cars, each girl seemed to fail him. Sooner or later they would say something shallow and crass, and be turned in for the next model.

Avery's, the makers of weighing machines that he'd worked for pre-war, offered him the job of sales representative in the Isle of Wight. He'd hoped that something else would come along; although Wootton Bridge might not believe it, he knew that, schooled by the jungle and the Japs, he *did* have patience and an accumulated knowledge of men that could surely be put to use somehow, somewhere.

But nothing else turned up so John put his pent-up energy into selling scales. Having flogged suspect goods to the guards of Changi, selling reputable stuff to British shopkeepers was child's play to him. Soon nearly every shop, business and factory on the Island that could possibly use Avery's products, and even some that couldn't, found themselves ordering the equipment.

What would have happened to him if he'd gone on like this is anybody's guess. He was certainly ripe for disaster. But, just as he'd met Marquita at the point where he was going to need her most, he now met Alyson, and in much the same way.

It was April Fool's Day, 1947, and he was driving fast, as usual, through Ryde in his latest car, a green Morris coupé, with his dog Skipper in the back. Walking towards him along the pavement by the Ryde cemetery he spotted an unusually attractive girl. The coupé jolted to a stop and John went into the old routine of pretending to ask for directions.

War work had taken Alyson to the Isle of Wight as a secretary to Saunders Roe, the aircraft firm, a job she enjoyed and held down with efficiency. Even more outstanding than her looks was her calm. At twenty-two she had a deep steadiness that seemed to slow down the most hectic of situations and people. She was exceptionally shy and not at all the sort of girl to be picked up by thirty-year-old salesmen in green cars; besides which her life on that April day was planned and settled. There was another John, a nice, uncomplicated red-haired young man who wrote poetry and whom she had every intention of marrying.

It's a measure of John's persuasion that he induced her to go out with him on the following Thursday.

He took her to Brading Down to a viewpoint overlooking the countryside and there, typically, he talked and she listened. She didn't really like him very much. She thought he was too full of himself but, as she confessed to her friends at work the next day: 'There was something about the brute.'

The evening ended in mild disaster when they found that John's dog had wandered away unheeded and couldn't be found. They spent an hour before dark roaming round, whistling and shouting 'Skipper', but eventually had to leave without him. (Early the next morning John went back and found the dog.)

It needed all Alyson's calm to cope with the disruption John brought into her life. Without quite knowing why she allowed him to take her out fairly regularly. She found him argumentative, sometimes infuriating and always restless, but even then she recognised something that potentially was of great value in him. At the end of six months she found, to her surprise, that she was torn between the two men who were courting her.

She was facing a spiritual crisis of her own just then. A group of friends at Saunders Roe had interested her in Christianity and, partly to discover more, and partly to find help with her dilemma, she began to attend a different church or religious meeting every Sunday. John tagged along, too, wanting Alyson's company.

In the autumn he invited her to join him on a brief holiday by car in the Lake District. Believing it would resolve her feelings towards him one way or the other, she accepted.

It was a disaster.

Alyson was enchanted by the mountains with their falls and lakes and didn't care how long it took or how lost they became as long as they saw the countryside. John, as always, wanted a definite destination to get to as fast as possible, and he found the vagaries of the hilly tracks and Alyson's casual map-reading insufferable.

'Where are we going?' he asked as they turned the car down a particularly beautiful lane.

'I don't know,' said Alyson, vaguely. 'It's on the map.'

A few minutes later they found the way barred by a cattle gate. John loathed gates; like petty bureaucracy they reminded him of Changi and impeded his progress—a cardinal sin in the animate and inanimate. He flung out of the car, shoved the gate open, stamped back to the car, roared it through and hurled himself out to close the gate again.

In another few minutes they came to a stream in full flood, too deep to be forded.

Alyson reminded herself of the years the locust had eaten—it was a phrase she had come to know well—and kept her patience as John crashed the gears to turn the car round and face the gate again. But on the journey home they quarrelled so badly that when they reached Stratford-on-Avon, where rooms had been reserved for them, Alyson went in to the Lamb Hotel alone while John spent the night, fuming and uncomfortable, in the car outside.

The holiday had resolved things for Alyson, however. Cross as she was that night, she realised that this exasperating John was the man she would marry, but that she couldn't marry him as he was.

Gritting her teeth, she got down on her knees and prayed for him.

Good Friday, March 26, 1948, found them both crammed into the Commodore cinema in Ryde, listening to a young singing group heralding the arrival of the Billy Graham team on one of its crusades. The auditorium was packed and hot. Those who couldn't get seats were standing down the sides and at the back. Alyson, determined to experience everything in her ever-growing faith, had gone and taken John along with her.

As it happened Billy Graham himself was ill and in his place as speaker stood a young naval chaplain. Afterwards they were unable to remember his name or exactly what he'd said except that he'd spoken gently and as if Jesus had been crucified and had risen only the week before. A hush fell over the auditorium and Alyson found peace of mind for the first time in a year. Like the quotation from *Dr. Zhivago*: 'And then, into this tasteless heap of gold and marble, He came, light-footed and clothed in light, with his marked humanity, his deliberate Galilean provincialism, and from that moment there were neither god nor peoples, there was only man . . .'

At the end the chaplain looked at his still audience and asked those who wished to give witness to their new-found faith to come up to the stage. Breaking out of its trance, the crowd began to surge forward. John saw young John Wadham going steadily along in the crush. Then, with a shock, he felt Alyson get up from beside him and step over his feet to join the procession moving up the aisle. Nobody knew better than he what it must have cost the retiring Alyson to make so public and dramatic a declaration. He was moved by her gesture, he even felt the urge to join her, but he fought it down. He didn't need God. If he could get through the jungle, torture and Changi without God, he could surely get along without him now.

He remained obstinately in his seat.

Later that year he took Alyson, his father and his mother to Paris to pay a surprise call on Marquita. They had corresponded regularly and he knew that Marquita had found her husband but that the war had been too great an interval for the marriage and they had agreed to separate.

She was exactly the same, looking a little more worn perhaps, but with the same vitality and disregard for authority. She shouted with delight on seeing John and ushered them all into the sitting-room of her flat, the floor of which was littered with banknotes. She was, she explained, busy sewing them into a corset in order to smuggle the money into Italy.

'You see I have this dear friend in Java who is a stateless refugee and the French government won't allow him into the country. But I have been in touch with some bandits in Italy and I'm going to pay them to smuggle him across the border.'

She saw no difference in doing in peacetime what she had done for John and others in wartime and was quite as prepared to flout the Italian and French governments as she had been to flout the Japanese. When Marquita made a friend smaller loyalties went by the board.

Inevitably they talked of the war. Some time after John's capture Martin, the plantation owner, was interned, leaving Marquita and Phiphine unprotected among the native workers who had grown hostile. 'Then that bitch, Martin's wife, went off with all the food and my brooch—Martin returned it to me after the war. We nearly starved. We had to go into the jungle and find roots and fungi to eat.'

Somehow they had got back to Batavia and persuaded the Japanese to give Marquita back her house.

'I became great friends with an officer in the Kempei Tai who was very good to us—not all Japanese are bad you know, Johnny.'

It was through this officer that they had been informed of John's progress. He had told them that John was being brought to Batavia by train and Phiphine had gone down to the railway sidings every day to wave at every train that passed.

From the same source they had learned that if they waited on the road to the docks they could probably see John being taken on one of the work parties. 'Do you remember, Johnny, how you leaped up? And how they beat you? It was terrible.'

She had actually got plans under way to effect John's rescue, when the Kempei Tai officer told her that he had been moved to Singapore.

'Because he had been so honest with us, we believed him when he said you were dead.'

Like a magnet her bungalow in Batavia had attracted anybody in danger from the Japanese authorities. Towards the end of the war she was concealing an Englishman, a German and a Japanese deserter, all of whom were on excellent terms with each other.

'Then one day a Jap officer I'd never seen before forced his way through my door. He was drunk and thought the place was a brothel—the Japs aren't used to women owning their own houses.

'I was very cross and worried that he would see those poor boys I was hiding, so I hit him on the head with a heavy table lamp that was standing in the hall. It broke, which made me very, very cross. I rang up my friend in the Kempei Tai and said: "If one of your men broke into my house and made himself unpleasant, would I be safe in knocking him out?"

'He said: "Indeed you would."

'I said: "Good. I've just done it. Will you send someone to please carry him away?" '

It was a marvellous day, and during the course of it Alyson and Marquita became firm friends. Outwardly very different, perhaps it was their faith in God that they had in common; Alyson's conversion was now complete and Marquita had always been a devout, if unconventional, Catholic.

'Miracles?' she said, shortly before they left. 'Of course there are miracles. One day on the Martin plantation when Phiphine and I were starving and out grubbing for roots to eat, I got down on my knees and said: "God, we are starving and must have meat. And please, God, we want it now." Then I sat back and waited.

'Almost at once a huge bird came flying overhead carrying a chicken in its beak. As it came near it dropped it—only a few yards away from me. Of course there are miracles, and of course there is a God.'

John returned to the Isle of Wight still with the odd feeling of being hunted. It seemed that wherever he turned somebody was trying to attract his attention to God. If he turned on the wireless the Bishop of Singapore was talking about God, the name was never long off the lips of his mother, Alyson and John Wadham, and it had pursued him even to Paris.

Then one day—and he can't even remember which day it was—it was all over. The long fight against God finished in the discovery that he had been fighting himself while God, absolute, stood waiting for the dust to settle. He saw that the Galilean had dragged his cross up the hill to Calvary for the sake of John Dodd as much as for everybody else.

Suddenly there was meaning in his life. There had been purpose in the impulse that sent him flying to take cover behind the ship's propeller on the *Empire Star*, there had been purpose in preserving him in the jungle, from the Japanese, in the hold of the Java hulk, in Changi. He couldn't imagine what that purpose was, knowing himself no better than the men who had died, but that it was there he had no doubt.

Thus John became a Christian. It was a switch of such magnitude that, with the possible exception of Alyson, it surprised everyone who knew him. In his own deathless phrase: 'It was like an Everton supporter becoming a Liverpool fan.'

CHAPTER ELEVEN

ALL THINGS NEW

In April 1949, Mr. Dodd died, slipping out of life as unostentatiously as he had lived it. He had been a quiet undemanding man whose great loves had been the countryside, his garden and choral music, but John had got to know him better since returning from the war. His strong bass voice was heard for the last time in the village chapel that Easter Sunday, the day before his death.

It was a personal tragedy that was not helped by the general feeling of depression, the strikes and the renewal of war in Korea. It left Mrs. Dodd leaning heavily on the shoulders of her elder son.

But, despite his sadness for his father, the austerity years that made life so dingy for most people in Britain went by John in vivid colours. Alyson had told him that the experience of conversion was like the sensation of flying. And so it was. Everything seemed changed and fresh. Yet it was not escapism. Bonhoeffer, who was executed in a concentration camp, had said: 'In Christ we are offered the possibility of knowing the reality of God and the reality of the world, but not the one without the other.' John saw life clearly, but he saw it as having meaning and hope.

Luckily he had around him Christians like Alyson, his mother and John Wadham, who accepted religion as part of everyday life and were neither surprised nor embarrassed when he talked about it. He was grateful for this—to have made such a discovery among uncomfortable, unreceptive people would have been like Alexander Fleming having to keep quiet about penicillin.

He found too that among the Christian community of the Isle of Wight there were outstanding people. He and Alyson were particularly drawn to Tom Foinette, Methodist minister at Ryde, who had become as thin as a lath through neglect of himself and work for others.

It was to Tom Foinette that John went, voracious for work that would serve both God and his fellow-man. He'd found meaning, but he still lacked purpose. It seemed impossible that he should have come through the war merely to sell weighing machines.

Tom Foinette *had* a job for him. In Havenstreet, a sprawling village near the centre of the Island, was an old, deserted chapel. Havenstreet had no Sunday School. How would John like to start up a Sunday School in Havenstreet?

The idea of himself as a Sunday School teacher made John roar with laughter and all the way home he kept grinning at the thought of what Ned and Rupe and all his other fellow-gamblers in Changi would have said. But if that was what God via Tom Foinette wanted, it was okay by him. He got cracking the next day.

It's doubtful if Havenstreet ever quite knew what hit it. John had become interested in the Wootton Bridge youth club and press-ganged some of its more enthusiastic members, as well as Alyson and John Wadham, into helping him clean up the chapel. Out of a clear blue sky they swooped into the sleepy stillness of the place, scraping away bird droppings, scrubbing, polishing, dusting and painting until the old two-storey building was shining and ready for business. Immediately John went out to drum it up.

He visited every house, farm and isolated cottage in that far-flung village, selling Sunday School as enthusiastically as he sold scales. 'Don't worry about transport,' he reassured the mothers in their lonely cottages, 'there will be a door-to-door service.'

He hired a Bedford van and every Sunday made a circular tour of the area picking up all the children whose homes were too far away to allow them to make it under their own steam. It became a Sabbath morning occasion to see the van, crammed with children, whizzing along the lanes, and to catch a burst of 'Onward Christian Soldiers' as it went past, rendered by a lot of high trebles and one deep baritone—John, like Winston Churchill, believed in hymns with some go in them. At the chapel it would stop and disgorge an incredible number of children and

John, like a large Pied Piper, would shepherd his flock inside.

The pattern for all the Sundays was set by the first. John gave the children short, punchy stories from the Bible and then they would all swing into a rousing hymn. The only element of criticism came from a minute five-year-old called Yvonne. 'You don't sing,' she told John sternly after the first hymn. 'You croaks.'

After the final prayer there was a pause and John waited, a little uneasily, for the children's reaction. Again Yvonne acted as spokesman. Sidling up to John, she nudged him in the knee with her elbow. 'All right,' she said, 'you're on.'

He ran the Sunday School at Havenstreet for the next ten years.

Keeping up his quota of selling for Avery's, running the Sunday School and the youth club were not enough for him. He joined the Christian Businessmen's Association and accompanied Alyson to Bible classes—another step that would have astounded Ned and Rupe. But these were no ordinary Bible classes run by no ordinary man.

Percy Rolf was, and still is, a distinguished solicitor in Ryde. He not only prepared the brief that eventually got Alfred Hinds out of prison but, more difficult, he convinced that gentleman that not all lawyers are crooks. He has an intensely logical mind which he applied to the Bible, on which he was an authority, questioning everything and finding satisfactory answers. Under his tuition the book came alive.

He formed a warm friendship with John Dodd whom he recognised as having been always spiritually aware, even when he was struggling against that awareness. His pity was reserved for those 'who are really in the devil's clutches, who endure no torment, who exist on a purely material level, who are no more than the clay from which they came and to which they will return'.

It was an uncompromising view of Christianity and later the faith of John and Alyson and John Wadham too, was to change in emphasis, becoming more liberal. But what Percy Rolf did for them was to put their first effervescence of belief on to a stable basis that could withstand all the inevitable doubts to come.

Alyson watched with approval as John's interests turned away from himself and towards other people. By 1958 he had another project in view. Tom Foinette had visited him one day and said: 'Have you ever thought of becoming a prison visitor?'

John hadn't, but began thinking about it.

He was discussing the idea with Alyson one day, wondering how he was going to fit everything in because, as he said, in September he was due to go on a special course at Avery's Birmingham factory.

'You can't go,' said Alyson suddenly.

'Why not?'

Alyson announced her decision calmly. 'We're getting married then,' she said.

Their wedding was on September 1, 1951, and they spent their honeymoon first at a tennis tournament and then at a succession of festival cricket matches where John alternately exhorted and barracked the players with the abandon of a football fan. Alyson, a little to her own surprise, found that she didn't mind at all.

Five months later John Dodd walked up to the gates of Parkhurst prison for the first time.

CHAPTER TWELVE

ET IN HADES EGO...

Originally built as a hospital for the wounded during the Napoleonic wars, Parkhurst has been a prison for habitual male offenders for one hundred years. Six hundred and eighty of them were kept inside its drab, hostile walls. Despite the difference in size, it reminded John irresistibly of the native gaol in Batavia where his fellow-prisoners had begun to die.

At the great iron gate in the wall he was met by the prison chaplain and introduced to the officers on the gate as a new prison visitor. There was a moment while they scanned his face, committing it to memory, then he was allowed to walk on to the next iron gate leading into the huge complex itself, where the same little ceremony was conducted.

Gate after gate, door after door clanged to behind him, stopping up his way back as he walked along reverberating landings to reach the men who had been allocated to him for visiting. Everything moved with implacable precision. Men had been being locked away here so long that it had become humdrum procedure and the men themselves mere components in a factory.

The prison was divided into three 'halls'. Each landing was designated by a number and each cell carried the number of its landing and its own number. They were all exactly the same, being lit by the light from a small barred window high and deep in the wall, and containing a bed, a table, one chair, a slop-bucket and a man.

His meeting with the first inmate on his list was not propitious. The number outside the cell declared it to be B.3.26. 'Smith,' said the chaplain, 'I'd like you to meet your new visitor, Mr. Dodd.'

Smith, who had been lying down on his bed reading the *Daily Graphic* when the two men entered, remained lying down and went on reading the *Daily Graphic*.

'I'll leave you two to get better acquainted,' said the chaplain and hurried off.

John remained standing at the door for a moment and then sat down on the only chair.

'It's a cold day,' he said, brightly.

Smith went on reading.

'Sad about the King,' said John.

There was more silence, broken only by the rustle as Smith turned a page of his newspaper.

A prison visitor is not allowed to see his visitee's record nor carry out any commissions for him outside, neither is he encouraged to discuss politics, religion or the circumstances of the man's conviction.

In desperation John turned to sport.

'Who's going to win the Cup this year?' he asked.

Silence.

John decided that any man who couldn't respond to that question wouldn't respond to anything, so he left.

'Are you sure that man wanted a visitor?' he asked the chaplian as they walked on.

'Oh yes, Smith made his application all right.'

But although John went back once more, Smith of B.3.26 remained silently just Smith of B.3.26

The second cell held no warmer welcome to begin with although it contained one of the most spectacular men John ever met in prison and one who had a great bearing on his future.

He was as tall and thin as John himself and sat on a chair, studying a heap of papers spread out on the bed.

'Do you know anything about this lot?' he demanded as John came in.

John looked closely at the papers; they were a correspondence course in advanced accountancy for a company secretary's exam. By virtue of his job John knew something of accountancy, but this was beyond him.

'I'm afraid not.'

'Then shove off.'

It was typical of John that he began to roar with laughter—his lack of success as a prison visitor struck him as funny.

The man looked surprised, as if hearing an unaccustomed

sound, and then said grudgingly: 'I suppose you'd better sit down.'

By the time John left, forty-five minutes later, he and Bob Tullett had become friends, and in time they came to know each other well.

Bob was a strangely mixed man; of high intelligence, he was a con-man par excellence with a golden tongue that could draw money from a miser's purse. His father had died young, leaving Bob to be brought up by a strong-willed mother and some uncles, one of whom thought it amusing to teach the boy to drink whisky. By the time he was nineteen Bob was drinking a bottle a day and couldn't do without it.

Desperately in need of money to buy whisky, he found he had a talent for tricking people out of it, which was easier and bought more bottles than working for it.

By the age of twenty-one he had already done the round of Approved School and Borstal and was starting his first prison stretch ... he was taken into the usual prison reception room for the symbolic ritual of being stripped of his own clothes, bathed and dressed in coarse prison uniform.

'Then they take you and lock you alone in your cell, and if they'd only come to you then and say: "Son, you've had a taste—now hop it," you'd run straight back to your mother and never go wrong again.'

In fact you wouldn't—not if you were Bob Tullett. The old warder who released him at the end of that first term knew better. 'See you soon,' he said, cracking the weary old joke that is no joke at all.

Bob ignored him. He had every intention of going straight and had lost the craving for whisky.

But this is how prison perpetuates its own myth. Bob had stopped drinking in prison because there was no drink to be had. Outside, pressed by a hundred problems, every pub had called to him as relentlessly as the Sirens sang to Odysseus.

Within three months he was back in prison. On release the same thing happened. Out, then back, out, back. By the time John discovered him in Parkhurst he had qualified for P.D.

Preventive Detention had been re-introduced in an altered form by the Criminal Justice Act 1948 and was detested among criminals, not only because of the time it carried—anything from five to fourteen years—but because it was felt to be unfair. A man qualified for P.D. because he had a long record of crimes for which he had already served prison sentences. If the record was bad enough he could steal as little as two shillings and be sent down for ten years. It was a bitterly resented form of paying twice, particularly since it punished most the alcoholics, the inadequates and the homosexuals who had shown themselves incapable of staying out of prison.

In his long prison career nobody had yet discovered that Bob Tullett was an alcoholic. He didn't know it himself; conning to get money for drink and going to prison for conning was just the way life had worked out for him and he was hardened to it. When, this last time, he had been sentenced to seven years, he had merely looked the judge in the eye and said, pretending a hardness he did not feel: 'Is that the best you can do?'

He had applied to take the correspondence course in accountancy merely to make him a better con-man when he came out. The primary and intermediate papers had been child's play for him, but he was having difficulty with the advanced course, so he'd applied for a prison visitor or, as he put it, a 'mug', to help him. That was how the human race divided itself to Bob at that time—into mugs and con-men.

Fate had played a nasty trick on the occupant of C.2.14, the next cell on John's list. It had deformed him, hunching his shoulders, and set on them an ugly head that was not enhanced by a prison haircut. As a final touch he had bad breath. He was the most unprepossessing man John had ever seen.

Yet Claud's welcome was the most sociable so far, almost pathetic. He insisted that John sit on the bed while he himself took the hard chair, poured half his mug of tea, which had just been delivered, into a jam jar for John, and even offered him half his supper—two slices of bread and margarine. He talked and listened with a frenetic eagerness that argued a loneliness uncommon even in this isolated place.

There were moments when he reminded John of Ben Gunn and others when an expression or movement took John back to the war years. He was puzzled by this for a while until he realised that Claud reminded him of a homosexual in Changi.

By contrast, Scouse Jones in C.4.36, was normality itself. A stocky man who looked older than his forty-two years, he had endured a wretched, poverty-stricken childhood in Liverpool with a drunken father and a timid, frightened mother. He had Gothic early memories of his father coming home from the pub and kicking his mother unconscious.

Scouse had become a burglar almost as a matter of course; it had seemed the only short-term method of alleviating the poverty that tethered him to the slum.

He had spent more years in prison than he had out of it; the crime that qualified him for P.D. had been committed with a mate, a fellow-burglar who had got away while Scouse struggled in the arms of the police. The police had put pressure on Scouse to find out his accomplice's name, but Scouse's code of ethics would not allow him to split. At his trial he had asked for seventy-seven other cases of burglary to be taken into consideration, eleven of them committed in the same night in the same Liverpool street—he'd reckoned himself fortunate in getting away with only ten years P.D. He showed no inclination to go straight on release and was operating in Parkhurst as a bookmaker and tobacco baron.

He and John liked each other at once and spent the first interview talking football until it was eight o'clock, time for the night staff to come on and John to go.

John Dodd walked out of the prison a thoughtful man. His three hours in Parkhurst had swept away the seven years since Changi as if they'd never been and he was back again, reliving the fear and boredom.

Not normally a fanciful man, he'd experienced in Parkhurst an overwhelming sense of *déjà vu*, brought on by the look in the eyes of Bob Tullett and Scouse Jones as they'd asked him for a smoke—he'd given up cigarettes and couldn't help them—by the way Claud had looked at his supper of bread and marge, by the old memory of being cut off from the outside world as surely as if they were all encapsulated in space.

For better or worse he was involved with those men, not because he was sorry for them—it went deeper than that—but because down to the marrow of his bones he knew how they felt.

CHAPTER THIRTEEN

INSIDE AND OUT

Where most prison visitors made their visits once a week, John went twice, impelled by this extraordinary sense of recognition.

His consistency was valuable to men who, sometimes with justice, felt that they had been let down from birth. He was reminded again and again of the jungle as men like Bob Tullett stretched out their hand for his friendship and then drew back, afraid of trusting him; much as the monkeys had stretched out a wary paw for fruit.

Their mistrust became understandable as, gradually, they allowed him to come close and he discovered the common factor in their varied lives—a deprived childhood. There were times when their stories of neglect, rejection and cruelty, even when taken with a pinch of salt, made John wonder how some children survive at all.

Even as his list grew to take in other men that denominator remained appallingly constant.

The childhood of Jack Long in A.3.22, for instance, was typical in its poverty and twisted development. He came from the sort of family which considered any attempt to abide by the law as a sign of degeneracy and had taken to crime as a matter of course. He had married a wife from the same mould and brought up his children in the tradition. His stretch in Parkhurst had been for knocking down the tally man when he called and, with his eldest son, tying the man up, stealing his takings and going off on the spree.

Despite all this there was a sort of innocence about him that John found both pathetic and likeable.

Out of all the men that John eventually got to know well in Parkhurst, only one came from an apparently normal home— Percy Draper. John liked Percy very much—nobody could help it—but the man puzzled him. He wasn't too bright, but he was very gentle and talked lovingly for hours about his childhood in

Lincolnshire with affectionate parents. This seemed to be borne out by the fact that Percy was about the only prisoner who got regular letters from home. Yet from puberty onwards this apparently adjusted boy had committed an ever-increasing number of petty thefts, leaving so many clues that the police never had any difficulty in picking him up.

John wondered at a system which spent a lot of money in keeping Percy in prison and none at all on discovering *why* he was there.

In those days John felt that his mission was to convert the men in Parkhurst. This wasn't purely evangelistic zeal: having been desperate himself, and having been rescued by a realisation of the presence of God, he badly wanted to dispel the isolation of each cell in the same way.

He was prepared, despite what the Prison Commissioners might say, to bring the conversation round to religion himself if necessary. It rarely was. With all the time in the world to dwell on things that hadn't concerned them at all outside, the men almost invariably brought the subject up themselves. 'What do you think the point of it all is, John?' he was asked over and over, and John would tell them simply what had happened to him. His approach was so matter-of-fact and unembarrassed that quite frequently men who were usually uncomfortable discussing religion would ask him to say a prayer before he left.

But even at that time he realised he was treading delicate ground. Prison gives a distorted image of religion as of so much else. Often a man equates the church with the establishment that is punishing him and, bitterly, adds God to the long list of people whom he has 'let down'.

Or else the loneliness and fear act on him to bring him literally to his knees. God, he thinks, may have been the missing piece in his life's puzzle. Just fit God in and all will be well.

'Prison conversion' has become suspect, especially among prison officers who had seen more than enough men go out breathing spiritual fire on discharge, only to be re-admitted a few months later having found that a profession of faith does not automatically solve problems.

John was fortunate that, as a prison visitor and a Methodist, he wasn't regarded as part of the prison establishment. But he was concerned at the facile approach of men like Claud to religion. Claud had 'seen the light' while in Parkhurst and kept insisting: 'When I come out this time I'll be all right.'

John now knew what Claud was inside for—prison rumour being as efficient and fast as borehole in Changi. Life-long burglars, pickpockets and con men were quick to tell him about 'that nasty little bastard in C.2.14'. Claud, apparently, had a long record of sexual assault against small boys.

This knowledge, combined with Claud's appearance, proved the biggest challenge John's Christianity had encountered so far. But he was determined to overcome his natural revulsion and treat Claud exactly as he treated the others. And actually, after one evening in which Claud told him about his crimes and the compulsion, guilt and terror that went with them, it wasn't quite so difficult.

About this time the evangelical film 'Oiltown U.S.A.' was being shown in Parkhurst and making a big impact. To the men who had been exposed to John's considerable personality the effect was decisive. One after the other Scouse the burglar, Jack Long the knocker-down of tally men, and the gentle Percy were converted, and changed almost overnight into happier, more confident men.

Bob Tullett, on the other hand, could neither take Christianity nor leave it alone. He had refused to see 'Oiltown' but would spend hours questioning John closely and often offensively about the Bible. It intrigued him that John, whom he respected, should believe in what Bob had always regarded as a fairytale. Eventually he reduced everything down to a basic alternative.

'Either this Jesus was what he said he was, right?'

'Right.'

'Or he was the biggest con man who ever walked the face of the earth. Right?'

'Right.'

There were times when John wondered in which capacity Christ appealed to Bob Tullett most.

In 1953 Alyson had her first baby, a little girl they called Rosalyn. Within months she was being carried into the Bedford van by her father to be raced round the lanes on the Sunday School pick-up and was loving every minute of it.

Those should have been contented years for John, a proud father, active and respected in the community, and, indeed, when he was with his family, his Sunday School or his prisoners he was happy enough. But there was a fly in the ointment—his job. Selling weighing machines, he felt, contributed to nobody's welfare but his own, and even he wasn't being extended or fulfilled by it. Furthermore he was gradually exhausting the Isle of Wight as a market. Everybody who needed scales had now got scales, and in order to keep up his quota he was forced to offer a better trade-in price than Avery's rules allowed. Not that John cared about breaking rules, nevertheless his family and friends were dismayed to notice a return of the old restlessness.

However, there were highlights.

The first was provided by his mother. Since the death of her husband she had been a semi-invalid, and John and Alyson had set up their home in the Wootton Bridge bungalow to be with her—now that her usefulness seemed over even her faith couldn't halt the beginnings of a running-down process.

But she loved hearing John talk about his men in Parkhurst, which he did almost incessantly, and one day surprised him by saying: 'Do you think those poor boys would like it if I wrote to them sometimes?'

Knowing how few letters most recidivists receive, and how important to them they are, John said he was sure they would be delighted.

And that is how a retired, gentle and elderly lady on the Isle of Wight began a correspondence with a number of life-long criminals, and came to be known as 'Mother Dodd' throughout the length and breadth of the British prison system.

The activities of some of her correspondents must have appalled her, but as she said: 'We don't know what sort of things we might have done if we'd been brought up in different homes, dear,' and went on writing. What started as a very part-time occupation grew, as John's prison acquaintanceship increased, into almost a full-time job involving the writing of some thousand letters a year.

She became a mother-figure for hundreds of old lags whose real mothers had been so different from the ideal, silver-haired old lady they now adopted. She was invariably pleased and hopeful when one of 'her boys' finished his sentence, and kept in touch with him outside. The fact that so many later returned saddened but did not discourage her, and there was always one of her letters awaiting them in Dartmoor or the Scrubs or wherever it was, to make them feel less isolated.

She sent Bob Tullett a copy of the *Life of Wesley* and, what's more, he read it and enjoyed it.

The conversion of Bob Tullett was another highlight. One evening when John went into his cell he was met with: 'I've done it.'

'Done what?'

'Jesus made certain promises, didn't he? Well, I'm taking him up on them.'

It didn't sound a propitious attitude to a life of faith, but John felt it was sincere. Certainly there was no doubting the change that came over Bob. His usual bitterness dropped away and serenity took its place.

About this time both Scouse Jones and Bob Tullett began talking about 'coming up before the Board for the third'.

'The third' was the hoped-for remission of a third of their sentence. In P.D. this remission was not automatically granted for good behaviour, as in ordinary sentences; it depended entirely upon the decision of a Board, which included the governor, the chaplain and a representative of the Central After-Care Association and which met in the prison to interview men halfway through their sentence. On this interview and on a man's record rested the Board's irrevocable decision to grant or withhold the third.

For a man doing, say, twelve years P.D. it meant that the Board could free him after eight years, or, as he saw it, condemn him to another two years by allowing only one-sixth remission.

As only a very small percentage of men got their third, the Board was not popular.

John was anxious to see Scouse and Bob out of prison as soon as possible and did what he could by writing to the Board on their behalf.

Bob Tullett, who impressed the Board during his interview by saying: 'If it's God's will that I get out of here, I'll get out—not unless,' was granted the third. Scouse, less silver-tongued, was not.

John couldn't see what difference had been found between the two men whose records were equally bad and whose determination to go straight from now on was equally valid. He was relieved, as the weeks went by, to find that Scouse's faith survived his disappointment.

Then, one morning, Bob Tullett was discovered collapsed on the floor in his cell where he had lain most of the night haemorrhaging from a perforated duodenal ulcer. The prison surgeon pronounced him inoperable, but he was sent to the County Hospital at Ryde. It was the first time he had been outside Parkhurst for four years and by a nice coincidence the men's surgical ward was alive with Christians; nurses, patients and the surgeon who operated on him, creating an aura of goodwill he had never known before. John and Tom Foinette visited him regularly, to find him happier than they had ever seen him before.

But if the hospital impressed Bob Tullett, he also impressed the hospital. At the end of eighteen weeks the surgeon apologised for finding him so fit that he must be discharged back to prison, and two of the nurses approached him with a plan of escape which, deeply touched, he turned down.

He got back to Parkhurst to find he had been picked for the 'Bristol Scheme'—a relatively new experiment in which some men were allowed to serve the end of their sentence living in a hostel inside prison, but working at an ordinary job outside. It had not been envisaged for recidivists and Bob was one of the few men from Parkhurst to be tried out: he was one of its greatest successes.

He was transferred to Bristol and given the job of sweeping the yard at the potteries there.

Now, although most men in prison protest loudly and often that all they'll need to go straight when they get out is a steady job, in reality it is rarely that simple. Partly through being institutionalised, partly through an inadequacy that made them

criminals in the first place, they find it difficult to stick at anything.

Often they irritate those who don't understand and are trying
to help them by their excuses—the job's too menial/responsible,
too easy/hard, they don't like the look of the foreman, a work-
mate asked them where they spent their holiday last year. In
actual fact, they are raw with insecurity and fear.

Bob Tullett faced hard manual work for the first time in his
life. On top of everything he became acutely aware of the invitation issuing out of every pub he passed on the way to and from
work. He rejected it, however, and did his sweeping so
thoroughly that eventually he was offered promotion and put in
charge of a kiln.

On the Isle of Wight the Dodds, now with a second daughter,
Diana, had moved, taking Mother Dodd with them, to a bigger
house high on a hill overlooking the Solent—and Parkhurst.
The prison was taking up more and more of John's thought and
time. He had become deputy to the visiting Methodist chaplain
at Parkhurst, entitled to come and go almost as he pleased, and
was keeping in close touch with about eighty men.

On Wednesday evenings he held a Methodist discussion
group with some of the men, a lively affair, and occasionally
preached on Sunday mornings in the chapel.

John's sermons were unconventional and enjoyable. One
morning, wanting to prepare his congregation for the fact that
life outside wasn't going to be roses all the way, he told them
about a recently discharged old lag, a converted Christian,
whose wife had been so disgusted at his new-found piety that
she banished him to sleep in the garden shed. From the back of
the chapel came a deep, North country voice, 'A right bloody
charlie he must have been,' it said and John, in the pulpit,
collapsed into laughter.

In fact, the converted old lag of John's story was his friend
Jack Long, and John was worried about him. After Jack's discharge, John had crossed to the mainland to visit him at his
terrace house in Brighton. The door had been opened by
what John later described as 'a female gorilla' who, with a voice
booming from down in her stomach, had declared herself to be
Mrs. Long.

'Is Jack in?' John asked, politely.

'He's down on the bloody beach, singing with the Sally Army, and as far as I'm concerned he can bloody stay there.'

When John eventually found him, Jack was in a real dilemma. His wife, proud of her criminal heritage, had been shocked at his changed outlook. A poker school was being run in the front parlour, his daughter showed every intention of becoming a prostitute, and his younger son had reacted to his father's conversion by loosening the brakes on his father's bike.

John gave what encouragement he could, told Jack to come and visit him whenever possible and left, wondering how much longer Jack could struggle against the tide, and even—in one black moment—whether he should.

In the summer of 1956 Avery's discovered about the trade-in price John was offering his customers on their old scales, and he found himself without a job.

Within the month he had been offered four different jobs, all in selling, including greetings cards and marzipan. Undecided, he went on a week's intensive training course run by a firm called Tack which specialised in heating and air-conditioning.

The sales manual of Tack read something like the Sermon on the Mount with a price tag in small print at the bottom. Foot-in-the-door methods were scorned—human relations was the emphasis, the consumer and his benefit the only consideration. Hot, steamy, fly-ridden kitchens and restaurants, stuffy factories and smoky bars were to be transformed by the installation of Tack air conditioning.

The firm was run by two Jewish brothers, Alfred and George Tack, who, with brilliant success, were applying their advanced selling methods to the British scene. Nor were they insincere. Tack believed in its products and sent out its salesman—on commission only—armed in the same belief. It was a first-class firm to work for if you were a first-class salesman; those who weren't left after the first fortnight.

In John Dodd the Tack brothers found a man after their own heart, and he quickly became their representative on the Isle of Wight.

Within the year the Island was buying air conditioning as enthusiastically as it had once bought scales. With the conviction that he was giving customers a real service John became an invincible salesman. He also became affluent—frequently earning a commission of twenty or thirty pounds a day.

This, perhaps, is where John's story becomes extraordinary. With a hard war behind him he had struggled through to a certain peace of mind, a rewarding job, a comfortable home, a loving family and a status in his community. Not only that but, with his work for prisoners, he was contributing to an underprivileged section of society, enough to satisfy any ordinary conscience.

It was a life sufficiently full of all the riches to carry most men contentedly through to the grave. He thought it would.

Only Alyson, who only knew him better than he knew himself, enjoyed the material benefits while she might, and waited for her husband to find his purpose.

PART FOUR

TIME TO SERVE

CHAPTER FOURTEEN

THE OTHER SIDE OF THE LOOKING-GLASS

Christian Teamwork was a voluntary organisation of professional men and women giving assistance where they thought it was most needed. Already it had helped to set up the Richmond Fellowship, a scheme to aid those recovering from mental illness.

Now it had formed Team K to try and answer the question: 'What shall we do about Richard?'

Richard was a released prisoner who had approached Christian Teamwork with the idea that they should help to rehabilitate men like himself by providing them with a car with which to run a small business such as a taxi service or window-cleaning, etc.

Team K, new as it was to the field, rejected that idea fairly smartly; they weren't too new to realise that cars would solve nothing for such men—except, perhaps, the problem of getting from one crime to another.

Instead Team K, began looking round for a better way to help.

It is never easy for men and women, safely built into a social complex of family, friends, neighbours and business colleagues, all dependent one on the other to a greater or lesser degree, to imagine the hideousness of life without any such responsibilities. Team K tried, because in general that is the sort of existence that waits for most men coming out of prison. It is the other side of the looking-glass. Wives and children have probably faded away, a landlady has died, friends have moved or are in prison themselves. There is no money, no status, no reflection, in anyone's eyes but one's own.

There is only the cold welcome of the spikes and dossers where the beds stretch in gaunt rows, and the shuffling queue of homeless men across the stone floor to the canteen leads as surely back to prison, because prison is less terrible. Crime, after

all, can be a way of establishing identity or acquiring security—
at least the magistrate addresses you by name.

As Christians, Team K came up with the idea of providing a
home, a real home, with a built-in family to which the offender
could come straight from prison to find support, assistance and,
above all, love—a commodity all prisoners are short on—until he
could face society as a contributing and comparatively adjusted
human being. House parents would attempt to replace the security and affection that the men had missed in their first five, vital
years of life.

The idea was not new—Merfyn Turner, who had been in
prison himself as a conscientious objector, had just such a
scheme under way with his Norman House—but it was still revolutionary. Until now there had been no halfway houses, only
hostels.

Ostensibly Team K was made up mainly of successful and
hard-headed business men and women. There was Jack Wallace,
a Lincoln's Inn solicitor, Agnes Brownlow, a company director,
Roy Calvocoressi, a very English young man despite his name,
who had become a barrister via Eton and Cambridge, and Robert
Nuttall and Oliver Stott, two more company directors.

In fact they were idealists, or, as some might say they were
mad. At this point they had no money and no house for their
project but this worried them a great deal less than finding the
right man to stage-manage it. He had to be a Christian, a realist
experienced with prisoners, with great organising ability, yet
prepared to work for the small salary that was all Team K could
offer.

The finest computer ever devised would have had difficulty in
turning up such a man: God, as they all believe, did better.

Back in November 1956, Oliver Stott had given a lift to a
fellow-speaker at a Christian Businessmen's dinner in Richmond. The two men had never met before but Oliver Stott, who
had done a great deal of film evangelism in prisons, had been
impressed by the man.

Naturally enough, when Team K began discussion on the
form of rehabilitation it was to set up, Mr. Stott remembered
the man who had talked so understandingly about prisoners
during the drive to and from London.

Thus John Dodd met Team K. Although none of them

realised it at the time it was a meeting on a par with Wellington encountering Blucher or Rolls being introduced to Royce.

Within a short time Team K realised it had found its man.

John was in on the discussions almost from the first and brought with him some of his ex-convict friends, Bob Tullett among them, to give their first-hand knowledge of the needs of prisoners.

By March 1958 Team K had decided to pop the vital question. John was asked officially if he would take up the post of warden in the still non-existent house, to become house father to about fifteen old lags at less than one third of his current income.

With a sense of inevitability he realised that he was meant to accept this work as surely as if a sign in the sky was saying so. It gave his life meaning and shape. It was why he had been sent to Singapore, it was the purpose behind his narrow escape on the *Empire Star* and the uncountable escapes from death afterwards. It was the reason for the jungle, for Changi, and the two terrible years following liberation.

'I will restore unto you the years that the locusts have eaten ...' the full quotation from Joel came to him and he experienced a sense of immense gratitude that, after all, the operative word was 'restore'.

The years of the war and its aftermath had not been lost at all.

They had been a training ground.

Obviously the decision to take up the work couldn't be his only. Alyson was concerned quite as much as he; so were the children. All of them would be living twenty-four hours a day with some of the most notoriously difficult characters around. Alyson would have to be not only willing but eager to do it, or it could not be done.

There was another consideration—money. John was content to give up a large income, but he could not automatically expect Alyson to do the same thing.

He went straightaway to the Isle of Wight nursing home where Alyson had just given birth to their third daughter, Lorraine, and put it to her.

Alyson had seen this coming for more than a year.

The cause of ex-prisoners was dear to her heart but, as with most women, the cause of deprived children was dearer, and she had always secretly hoped that when John found his vocation it would be among them. But it was typical of John that he should champion a cause that attracted the least public sympathy of any.

At the moment of John's question Alyson was surrounded by flowers sent from Tack who believed in being considerate to the wives of its top men.

So, all in all, it was perhaps courageous of her to say, as she did without hesitation: 'Go ahead.'

CHAPTER FIFTEEN

'IT ISN'T GOING TO BE EASY . . .'

They moved, all of them, quite blindly in the year that followed, like men under unseen direction.

As an act of faith John and Alyson tore up their roots from the Isle of Wight and moved with the children and Mother Dodd to the mainland, to a house at Compton quite near Oliver Stott's on the outskirts of Winchester. It meant leaving all their friends, their beloved Sunday School and a paradise for children.

Still without *the* house and still without the money to buy it, planning went on. It became apparent fairly early that to be house parent, administrator, fund raiser, selector of residents etc., would be too much for one man, even if that man were John Dodd, and it was decided that another couple should be found to live in and be the actual house parents while John assumed the role of general secretary and overall administrator.

Another decision restricted the selection of men to those who had been converted to Christianity in prison. It was a limited conception and later they were to realise its short-sightedness, but at the time they genuinely thought that belief in God would not only provide a man with an incentive for a better life, but would solve his problems too.

Then they found a house—called Langley House, it was a farm on the coast near Fawley oil refinery but miles from anywhere else. Alyson thought it was awful and said so, but John and the rest of Team K were prepared to take anything. They registered themselves as a charity under the name of The Langley House Trust, raised sufficient money, and set about trying to buy the place.

But, unknown to them, someone stepped in with a better price, and Langley House was sold over their heads.

It was a blow at the time. Later they regarded it as providential. The farmhouse was off the map and men being integrated into society need a thriving community around them to help that integration.

They now had a name, but no house.

The first Langley House they actually acquired, turned up almost under John's nose in Otterbourne, the next village to his. It was a private hotel called Elderfield, owned by an old lady in her nineties who had, understandably enough, allowed it to become dilapidated. But it was large enough to house a family of seventeen or more, was in a pleasant village community, had a quiet garden at the rear and an atmosphere of tranquillity. Furthermore, it was available on a four hundred pound a year lease. The former Team K, now Trustees of Langley House, snapped it up.

They now had a name and a house—but no furniture.

While the others devoted themselves to scrubbing out and painting Elderfield John went into the highways and byways to scrounge something to put in it. He came back with a lorry load of old but serviceable beds, throw-outs from a holiday camp, an ancient dining-room suite, a second-hand fridge, and a clapped-out television set.

Researching the origins of Elderfield, Alyson and Mother Dodd discovered that it had once been owned by Charlotte Yonge, the nineteenth-century novelist and moralist. Further research uncovered a heartening coincidence—that among Miss Yonge's books were a series of works called *Langley Tales*.

It seemed a good omen.

They had need of some heartening just then. None of them had ever thought that the work they were undertaking would be easy but, as Elderfield was being got ready, they were given a demonstration of just how hard it was going to be.

It happened through, of all men, Bob Tullett.

To John, Bob Tullett had become a symbol for Langley House; an example of what a discharged offender converted to Christianity could achieve.

At the end of his sentence Bob had left the Bristol pottery, to the regret of his manager, and returned to his home in the Midlands to rejoin his wife, a long-suffering woman who at first took Bob's protestations of reform with a large pinch of salt. Like the wives of most recidivists, she had heard that before.

Gradually, however, she was forced to believe it. Bob had become a dynamo of energy and Christian zeal.

He got himself a job at an iron foundry, and kept it. He became a local Methodist lay preacher and started a youth club. At weekends he travelled the country preaching and raising money for Langley House. His success rivalled even John Dodd's, who was talking himself hoarse about the scheme at every opportunity.

Bob brought all the charm and technique of his old confidence tricks to meetings of Christian men and women, except that this time he was telling the truth. He told them frankly about his life and his belief in what Langley House and God could do for others like himself. When he sat down his audiences would, quite literally, empty their purses and within a matter of months he had raised eight hundred pounds for the Trust.

During the planning stage of Langley House he contributed many ideas which were adopted and won the respect of all the Trustees. He visited John and Alyson regularly, preaching at their local church, and became godfather to their daughter, Lorraine.

In all this time he never forgot the friends of his prison days and was on hand to help them when they were released—a forerunner of the 'associate' system, later to be suggested by the Working Committee on Voluntary After-Care.

John encouraged Bob in his public speaking, knowing that Bob's oratory combined with Bob's past was irresistible in furthering the cause.

Just after the 1958 Christmas Bob visited the Dodds in the Isle of Wight where he was due to meet a man being released from prison. Alyson wanted him to stay on; she thought he looked tired, but Bob insisted on returning home to see the New Year in with his wife. So, on New Year's Eve, John saw him off at the station ...

The train was packed and Bob was lucky to find a seat in a carriage filled with some boisterous undergraduates returning to Oxford for the New Year celebrations. They were attractive young people, full of optimism and dogmatic opinions, and he was drawn into their conversation.

Very soon they were asking him about himself and he told them about his work. He had made an inviolate rule for himself that at this point, when meeting new people, he always added: 'But before that I was doing seven years' P.D. in Parkhurst for false pretences.' This time, however, he stopped short. Perhaps he was tired of exposing his sores, or couldn't bear to see on the boys' faces the look of delighted horror that most people display when, for the first time in their lives they are in the presence of a 'real criminal'.

Anyway, he didn't tell them.

By the time they reached Oxford an anonymous bonhomie that can only occur on trains had grown up between them. The boys were determined not to lose it. 'Come and have a drink with us for the New Year,' one of them asked Bob, and the others fell on the idea with gusto. Bob shook his head: 'I don't drink.' But the students insisted and Bob gave in. He hadn't touched alcohol for over ten years; prison had dried him out and he felt that his subsequent four and a half years of teetotalism proved that he was no longer susceptible. He could take it or leave it alone now, like anybody else.

'Just one drink,' he agreed. He went with them to the bar of the station buffet and ordered a round of whiskies.

'Here's to 1959,' said one of the boys.

'To 1959,' said Bob and drank.

He didn't get home that night nor the next, nor the next. When eventually he did arrive it was to pick up some cash and disappear again. In the months that followed he would turn up in different parts of the country to borrow or con some money and then go off into the blue with it. As he looked sober, nobody suspected that he was spending ten pounds a day on whisky.

A typical incident was when a fellow lay preacher opened his front door to Bob who said he was on his way to meet a man coming out of Gloucester prison and wanted to give him money, but had left his wallet behind. The friend gave it unquestioningly—it was a well-known fact that Bob had given a great deal of his own money to discharged prisoners.

He turned up at John Wadham's house—the two had met through John Dodd and become friends—and conned money from him on the pretext that he had become a shirt salesman. John paid out for some shirts but they never arrived.

John Dodd he didn't visit, but used his name to stay at a hotel and later John got the bill.

What happened in between these emergences into the public gaze nobody knows. He isn't sure himself. 'It was like being a different person,' he says.

He can remember that towards the end of what he calls 'the skid', he fell on the steps of a public lavatory, slithering down the metal-tipped stairs to lie on the cold, wet stone at the bottom. When he opened his eyes there were men staring at him, asking if he were hurt. He had broken his thumb, but he didn't feel it. He got up and crawled up the stairs, away from the eyes. He remembers the blackness of the street and his own screams. Then there was the blue lamp of a police station and some steps. Bob Tullett climbed them and gave himself up.

Immediately he was a criminal again. The last four and a half years had gone for nothing. The Inspector who interviewed him cared little for Bob Tullett, respectable citizen, and not at all for Bob Tullett, lay preacher and voluntary welfare worker—that was just another fraud he'd put over on the unsuspecting public —he was Bob Tullett, con man.

When eventually he was allowed to go, pending further investigations and charges, he left with the Inspector's grin hanging in front of him like the Cheshire Cat's, issuing the words: 'With your record, you'll get ten years for this little lot.'

The news hit the Dodds hard. John blamed himself, feeling that he had put Bob on display, using him as a trophy. Busy though he was, he dropped everything to give what help he could.

But Bob had disappeared again, and it became a race for his friends to find him before the police did. From the North to the South of England phones rang, passing the message: 'If Bob turns up, keep him there—and call Dr. Lake.'

Dr. Frank Lake, author of *Clinical Theology*, is one of the best-known Christian psychiatrists in the country, but for Bob's friends just then his most important attribute was his knowledge of alcoholics, whom he treated in a clinic near Otley, Yorkshire.

Then, suddenly, there was Bob at the house of a friend, pale but plausible, with a tale of needing money. The friend gave him the money, but also saw that Bob waited while he rang Dr.

Lake. It was arranged that Bob should be put on the next train for Otley.

Bob allowed himself to be put on the train. 'I planned to go to the buffet car as soon as they'd waved me off,' he says, 'but they'd been clever. There not only wasn't a buffet car, there wasn't even a corridor.'

The only stop was the station where he was due to change trains. He was heading for the station bar when a man he'd never seen before came up and said: 'Mr. Tullett? I've been asked to help with your luggage.'

There wasn't any luggage, only first-class organisation.

Bob was safely delivered to Dr. Lake.

At the trial the prosecution laid emphasis on Bob's record and the fact that there was no evidence to show he was drunk when he obtained the money.

But for the defence, Dr. Frank Lake said: 'This man has been a chronic alcoholic since before he was twenty. His uncle taught him to drink when he was a child and he became a compulsive addict. The amazing thing is that he did not know it.' He went on to describe how such an addict would use 'the lowest and meanest form of deception to satisfy his craving for drink, and yet never appear drunk'.

Then John Dodd spoke for Bob. He told the court of the last four and a half years and the work Bob had achieved during that time. 'I still have faith in him,' he said.

Giving his verdict, the Recorder said: 'It seems to be a choice between ten years' preventive detention or a very bold and courageous decision by this court.'

He chose the latter. Bob was put on two years' probation.

It has been estimated that of the 33,000 men in British prisons at this moment, at least half have a drink problem. Among those whose stories are known because they have submitted to some form of rehabilitation there are rarely conclusively happy endings. Alcoholism plus criminality plus whatever caused both in the first place form a combination that is very nearly happy-ending-proof.

It would be nice to say that Bob went back to his wife and lived happily ever after with her. In fact, he did go back and lived quietly with her for two and a half years, continuing his work. But then she died, and Bob went on another skid, came out of it, took up the threads again, and went on another.

Bob's friendship with John, despite many troubles, has remained a valued factor in both their lives. Bob never lost touch with him or Langley, often spending time at one of the houses when things got too bad. He never returned to prison. He's married again now, drawing his pension and settling, not unhappily, into a calm, confident old age.

Bob had provided them with a warning but, as nobody can know the difficulties involved in rehabilitation work without actually doing it, they still believed that a six-weeks' stay at Langley House, a job, clothes and the confidence provided by a family setting, would be enough to turn former criminals into ready-made citizens. In June 1959 John gave his notice to Tack, who were surprised and sorry at his going, and the first Langley House opened its doors to its residents.

CHAPTER SIXTEEN

. . . AND IT WASN'T

The size and scope of their early mistakes approached magnificence.

In the first place the restriction of residence to professing Christians meant the house was filled with old lags—criminals apparently, turn to religion mainly as a last resort.

It was natural that John should accept released men he had known in Parkhurst, but it over-weighted the home with disturbed recidivisits in their middle age.

Elderfield quickly became a hotchpotch of clashing personalities. Among them was Claud, as unprepossessing as ever, but insisting that his conversion had cured his homosexuality, so that John took him in, much against his better judgement.

There was a bigamist who looked every inch a fairground boxer, which was what he was. There was Little Arthur, a worn shadow of a man with a limp handshake who seemed to be under permanent sedation and did everything he was told.

Then there was Henry, a con man with a genuine public school accent, who drove everybody mad with his insistence that they were beneath him. Working, it appeared, was beneath him too, and he would lie in bed in the mornings, clutching the sheet as if it were his lifeline and protesting that he was ill. John was sorry for him—over-ambitious parents had refused to recognise Henry's limitations and had driven him to the point where he dropped out rather than face more competition—but the man was a strain.

There was Jack Long, finally broken by his family's hostility and the nights in the garden shed. There were Scouse Jones and Percy, gentle as ever, all three appearing refreshingly normal against the bizarre background of their fellow-residents.

And, finally, there was Buck, younger than the rest, with a passion for the Wild West which he assuaged by dressing in chaps, a Stetson and holster complete with toy guns. His one ambition, for reasons which John found obscure, was to kill his uncle.

There were times when John, walking into Elderfield, felt that he had entered the back lot of some multiple film set filled with bit-part actors; an impression that the inevitable 'pow, pow' from Buck, snaking a toy gun from his hip, did not dispel.

The idea that such men would be fitted for society after just six weeks, like sausages coming out of a machine, proved to be their second mistake and was, in fact, never put into operation.

Little Arthur taught them that.

Little Arthur's air of defeat and utter weariness were not without cause. His life story made John wonder how society could expect a man to hold down a job and keep out of trouble after such ill-usage. He had been born in Holloway prison, the son of a prostitute who had him put into an orphanage, which had transferred him to foster-parents, who had handed him back. The viciousness of the circle had taken away all confidence and personality from him until he stumbled, in a lack-lustre sort of way, into trouble—at which point he was promptly sent to prison.

John allowed him to stay at Elderfield for fifteen weeks and then, reluctantly, found him lodgings outside, feeling that even this divergence from the six-week rule was little enough to set against Arthur's thirty-five years of ill treatment.

Within a few days Little Arthur had lost his job, and within another week he had stolen fifteen shillings from a newspaper stand and been caught. Touchingly enough, on arrest he gave his address as Elderfield and John was contacted. At the hearing John spoke for him, saying that if Little Arthur could be allowed to return to Langley House he would keep an eye on him himself. The Recorder said that he had made up his mind to give the defendant ten years P.D., but after listening to Mr. Dodd's pleas he would allow Little Arthur one last chance by putting him on probation for three years instead.

When they got him home to Elderfield Arthur, as usual, said nothing. But the next day he walked up the road to the Dodds' house and washed John's car—the first positive action he'd taken on his own since they'd known him.

It was another year before John felt that Little Arthur was

strong enough to live on his own, and even then he made sure that the man's lodgings were close enough for Arthur to visit Elderfield and remain within its circle of support. Little Arthur visited them regularly for two years after that, staying out of trouble, before moving away so that they lost touch with him.

They felt justified in hoping that, having survived for two years—a time presenting the greatest risk of return to prison—Arthur would cope for the rest of his life. The trouble was that, as with so many men, they never heard of him again and so will never know.

Those first six months at Elderfield were a cauldron brewing trouble, bubbling up occasionally and at last spilling over.

The house parents whom John and the Trustees had chosen were a kindly couple, previously officers in the Salvation Army, but they were first and foremost evangelists—elated when a man joined them in prayer, depressed when he showed no interest—and this particular job was beyond them.

Physically, it was tough enough. Money being extremely short, Langley was run on a shoestring, and the house parents did all the cleaning, cooking, provisioning and washing for themselves and their family of fifteen.

Their day began at five-thirty a.m. when men on early shift had to be given their breakfast and seen off to work with their lunch boxes, then there was the clearing up and preparing for the return of the 'family' and its evening meal, after which the house mother and father devoted themselves to the men, sharing their games, chatting, listening to their problems.

The men were free to come and go as they liked in the evenings. Most stayed in, but some who were out returned so late that it was often one a.m. before the house father could lock up and go to bed. John, realising something must be done if his staff were to have adequate sleep, instituted the rule that all residents must be in by eleven-thirty p.m. unless they offered a valid reason in advance for being late, in which case they would be given a key. It was a rule that caused much grumbling, especially among the freer spirits, but it proved so wise that it has stood ever since.

On top of all this was the strain of living cheek by jowl with unstable personalities, the daily fight to get Henry up and off to work, the bickering, demands for attention, the gangings-up, the complaints and counter-complaints. Scouse quarrelled with Buck, who got on his nerves, Henry complained about everybody, and everybody complained about Claud, the most unpopular man in the house.

In fact, a small deputation went to John, asking him to throw Claud out. 'Once a poof, always a poof. He'll get us a bad name.'

John was pleased at this first sign that the men were beginning to worry about their collective image, but he refused to evict Claud who, until there was evidence to the contrary, had as much right at Langley as anyone else.

Unfortunately such evidence came within the week in a telephone call from a Winchester resident who complained that Claud had been seen pestering the boys at the swimming baths.

John faced Claud with the complaint privately. Claud broke down and admitted it, but when John suggested psychiatric treatment he refused, and left Elderfield of his own accord the next day. When John next heard of him Claud was once more in prison, for assaulting the son of a couple with whom he had found lodging.

After two more incidents involving homosexuals, one a gipsy who made a nuisance of himself to the other men, and one a desperately unhappy youth who attempted suicide at Elderfield by drinking disinfectant, it became obvious that Langley House was not the place for them.

Although John and the Trustees disliked closing the door on such tragic cases, they agreed that future selection must exclude men with that particular problem.

The house mother at Elderfield found that not only were the men bickering but that most of the bickering was over her. She was the first woman many of them had met since their imprisonment, a mother-sister-sweetheart substitute, a role requiring a great deal of tolerance, experience and tact.

One night she found herself in the kitchen alone with Jack Long, who attempted to kiss her. This might have been all right except that at that moment Scouse Jones, who'd been wanting to do the same thing, came in.

With a cry of 'Traitor', Scouse leaped on Jack, there was a

scuffle and an emergency telephone call to John Dodd to come and cope with the situation.

It was too much for the over-strained nerves of the house parents, who left. They had lasted just over three months.

It was a nasty moment when John found himself with a house full of discharged offenders and no one to look after them. He himself was already working at full stretch, talking at meetings all over the country, raising money and selling the idea of Langley House, visiting prisons, interviewing prospective residents and finding jobs for the men. Alyson, besides looking after her own family, was tackling the exacting job of the trust's clerical work.

A volunteer came from an unexpected quarter. 'I'll do it, dear,' said Mother Dodd.

John was doubtful. His mother was now seventy-three and suffered from a bad heart. He was worried that the physical effort of looking after fifteen men, let alone such mentally demanding men, would be too much for her. Mother Dodd insisted, however, and John decided to let her try until replacements for the house parents could be found.

It was surprisingly successful.

Through her letter-writing to prisons Mother Dodd knew most of the men already. To them she personified the sort of mother they would like to have had—gentle, white-haired and loving. The house became imbued with a determination not to let her down.

'Oh, but they were good to me,' she said.

The house was not only chaotic but in sore need of repair and decoration, and Scouse, who had learned the trade in prison, became its full-time maintenance man. His hours were erratic, beginning at five in the morning until lunchtime, taking the afternoon off and starting again at night, continuing sometimes until the early hours.

It was an odd way of working but it suited Scouse who was consistent if unconventional and John saw the wisdom of letting him go on as he pleased.

The other men rallied round keeping their rooms as neat as they could and helping with the washing-up, while Joe Dean undertook to do the cooking.

Joe was a newcomer, a replacement for Buck who had left of his own accord to marry a girl of an even lower intellect than his own; a disastrous union which led him eventually into more trouble than Langley House could get him out of.

John was disappointed; he had hoped that Buck would be persuaded to attend the local mental hospital as an out-patient, but was relieved at least that his mother wasn't going to be jumped out on and pow-powed at. There were times, however, when Joe Dean made him long for Buck's return, Stetson and all. Joe was a garrulous and troublemaking old man who had spent more than half his life in prison, who would argue with anybody about anything, disputing questions of theology with the vicar. He claimed to be a chef by profession and had, he boasted continually, cooked for the Prince of Wales and the Governor of Parkhurst—it was difficult to know which afforded him the most pride.

His first supper was an occasion and everybody held their breath when Joe, napkin over arm, served up with a confident flourish. They ate in silence for a few minutes and then Scouse spoke for them all: 'You mean the Prince of Wales and the Governor of Parkhurst ate muck like this?'

Undeterred, Joe announced his intention of cooking for them every night. Something had to be done. The evening meal was an event to which everybody attached importance. It was the only time they were all together and John had already seen its possibilities in making contact. He dared not have it marred by bad food—the men had enough of that in prison.

Tactfully, he suggested that Joe shouldn't overtax his strength on top of a working day, but should cook for them instead just one night a week. Reluctantly Joe agreed.

'Joe's night' became a time when most of the men excused themselves from the supper table because of previous engagements, and John noticed that even the greatest enemies banded together against Joe's cooking. It became a joke which they shared with John and each other—the first indication that they were becoming a family.

At moments like these John saw what Langley House could create for its men if only they would let it.

He saw it again in the interest everybody showed in the cliffhanger that was Scouse's attempts to find a wife.

Scouse was settling down well and working hard, although his quick temper showed how difficult he found it. Unlike many recidivists he was a marital animal; both he and John felt that a good wife would go a long way to solving his problems accordingly, Scouse went out to find one. His method was to correspond with a Lonely Hearts Club and through its auspices he got replies from lonely women all over Britain.

Each letter with its accompanying photograph convinced Scouse that he had found *the* woman for him and every weekend he would ride off on his little two-stroke motor cycle to visit her. Distance did not deter him—he went to Cornwall, Durham, to Snowdonia and Herne Bay.

In the early hours of each Monday morning he would puttputt home to Winchester in bitter mood, saying: 'She didn't look like that at all,' from which John gathered that the photograph had either been someone else's or quite a few years out of date.

But the shouts of, 'What was she like then, Scouse?' and the invariable reply, 'She was horrible,' at the Monday night supper table created a bond of interest that was valuable, taking each man out of his own troubles and involving him in someone else's—a big step in their rehabilitation.

Just as Joe Dean had volunteered to do the cooking, Jack Long volunteered to do the praying, and once again John's tact had to be brought into play. Jack was a sincere Christian and in all his troubles with his family and his difficulties in holding down a job his faith had remained steady. But his prayers ran to length. Every evening at Langley House there was a prayer meeting, and the first time Jack conducted it he stood for forty minutes in verbal contemplation, and opened his eyes at last to find that everybody had slipped off to bed except Mother Dodd, and even she was nodding.

Jack's prayers gave rise to fury, particularly in Alex, a red-haired newcomer who was one of the most temperamental men in Langley House at that time. His elation was so powerful it could drag everybody's spirits up with it, but his low points were extremes of depression and tantrums usually found only in children. He had an irrational jealousy of Jack Long and the situation between the two men was fraught with tension—Jack's own predisposition to violence was very near the surface; his lengthy prayers were, in part, one way of talking out his aggression.

When it did come to a head, however, it was resolved not through violence, but in an even more childish way . . .

Jack Long was very deaf and for years had worn a National Health hearing appliance. One day at Elderfield his eye was caught by an advertisement in *The Reader's Digest* for a sixty-guinea hearing aid which, apparently, could do almost everything except tell the time. At this stage Jack was out of work and living on National Assistance which left him with spending money of ten shillings a week, but he wrote up to the address in the advert and a few days later an alert salesman in a white sports car drove up to Elderfield, got Jack's signature on an H.P. agreement . . . and a brand new hearing aid was adorning Jack's ear.

The story seeped out and Alex writhed with jealousy. Within two more days the salesman had paid another visit to Elderfield and this time the agreement he took away with him carried Alex's signature and the hearing aid he left behind adorned Alex's mantelpiece.

There can be few secrets in Langley House, where every man shares a room; the lack of privacy is compensated for by the general airing of everybody's problems—and in a short time John had heard about the two hearing aids.

'But you're not deaf,' he said to Alex.

'Of course not.'

'Then what did you want it for?'

If Alex had possessed self-insight and a certain fluency of speech he might have said: 'Because the thing was a symbol of what Jack's got—a longer acquaintanceship with you and Langley House, and the beginning of a settlement to his problems.'

But if Alex had possessed such insight and the means of expressing it he wouldn't, in all probability, have been in prison in the first place. So he just said: 'I don't know.'

John turned to Jack, 'And how do you think you're going to pay for a sixty-guinea set on Assistance?'

Jack didn't know.

'Well, this nonsense has got to stop. They're both going back.' and John saw to it himself, in a forthright conversation with the general manager of the firm concerned in London.

The incident marked a new approach by John to his men. He had hoped that Langley House would be a democratic institution where men could run their own lives with the discreet help of the house parents. Now he had cut across that democracy and imposed his own decision; but he noticed the air was clearer that night and that Jack and Alex, despite mutterings beneath their breath, shared a sense of relief—Jack because he had indeed been wondering how to pay for the thing, and Alex because his rival had been treated exactly the same as himself.

Langley House, John realised, could not be a democratic institution *and* a family home; if it was to recreate the parental environment then it would not have to be afraid of providing the discipline and control that went with it.

The deaf aid incident produced a progression in the life of Langley House and it did something else—it made Little Arthur laugh, probably for the first time in his life.

On the day that Mother Dodd took over at Elderfield she was alone in the kitchen, a frail Hercules facing the Augean Stables, when there was a knock on the door and Gerry walked in. He was a good-looking young man in his twenties and he had, he said, come to stay.

John was wary of men who turned up out of the blue and refused anybody whose record was unknown to him, but Gerry was installed before he could do anything about it.

He was a silent boy whose only affection seemed to be given to Mother Dodd, and for her he worked like a slave. Nobody ever did find out who Gerry was or why he had come; they were merely grateful that he had. For a month he scrubbed floors, changed beds, washed paintwork and generally helped to reduce the house to order. Then he left without saying goodbye and was never heard of again.

Mother Dodd, who believes in miracles, thinks he was a gift from Heaven, like the fact that for the seventeen weeks she was at Elderfield she was untroubled by her usual rheumatism.

To John, Gerry was like countless other men who were to come under the influence of Langley for a short while and then disappear, leaving a question mark hanging in the space they left.

Despite the general helpfulness, Langley House had so stacked the cards against itself that trouble was inevitable.

Murdo had appeared on the scene. He was a dark and swarthy Scot who looked like a 1930s image of a white slaver; certainly nearly every other crime from pimping to jewel theft was on his record. His profession of faith, however, was enthusiastic, even if it sounded odd issuing from under so villainous a moustache.

God, he said, had come to him in his cell and altered his life. The trouble was, he added, that in doing so God had stuck him on the horns of a dilemma. Back home in Scotland he had a wife and five children for whom he didn't care very much, while down here in the South he had a mistress and a child for whom he cared a great deal. The dilemma was between returning to the wife or to the mistress. Murdo's God was the righteous Jehovah of the Old Testament and was pulling him towards marital fidelity in Scotland, while his own inclinations favoured the set-up in the South.

All his resentment at having to make such a decision was directed against the Inland Revenue. The Tax Commissioners made an allowance for Murdo to send money to his legal wife but, siding with Jehovah, they made no such provision for his mistress. 'If I could get my hands on those Commissioners,' Murdo would say, evilly, 'I'd throttle the bastards,' and those who heard him knew he meant it.

Murdo's arrival coincided with the preparations for a big day at Elderfield. Joe Dean had bought a huge Bible which he wanted to donate to Langley House. 'It's my endowment,' he said to John. 'Endowed by Joe Dean, that's what it is. Shouldn't we have it blessed or something?'

John, touched by the little old man's gesture, couldn't see why not and decided to make it an occasion. The Reverend Arnold Bellwood, a founder member of the Otterbourne Langley House committee, was asked to conduct the ceremony at Elderfield to which the Trustees, friends of Langley and other interested people were invited. This, felt John, should be an opportunity to show how Langley House was progressing.

It was.

As the day approached, Joe Dean became more fussy and nervous. Everything must be just right, as befitted the donation of a Bible by a man who had cooked for the Prince of Wales and the Governor of Parkhurst. He pestered John with suggestions ranging from inviting the Bishop of Winchester to providing delicacies for the tea that would follow.

'And another thing,' he announced, 'I don't want Eric to be there. Come to that, I don't want to share a room with him any more either—he smells.'

This was undeniable. Eric had arrived with Murdo and from the same prison—though what society was doing in sending him there John could not understand.

Eric was an illiterate of very low intelligence. In rural England he would have been termed a village idiot and accepted as such, with people to wash him and point him in the right direction. But Eric had been born in a slum and, stumbling through the fog of his own mind had wandered into crime on abominably smelly feet and with his trousers falling down.

There was no harm in him, if you could stand his B.O. and his chatter, for Eric was a talker who loved spending half the night in an inane monologue on any misty idea that drifted into his head.

Joe Dean, who was both intolerant and personally clean, couldn't stand him. John decided that Jack Long's adjustment had now reached the stage where he could take on responsibility, and put Eric in to share his room. Jack accepted his room mate as a sort of penance such as the martyrs endured, and would switch off his hearing aid when Eric began his nightly ramblings.

'But he's got to come to the service,' John explained to Joe, 'he's one of the family.'

'Not mine he isn't,' said Joe. 'Well, see he smartens himself up a bit.'

Smartening Eric up was a task that boggled the mind, and anyway John had enough to do; the other residents had become enthusiastic over what they regarded as their moment in the limelight, and he was having to turn down helpful suggestions which included the building of a full-scale lectern in the dining-room to the pinching of hassocks from the nearby church.

In all the excitement he noticed that Murdo's hatred was turning away from the Commissioners of Inland Revenue and concentrating on him, John, but he was unable to do much about it. Murdo had wanted him to make the choice between the wife and the girl-friend and this John declined to do—the decision could only be Murdo's.

The day came and so did the visitors. Joe Dean greeted them and ushered them into the dining-room where his Bible was to be blessed. It wasn't until everybody had gathered and the service about to begin that Eric made his appearance. Jack had done his best to clean him up and forced him into a new shirt, but the whole beautiful effect was negated by the fact that his flies were undone and gaping to the world.

Unaware of his condition, Eric moved graciously among the guests, slapping ladies on the back and winking proudly towards Joe Dean, who could have killed him.

The service was going well when, at the top of the stairs leading down to the dining-room, Murdo, who had been conspicuously absent until now, made *his* entrance.

He was wearing a crimson dressing gown and smoking a cigarette. The Rev. Arnold Bellwood's voice faltered in its blessing and then carried on. Like Cinderella arriving at the ball, Murdo descended the staircase, swept through the assembled company and went to the television set on the other side of the room. This he switched on, waited until it had warmed up and then turned it to full blast.

Then and only then did he turn round and open his mouth. 'Call yourselves bloody Christians,' he screamed at them.

Because they did indeed call themselves Christians Murdo stayed on at Langley House. It was Eric who had to go, after Jack Long went to John and said he couldn't tolerate sharing a room with him and his lack of personal hygiene any longer, and nobody else was prepared to take him in.

He was the first man they had ever turned away and it was not without a certain agony that John drove him to Southampton where he had got Eric a bed at the Salvation Army hostel, and watched him shamble off to it. But it was becoming increasingly clear that if Langley House was to be effective its selection of residents would have to be narrowed still further.

Langley House is essentially a place of transition and the Erics of this world are never going to move on. Their need is for something different, a permanent home with specialised and intensive care where they can find shelter.

So Eric went to Southampton and the next day he made his way to the busiest street of that busy city, stood in the middle of it and began to direct the traffic.

They put him in prison because they didn't know what else to do with him and he has remained there on and off ever since, not unhappily. But the picture of Eric waving his· arms as his trousers fell down, smiling his amiable, foolish smile at the furious traffic, has haunted John Dodd to this day.

Eric went . . . and Scouse went.

Scouse's search for a wife had become increasingly frantic and was carrying him further afield than ever. Eventually John could stand it no longer; he spotted an advertisement in the *Hampshire Chronicle*: 'Respectable widow seeks friendship of middle-aged gentleman with a view to matrimony,' and answered it himself on Scouse's behalf.

The result was a meeting between Scouse and Kitty, who turned out to be an attractive and sensible woman of forty-eight with a son at grammar school and a married daughter. She and Scouse took to one another at once. On John's advice Scouse told Kitty the truth about his criminal record—a revelation she took in her stride—and then brought her home to Elderfield, 'to meet the family'.

John told her, 'Scouse is ready to settle down, I think he'll make a very good husband.'

Kitty agreed and the couple got engaged. John is convinced that, left to themselves, they would have been happy; but life is rarely simple for the discharged prisoner. They had nowhere to live since Kitty was resident cook at a boys' prep school and had no home of her own. Prices were high and accommodation scarce. Scouse took on a second job in order to save more money. Despite his Liverpudlian love of town life, he even applied for a job on a farm in the hope of getting a cottage, but was turned down.

The delay was fatal. Kitty's family got cold feet about the affair and began to apply pressure to make her give Scouse up. He had been a criminal, they pointed out, they would never rest easy in their beds if she married him and anyway what would people say?

The problems became too intense, the struggle to overcome them too great. Sadly, Kitty called off the engagement.

Scouse's hurt and bitterness were pitiful to see. The only way he could bear them was to find a scapegoat.

On the night that he and Kitty parted for good he arrived at John's house full of abuse and with his bags packed. 'You lousy bastard,' he shouted at John, among other things. 'It's all your fault.' Then he turned and ran away into the darkness and disappeared.

John had lost a friend, and Langley House had lost a first-class maintenance man: Scouse's losses and gains remained to be counted.

It was Christmas time and one or two of the men were making plans to spend the day with their relatives, others had been invited to the homes of local families, but most were staying at Elderfield, and the Dodds were busy decorating the house, putting lights on the tree and buying presents for each man.

John had decided that there must be two Christmas dinners, one on Christmas day, and one a few days before it so that the men going out could carry a sense of belonging with them.

Murdo had decided to spend Christmas away but he still couldn't make up his mind with whom to spend it, his wife or his mistress, and was in a torment of indecision. When they all trooped into the dining-room for the pre-Christmas dinner, he was ominously silent.

It took a bitter man not to be moved by the sight of the table which was laid out as even the Prince of Wales and the Governor of Parkhurst might have wished, while by the side plate of each man going out for Christmas there was a present—the first some of them had ever received. The others were to get theirs on Christmas morning.

They worked their way through the turkey and reached the Christmas pudding.

Without warning, Murdo crashed back his chair and leaped for John's throat. Everyone sat immobile for a second as the two men struggled, and then the volcano that had been threatening for weeks erupted.

Four men hurled themselves on John and Murdo with, as they said later, the intention of parting them. Others took the opportunity to pay off old scores—Alex immediately swung a punch at Jack Long. Soon the table had been overturned and men were struggling on the floor in the remains of the Christmas pudding and a release of pent-up violence.

Alyson called the police. Mother Dodd fainted and in the excitement was revived, a total abstainer all her life, with brandy.

Within minutes the police had arrived. John and Alyson went to meet them, still wearing their party hats.

CHAPTER SEVENTEEN

THE FIRST FIFTEEN

Almost anyone but John might have thought the project a failure.

Six months of the most intensive work of his life, in which he had hardly seen his wife and daughters—and John was devoted to his family—had ended in fiasco.

Murdo had gone, with no charge laid against him. Henry had gone, and was in prison, so was Buck. Scouse seemed well on his way there, and Little Arthur was still clinging to Langley for support. Their Christmas had been wrecked and so had the dining-room, and all they had left was a houseful of unsettled old lags.

It was not exactly a promising start.

But John's belief that God intended him to do this work was not just a happy thought that had popped idly into his head one day. It was a profound conviction. Furthermore the progression of events that had given him this certainty had also endowed him with a determination not to be beaten. The Japs hadn't been able to make him give in and neither could anything else. As usual, he was backed to the hilt by Alyson and the Trustees.

He carried on.

He saw his mistakes very clearly and blamed himself for them, although it is doubtful if he could have acted differently. There were no training schools for projects like Langley House because there was no precedent for it, except, perhaps, Norman House and, as Merfyn Turner points out in his book *Safe Lodging*, that was busy making mistakes of its own.

The only way to learn was through experience.

But in realising his mistakes, John also saw their remedy and over the next year or two Langley House acquired a new format. Fresh house parents were chosen who placed less emphasis on evangelism and rather more on concern for the men's mental and physical welfare, and in his briefing John warned them that coping with bickering and constant demands for attention were an intrinsic part of the job.

John's selection of residents became more discriminating. He saw to it that there were rarely more than two old lags in the house at any one time, the other places being filled with less committed offenders. Obviously psychopaths and men with violent crimes on their record sheet could not be accepted, neither could anyone who had committed sexual offences. Neither, he reluctantly decided, could eneuretics. Eric had been a bed-wetter and John had seen what a strain the daily washing of a complete change of bedding imposed on the house mother. It was a shame because eneuretics are the most pitiable of criminals, badly disturbed, and often forced into crime by their disability —landladies and hostels refuse to take them and they are turned on to the streets. But John felt he must protect his house parents from as many additional burdens as he could.

But if Langley House's portals narrowed in this respect, from 1960 onwards it was open to Christians and non-Christians alike. In future, John decided, the only criterion would be whether a man needed help and whether Langley House could help him.

Other, less definable changes came about in the attitude of everyone concerned in the running of Elderfield, from the Trustees down. They began to see that the job they had taken on was very long-term work and that a man might need a year or more at Langley House before he could face life on his own, and even then the result might not be instant integration.

Gradually, they abandoned yardsticks like success and failure; apparent success could turn to failure and apparent failure become success over the years and, anyway, only God was equipped to assess a man's life in such terms. For their part they became less concerned with whether a man kept completely free from trouble after his stay with them, and more interested in how he resolved his personality problems. So they just kept casting their bread upon the waters ... and often after many days they found it again.

Murdo, for instance, was to turn up on the Dodd's doorstep five years after the disastrous Christmas, friendly and grateful. 'Just thought I'd come and say thanks for all you did for me.' He had been in prison since they'd seen him last, but had rid himself of indecision by returning to his wife and retrieving his children from the care of the local council.

As for Scouse, after shaking the dust of Langley House from his feet he returned to his old stamping ground Liverpool to live with his married sister, and there he met up again with Edith, an old flame, the sister of his former accomplice in crime.

Once an attractive woman, Edith, now a widow, had aged badly during Scouse's imprisonment. She was suffering from brainstorms and was very deaf which made her temper uncertain and caused her difficulty in providing for her teenage daughter.

Scouse could not bear to see her in such straits and went to live with her, making a home for her and her daughter, and getting a job at an iron galvanising works to do so.

The work was hard for a man who had never worked consistently, and a disruptive home life, with Edith throwing frequent tantrums and even smashing up the new furniture Scouse had bought for her, did not help.

These were heavy burdens for someone like Scouse to bear, and the strain could have sent him back to burglary. But Elderfield had given Scouse more than just the opportunity to practise painting and decorating, and he didn't go back to screwing. What he did do one day after a quarrel with Edith was to slam out of their flat, carelessly picking up their landlord's raincoat on his way out. And the landlord informed the police and preferred a charge.

Luckily the C.I.D. sergeant who handled the case turned out to be one of the best. He knew Scouse and had heard of Langley and was sympathetic to both. He contacted John and told him of Scouse's approaching trial, which was to be before Judge Laski, renowned among the criminal fraternity for his tendency to 'hand out porridge like it was breakfast'.

But the attitude of the police, John's plea on Scouse's behalf, and Scouse's heroic attempts to go straight were impressive; Judge Laski gave him a conditional discharge.

Seven years were to go by before they heard from Scouse again and then, one breakfast time, the familiar putt-putt of his two-stroke motor cycle sounded in the drive of the Dodds' home. It was as if he'd never been away. There'd been one hell of a row with Edith, he told them, and he'd felt he couldn't stand it any more, so he'd hopped on the bike and driven down the M.6 all night to see John.

He was still working as a galvaniser, was still keeping straight and, after a day talking it out with John and Alyson, he went back to his Edith.

He is another man who has reached honourable retirement without any more trouble. He keeps in close touch with the Dodd family and Langley by visiting one of the houses where staff and residents alike are helped by his calm assurance. John remembers an official report on Scouse from a prison governor who wrote: 'This man was a Salvationist, is now a Methodist, and is on the road to hell.'

But all these things were unknown to the men and women of Langley House in 1960 when they settled down to do their job because, like Everest, it was there.

There was one more devastating blow to come, the worst of all, and although they were not to blame for it, they couldn't have felt worse about it if they had been . . .

. . . In all this time Percy had been a model resident, his calm personality in strong contrast with the violently disturbed men who had blazed in and out of the house like twisted comets in the early months. Percy was at his happiest doing odd jobs for Alyson and John and adored the three Dodd girls. He had given them a present of a baby rabbit each which, he assured Alyson, were of the same sex. (The fact that they later came back from a holiday to find the garden cropped to the bone and hopping with baby rabbits proved him wrong.)

It was difficult to remember that Percy had a long record of senseless petty larceny, so trustworthy did they find him. One of his many inexplicable exploits, for instance, had been to steal the car of his local minister when it was standing outside Percy's own house—the minister having called on his mother.

When Percy began courting everybody was delighted. Marriage to a sensible woman had been the saving of more than one discharged offender, and will be the saving of many more, and Percy had chosen a nice, red-headed girl, a local youth leader.

The Dodds were delighted for him and at Percy's and Jane's wedding, their youngest daughter Lorraine was bridesmaid.

The couple rented a country cottage nearby and, obviously

happy, frequently dropped in to see John and Alyson.

Then, one morning three months after the wedding, Percy got up and went downstairs to make his wife a cup of tea, as he always did. He filled the tea pot, laid the tray neatly, and took it upstairs.

At the door of the bedroom he stopped. The room was in chaos, with blood everywhere and his wife was lying dead in it, a hammer on the floor nearby, which he had been using to mend the window the night before.

Percy stood there in shock for a long time until he realised that he was the only person who could have done it.

He dropped the tray, ran out of the house and disappeared.

Three weeks later he walked into a police station and gave himself up.

The effect on everybody who knew Percy was one of incredulity.

But at Percy's trial for murder facts were brought to light that explained many things.

Jack Wallace, the solicitor and chairman of the Trustees, who was fond of Percy, took up the case and Sir Norman Skelhorn Q.C., was engaged for the defence.

Evidence was brought to show that the accused had suffered severe convulsions within a few hours of his birth. Then an eminent brain specialist from the Middlesex Hospital who had examined Percy went into the witness box to testify that the man had always been, and was now, an epileptic, subject to fits which, although they had passed unnoticed so that not even his family had suspected them, made him not responsible for his actions. The specialist had no doubt that the state of marriage had brought a latent violence to the surface.

The prosecution tried to counter this by producing the senior medical officer of Percy's prison, who insisted that he had studied the accused and could find no trace of mental abnormality.

Sir Norman cross-examined, trying to get the M.O. to change his opinion or at least admit to doubt in view of the specialist's evidence, but he refused to budge. John, watching him get down from the stand, thought: 'He's done Percy more good than harm.'

The jury evidently agreed. The verdict was 'Not guilty of murder, but guilty of manslaughter on the ground of diminished responsibility.'

Percy went to Dartmoor and was later transferred to Parkhurst where the medical facilities are better. Langley kept in touch with him all that time and Mother Dodd, now ninety-two years old and still flourishing, wrote to him regularly. It wasn't feasible to take him in again, but at the end of his sentence they managed to find a small epileptic unit in London which makes a home for such ex-offenders.

A little while ago the matron there wrote to John saying that Percy was becoming upset because he didn't know where his wife was buried. John made arrangements and a few weeks later she brought Percy down to Hampshire for the day and took him to see the grave. After he'd gone back he wrote to say he felt more at peace.

In January 1961 John got a letter. It was on plain paper, giving a Yorkshire address, and it was very short. It just said: 'I have recently read an article about the work of Langley House and I am interested in buying you another Langley House in Yorkshire.'

John drove up North the next day. Going through Manchester he got tangled up in the traffic of a rosetted crowd on their way to see United play Spurs in the Cup. Memories of boyhood visits to Old Trafford flooded back and for a moment he was tempted to turn his back on Langley and its heartbreak and go with them, but he fought it down and drove on.

The woman he had come to see ran a dental clinic. Then, as now, she wanted to be anonymous. She gave him tea, boiling eggs in the steriliser, ladling apricots out of an ointment jar and setting the instrument table for two. She had, she told him, some savings which she wanted to put to good use. She had thought of donating a Cheshire Home, but there was already one in the area.

'Whatever it is,' she said, fixing John with her eye, 'I want it here in the North where I can take an interest in it.'

She had been looking round for another good cause when

she happened to read an article about Elderfield in *Church Illustrated,* written by Geoffrey Howard, a B.B.C. friend of John's who had done a great deal to publicise the work of Langley House. It had impressed her profoundly.

'And so,' she ended, briskly, 'I have decided to buy you a house. Will you accept it?'

She bought them Box Tree Cottage, a large old house in a pleasant residential area of Bradford. It was furnished, as Elderfield had been, with varied gifts from well-wishers, inconsistent as to style, maybe, but creating an instant effect of home.

It opened in June 1961. The houseparents at Elderfield moved to Bradford to take charge, while another couple, the Herringtons, were installed at Elderfield in their place.

Into it, too, came Braddy, a twenty-one-year-old epileptic. John was refusing epileptics then. But as his skill as a selector increased he came to rely more on his own judgement than on a man's record sheet and was prepared to break his own rules occasionally. Selection, after all, is an art, not a science, trying to see the man not the label—and nobody ever needed help more than Braddy.

The son of a prostitute, he had never known his father—it is doubtful if even his mother could have told him whose son he was—and had spent most of his early years waiting in the street in all weathers until his mother had finished entertaining her clients.

His lack of confidence was reflected in an extremely bad stammer, not helped by the fact that his epilepsy barred him from a steady job. He had committed stupid, minor offences, so ineptly that it was obvious he intended to be caught and, at twenty-one, had all the hallmarks of a recidivist who found prison more congenial than life outside.

Box Tree Cottage was a revelation to him and during his first few weeks there, off work while he received out-patient treatment for his condition, he was in a constant state of surprise at the meals, the clean beds, the companionship and, above all, the fact that he was cared for.

He spent a lot of time in the kitchen watching the housemother preparing the meals and she realised he had probably never seen a woman cook before. Acting on an inspiration one day she said: 'Would you like to help me?' Braddy would, very much. He had a natural aptitude for cooking and the housemother, an excellent cook herself, taught him all she knew, starting with plain dishes, then pastry and puddings, bringing him eventually to *haute cuisine.*

They hardly dared hope so simple a key would open the way to his rehabilitation but the more proficient Braddy became the less he stammered. When he left them just over a year later it was to become under-chef at a large hotel in Blackpool.

John's case-book on him reads: 'Braddy—happily married. Holds down job as chief chef. Epilepsy under control. Stammers only occasionally.'

John broke his own rule again when he took Andy into Elderfield because, strictly speaking, Andy was a sexual offender. He had been found guilty of indecent assault, as well as having a long history of larceny.

The public image of sexual offenders is frequently of rapists, but Andy didn't belong in that category at all. He was a big, shambling, overgrown schoolboy of forty-eight whose elderly parents had 'protected' him from normal life, especially such wicked traps as girls, and had then died, leaving him to blunder about the world on his own.

His indecent assaults had never involved anything more than touching girls' legs which John judged, rightly, to be the fumblings of a delayed adolescence. It was the innocence and loneliness on Andy's round and simple face that decided John.

Andy loved Elderfield and particularly the housefather, Pop Herrington, with whom he shared a weight problem. Both of them were over eighteen stone and had been told to go on a strict diet. They would sit in the kitchen together, solemnly eating their ration of slimming biscuits, and then tuck into a three-course meal. It did nothing for their figures, but the shared wickedness of it did a great deal for Andy's morale.

By the time he left them, two years later, Andy had matured beyond recognition and they knew, with a fair degree of certainty, that he would be able to hold down a simple job, and wouldn't pester girls any more.

CHAPTER EIGHTEEN

NEW HOUSES: OLD ATTITUDES

It's mainly because of people like the lady dentist that Langley House Trust has become the biggest organisation of its kind in the world. It now has twelve houses, most of them bought through the generosity of Christians prepared to put their money where their faith is, so that the Trust can now accommodate 240 men at any one time.

It's running ahead of the story, but it's worth listing here how the houses were acquired.

After Box Tree Cottage at Bradford came The Chalet at Reading, which opened its doors to discharged offenders in August 1962. That was an acquisition entirely due to John's great friendship with Dr. Leslie Davison, general secretary of the Methodist Home Missions Department. Through him the Methodist Church became one of Langley's biggest supporters. In 1961 it had bought Elderfield outright for the Trust, relieving them of the £400 a year lease, and the next year gave them The Chalet, a pleasant house in a quiet, good-class residential street.

The following year saw the opening of a house in Cheltenham, provided by the Cheltenham Council of Churches.

In 1964 the Bournemouth Discharged Prisoners' Aid Society offered them a house in Poole, Dorset. Soon after came another, this time in Strood, Kent, bought for them once again by the Methodist Church.

It was a local group of Christians, energetically raising money by running a shop for the cause as well as more usual fund-raising methods, who bought them their next house in Lancaster.

In November 1967 the Home Secretary opened Langley's most ambitious project up to that date, the Coventry house for young offenders. This had been a dream of John's and Oliver Stott's from the beginning. It had never been satisfactory to include adolescent boys and young men, some of them with only one offence behind them, who badly needed a home influence, among older residents with longer records.

It came about from a report by the Principal Probation Officer for Coventry, Andrew Murray, in 1961 on the problems of finding accommodation for the very type of young person Langley was concerned about. 'The real need,' he wrote, 'is not for a training hostel, but for good, straightforward homely accommodation where people can stay and go out to work normally.'

The Bishop of Coventry, Dr. Cuthbert Bardsley, became interested and the Coventry Council of Churches took up his plea, turning to Langley for advice. The Trust agreed to accept responsibility.

The Council of Churches made an appeal for £10,000 towards the project, getting only £4000 and so went to the Coventry City for help and received an amazing response.

The City Council offered to provide specially-built premises costing £35,000, the first—and perhaps the last—time a local authority has financed new premises for such a purpose.

In those days £35,000 went a long way. The house had a games-room, music-room, sitting-room, dining-room, fully equipped laundry and sewing-room, flats for houseparents and assistants, bedrooms for nineteen residents and a sick bay. John called it Murray Lodge in honour of Andrew Murray.

Because of their adolescence its residents have always been more difficult even than the usual run of Langley House men. Now that unemployment has reared its ugly head in the area, they're more difficult than ever. To be out of a job for a long time is always degrading, but its especial evil for ex-offenders, particularly young ex-offenders, is that they can't ever acquire the self-respect which earning money can give.

The house at Coventry pounds with frustration and aggression. Nevertheless, John says it has succeeded beyond his expectations and the boys know that at least somebody cares and that, sooner or later, will stand them in good stead.

In 1969 another dream of John's materialised with the acquisition of Wing Grange in Rutland, bought by the Home Missions Department of the Methodist Church again and leased to Langley rent free. Up to then there had always been a certain agony for Langley selectors in having to turn down many of the men who needed them most, the grossly damaged, who would never be able to cope with the demands of society and who would, from lack of suitable provision, have to spend most of their lives in prison.

Now they were able to create a sheltered community in a house surrounded by some twenty acres with its own market gardens and workshops where residents could do a useful job of work within their capacity without having to face competition.

It was the sort of place where the type of men who were scarred on John's memory, like Henry the public schoolboy who was afraid to get up in the mornings, and Eric last seen directing traffic in Southampton, could come and find sanctuary.

The scheme was such a success that John wanted to expand the idea and buy another community elsewhere, so he turned again to the man he describes as his father confessor, Leslie Davison, who acted as go-between between him and Lord Rank who, as J. Arthur Rank, had created the film company and a large empire of many other things besides. Lord Rank was a devout Methodist who had already given enormous financial help to Langley.

Always a man who liked to see what good his money was doing Lord Rank decided to visit Wing. As a result John and Leslie Davison found themselves cruising up to Rutland with him in his Rolls-Royce, arriving in time for lunch. John had previously inquired what Lord Rank would like for lunch. The answer had come back: 'Salmon'. On being told this the staff at Wing protested in good democratic manner. Salmon? Why give him salmon? Why not the plain, sustaining everyday meal they and the men always had?

'Good grief,' said John, 'he bought the place. Give him salmon.'

So they did. Afterwards Lord Rank went all over the Grange, peering into the workshops, the greenhouses, asking questions of the staff, talking to the men. He was particularly taken by a little ex-burglar called Geoff, who, like Lord Rank, was a Yorkshireman but who, unlike Lord Rank, hadn't made it and was now happily ensconced at Wing looking after the pigs. During a long conversation Geoff the burglar told Lord Rank the capitalist what it had been like for him to find Langley. 'If it wasn't for Wing I'd be back inside,' he said firmly. 'It gives you a breather, see, away from pressure.'

Lord Rank walked thoughtfully back to the lawn in front of the old, red-brick house and stood staring out at the lovely Rutland countryside. As John and Leslie Davison came up he turned: 'Leslie,' he said, 'I think I'll buy them another place.'

He bought them Forncett Grange, another community with farm and workshops in Norfolk.

When both he and Leslie Davison died in 1972 John felt bereft.

Their next acquisition, in December 1972, was a house with four and a half acres of land near the village of Norton Fitzwarren just outside Taunton. At the beginning of the century it had been run by a local trust as a home for young wayfarers and then, much later, had been taken over by the St. Martin-in-the-Fields' social service unit as a place to send some of their homeless and destitute men. But it had proved too difficult and too far away to administer from London and had been offered to Langley.

John and Alyson went down to see it together. John has come to lean more and more on Alyson in Langley House work over the years and particularly on decisions about houses. She is an architect *manquée* with a feel for houses, and casts a very stern eye over possible properties. The one at Taunton looked terrible—a run-down old house surrounded by pre-fab buildings. 'It was really grotty,' she says, but she could see its potential and, several years later, with a grant from the Home Office, the biggest they've ever received—£45,000—the potential was eventually realised. With its apple trees, its poultry runs, its light and airy extension at the back, its workshops, greenhouses and fields, all set in view of the Quantocks, it has become perhaps the most attractive community house the Trust runs.

Their latest property, Hanby House, came through the kindness of Mr. and Mrs Lyonel Tollemache. Mary Tollemache, née Whitbread of brewery fame, had long been a supporter of Langley and early in 1972 she wrote to John saying they had a property in Buckminster, a village only sixteen miles north of Wing, 'which we'd be pleased to let you have if it's any use'.

John and Alyson drove up there not knowing what to expect. What they found was an enormous ex-stable block built round its own courtyard and then in use as a students' hostel. It opened as a Langley community in August the following year.

All this was not achieved without opposition. John says that as he's becoming older he's getting less resilient—he's sixty-one now. If he is, it isn't discernible to the naked eye, but there's no doubt that with the acquisition of each house he's had to spend more and more energy on winning the public round.

The first time they met such opposition was when the local Council of Churches offered them a house in Cheltenham. Planning permission to use it as a residence for ex-offenders had been given but when the news reached people in the area there was an immediate emotional reaction. Angry letters were written to the *Gloucestershire Echo*, protest meetings were held and John appeared on television in a confrontation with one of his opponents. Another said to him privately: 'We've already got a home for mentally retarded children, we don't want criminals as well.'

John explained and explained, pointing out that he knew the history of every carefully selected man in his houses and that to protect his own houseparents and their children, let alone anyone else, he refused anyone with a pattern of sex or violence on his record.

Writing in reply to the letters in the *Gloucestershire Echo* which had complained of the proposed Langley House's 'proximity to children and lonely old people', he said: 'It would be difficult to find anywhere that wasn't. Anyway, many of our staunchest supporters elsewhere are elderly ladies. Incidentally, perhaps the person who voiced a threat to "burn down the house" would like to add his name to our waiting list of residents. We could not, of course, guarantee to accept him.'

But the two sides were irreconcilable. Eventually the Borough Council stepped in and offered Langley another house in a different, more acquiescent part of Cheltenham.

Finally there was a cartoon in the *Echo* showing a convict sitting in his cell, looking up at a tweedy colonel and his lady and saying: 'No thanks, I'm choosy where I live—particularly as regards neighbours.' John has kept it to this day.

But if that particular incident was over, the fight has gone on. Time and again John had to appear at protest meetings. The most recent was one of the worst. It was in Leeds where John was attempting to set up some rather more independent housing for ex-offenders in a deprived downtown area. A disadvantage of some Langley Houses is that they are rather isolated and in countryside whereas, in the nature of things, their residents originate from and are used to big towns. The area that had been chosen already had a Corporation lodging house which contained 600 men and John thought that his modest housing scheme wouldn't be noticed or minded. He was wrong.

The anger and shouting coming at him from the body of the hall was an indication of how threatened the locals felt. Using some of the milder language of the occasion one large and vociferous lady yelled: 'We don't want those buggers here.'

John abandoned the idea, at least for that area.

Being John, I don't think he can quite understand the people who oppose him, although he tries. He sees only the appalling need of men like Braddy, Scouse and Eric and the fact that a truly decent society can't leave them without help. His opponents see only a threat.

However, the Reverend Arnold Bellwood, the Trust's chaplain, has some sympathy: 'We're facing a basic human fear, after all,' he says.

On the whole, though, that fear is not justified by the facts. It wouldn't be honest to pretend there haven't been incidents over the years caused by Langley men going off the rails. There have been one or two minor assaults and an occasional break-in. The men at Wing are banned from three of the four local pubs but then, Wing is a village which led a very sheltered life until the advent of a Langley House in its midst. When the same thing happened down in Taunton, Trevor Dunkerley, the young housefather, got the bans lifted by going and drinking with his men. (No alcohol is allowed in any of the Trust's houses.) Then there was the ludicrous incident at Forncett where a grossly inadequate young resident who'd been asked to shoo the hens into the henhouse for the night, panicked when he found they wouldn't go, knocked the truants on the head and covered up his crime by chucking their bodies over the wall on to a neighbouring farmer's land.

Nevertheless, considering everything, the houses are a credit to careful selection, the staff, and of course, the men themselves. There are times when people living around the homes positively benefit from having them there. In the recent bad February when the south-west of England was flattened out by snow, for instance, the men at Taunton saved the life of one man by finding him and digging him out of the snow where he had lain all night.

Then they carried milk to old age pensioners in the area, dug out other people's houses and rescued their own greenhouses and workshops from collapse by staying up for two nights shovelling the snow off.

The same thing was done by the men at Elderfield, who won themselves a commendation from Otterbourne's vicar in the *Hampshire Chronicle* for their 'cheerful hard work' in digging out stranded motorists.

Also the ordinary men and women who neighbour the Langley Houses often show great understanding and kindness by sending in gifts or proffering invitations to tea. There's a barrister who spends one evening every week at Elderfield just talking and listening to the men. There are local policemen who do the same.

It's not all hostility by any manner of means. Nevertheless, as Keith Best, Langley's deputy administrator for the northern houses, says: 'We're a non-respectable charity. Always will be. The attitude is: "You're doing a grand job, go and do it somewhere else." '

How they kept going financially in those early years when Langley was supported purely by voluntary contributions is a miracle in itself. It was one thing to acquire houses and another to keep them functioning and pay the staff. The men's rent went nowhere near covering running costs—even in those days each house needed an additional £2000 a year over and above the men's contribution.

Their greatest resource, of course, was John himself and his gift of salesmanship and when, in 1962, they were joined by Doug Healey, it left John freer to use that gift. Doug, a Quaker, was that unusual combination, a stern realist and a man of compassion. He and his wife Blanche were already experienced in after-care and to him John handed over the work of selecting, which, because of the extensive travelling it entailed to prisons, had become a full-time job.

They were a good team, Doug and John, because they held the same view that Langley's job, first and always, was to provide a home. As group therapy and trained social workers were being used more and more in progressive prisons there was a lot of pressure on Langley to use trained welfare workers as houseparents who would apply psycho-therapy in the homes.

This John and Doug, backed by the Trustees, steadfastly refused to do. Then and now some houseparents had previous social work experience, some had not. Regular in-service training has always been provided and has become part of the Langley scene, but both Doug and John maintained that loving care is the essential qualification for staff and that a housemother who sewed on a missing button, or a housefather who asked: 'How did you get on at work today, Alf?' and then listened with interest to the reply about the bloodymindedness of the foreman, are providing the real therapy.

'Langley House is not a clinic,' said Doug, 'it is a family in which a man can feel at home and secure and to which, if he is mentally or physically sick, the ordinary welfare services can be invoked from outside as they would be by any normal family.'

Anyway, with the advent of Doug, John was able to go around the country selling his unrespectable charity to respectable people, breaking down prejudice, raising funds and, just as important, persuading firms and organisations to employ his men.

At the start of the Trust in 1959 the Friends of Langley had been formed, a band of sympathetic men and women all over the country who supported the project with financial help and with what John regarded as equally important, their prayers.

Year by year the Trustees and John have built up their numbers so that they are now about 1400 strong and many make covenanted gifts of money to the Trust.

His personal contacts with people like Dr. Leslie Davison, Lord Rank and, later, with the powers-that-be at the Home Office have been of enormous value to Langley. People like Princess Alexandra have become interested in the project; in fact the Princess has visited both Lancaster and Forcett Grange houses and went on record as saying: 'Founded on truly Christian principles in the spirit of compassion and realistic idealism, this work demands the support and help of us all.'

The head of Community Service Volunteers, Mr. Alec Dickson C.B.E., is an admirer of John and Langley and it is a great deal due to him that nearly every Langley House has at least one C.S.V. helping alongside the Trust's staff.

It was Alec Dickson who quoted Goethe about John's empathy with ex-prisoners: 'Only he who has eaten his bread with tears can know my thoughts.'

And it was Geoffrey Howard, John's friend from the B.B.C. and unofficial publicist to Langley House, who told him he could best sell Langley by selling himself. 'You've got a good story to tell, why not tell it?' asked Geoffrey and arranged that the story go out on B.B.C. radio in 1963 in the 'People Today' series. He did the narration, brought in Oliver Stott and some of the Langley residents and left John telling his own, typically plain, account of his life to do the rest.

It had been years since John had thought deeply about his time in Changi and the jungle and he found, as he talked, that the memories had lost their sting.

The broadcast had an immediate impact and money and offers of help came pouring in. For two Christmasses running they received an anonymous gift of £1000. A battered Cadbury's Milk Tray box arrived containing £100 and a message: 'As unto the Lord'. What pleased John most was the fact that many people wrote to say that he'd given them a fresh slant on offenders, although one lady, who seemed to have missed the point, sent £50 with a note saying: 'This is for you and your dear family and is NOT to be used on those dreadful men.'

The other thing that happened was that John became a

subject of 'This Is Your Life'. He didn't know he was going to be, of course. Alyson, who went on the programme with Mother Dodd, Ros, Diana and Lorraine, had kept the secret for months. John, conned by Geoffrey Howard thought he was on his way to Wormwood Scrubs to take part in a T.V. programme on offenders. He couldn't understand why the taxi taking him and Geoffrey there was going so slowly, and kept saying so. (He's always loathed sitting still.) Geoffrey, who, knowing they had to time their arrival exactly, was perspiring a lot, said desperately: 'There's a traffic jam.'

John peered out of the window into a street that was clear for as far ahead as he could see. 'A traffic jam?'

'It's round the corner,' said Geoffrey, mopping his brow.

It was when they arrived at the Scrubs and were ringing the bell that the lights went up and Eammon Andrews stepped out of the shadows to announce that This Was John Dodd's Life.

Strangely enough, although I didn't know John then, I happened to see that programme and I remember thinking then that it was outstanding of its kind. Briefly as the story was told, it came over strongly that here was a man who, having endured terrible events, had turned them into good for his fellows.

John, after the first shock, realised it would be good publicity for Langley House. So it was. Jack Long was seen in silhouette and said that John had probably saved him from the gallows. Terry and Canon Noel Duckworth came on to talk of John's endurance in Changi. Oliver Stott gave his tribute, so did the voices of some of the men at the Reading house.

John guessed from the first that the climax would be an entrance by Marquita and was dying to see her again, their last meeting having been in France nine years before. What he hadn't anticipated and what shook him was when Phiphine walked out from the wings. It had been twenty-two years since he'd seen her, when he was marched off at bayonet point. She was now the mother of two children but she still looked very much the same, and the sight of her brought scents and memories of Java overwhelmingly back. But by the time Marquita came on, projecting her own tremendous personality, he was back in his stride and enfolded her in a bear hug.

In his peroration Eammon Andrews referred to John as a man of 'courage and compassion'. What made that programme last in the memory long after others had been forgotten was that it was so obviously the truth.

The work at the halfway houses gained a certain swing. At Cheltenham the men began a tradition of giving parties for old age pensioners. Box Tree Cottage did the same for deprived children. A shy, withdrawn resident saved 800 threepenny bits and presented them to the children's diagnostic unit near by. The Director of Education for Southampton, who lived near Elderfield, complimented the men on their neighbourliness.

They won some: they lost some. A case like Barry's would cause them joy only to be followed by one like Frank's.

Barry had been in trouble since the age of ten, when his mother died of cancer and he was taken into care. He had absconded often and had begun stealing early and was sent for corrective training. Eventually he had married and settled down to become a devoted husband and father. Then, after seven years, his wife left him for another man, taking with her their little girl. Barry was distraught, pleading with her to come back. When she refused he broke into the house where she and the other man were living and set fire to it. He was convicted of arson and sent to prison for four years.

Langley was asked to take him by John Williams, chaplain at Birmingham prison, in whose chapel Barry had been confirmed. The chaplain was convinced that Barry not only needed love but had an immense capacity for giving it.

John's growing circle of employers prepared to give jobs to ex-prisoners included the local hospital and there Barry was sent as a porter. Some time later the hospital secretary rang John to say: 'You haven't got any more like him, have you? If you have, we could do with a dozen.'

Barry's transition to the outside world was gentle. He stayed at Elderfield for eight months and then moved out to share lodgings in Winchester with another former resident. When he announced on one of his frequent return visits to Elderfield that he was again to be married, they were delighted, though somewhat taken aback to find that his intended was a widow with five children and that, because she had been having a difficult time, all those children were in care.

But Barry knew what he was doing. He married her, got the children out of care and made a home for them. With six people to look after he was in his element, and eighteen years later he still is.

Frank, on the other hand, seemed incapable of any emotion at all. He had been diagnosed as a chronic schizophrenic and was completely withdrawn. He was out on licence from an eight-year stretch of preventive detention, and his probation officer begged Langley to take him because nobody else would. 'He's been sleeping rough, and you know what that means.' It meant an almost inevitable return to prison.

He was sent to the Reading house where, it was hoped, the young houseparents would be able to establish some sort of contact with him. But it was like trying to contact a man layered in cotton wool; he was encased in isolation so deep it was impossible to guess at the personality beneath. He never spoke even to say 'Pass the salt' at mealtimes, and went for walks by himself, returning through the house as if it were deserted, making straight for his room.

The other men, usually quick to resent anyone who ignored them, were surprisingly tolerant of his silence and joined the houseparents in trying to penetrate the insulation with which he protected himself. Nothing happened; in a house full of people Frank behaved like the caretaker of an empty building.

This went on for four months and then one day Frank came home from work early. The young housemother was in the kitchen preparing the evening meal and keeping an eye on her eighteen-month-old daughter, Rosemary-Ann, who was in her playpen in the next room. Suddenly, through the half-open door, she saw that Frank had come in and was staring at Rosemary-Ann. Quietly she put down her potato-peeler and watched.

For a long time he stood still and then, slowly walked up to the playpen, knelt down and spoke through the bars. 'Hello,' he said, 'what are you doing?' It wasn't said in the way adults usually address babies, more as a serious inquiry from one individual to another.

Rosemary-Ann gave a polysyllabic and unintelligible reply to which Frank listened carefully. Just then someone came in and Frank moved away.

The next evening Rosemary-Ann was in her playpen again and her mother was in the kitchen—with the door slightly ajar. Frank went straight to the playpen and this time held out his arms. Rosemary-Ann, loving the attention, scrambled into them.

From then on it became a ritual and the other men got used to seeing Rosemary-Ann sitting on Frank's knee. They seemed to accept one another completely. John was there on the night that Frank carefully read her the entire Budget speech from the *Evening News*.

She became his baby. He helped to bath her, feed her and put her to bed and gradually, through their common interest, the houseparents were able to draw him right out of his introverted state to chat with them and, through them, to the other men. Before long he was taking a full part in the house activities.

But the time came when the houseparents, young and enthusiastic as they were, began to crack under the strain of their job. They had been offered a post at the Helen Keller Home in Jerusalem and decided to take it before they broke down completely. They went, taking Rosemary-Ann with them.

New houseparents came in, kindly comfortable people who wanted to help, but they were older and with no children. Frank was unable to transfer his new-found communication; it hadn't been in existence long enough to withstand the loss of Rosemary-Ann. Within a few weeks of the changeover he left Langley to take a bedsitter on his own. They did their best, but nothing would bring him back to the fold.

Some time later a neighbour realised she hadn't seen him around for a while and called the police. They broke the door down and found him lying in his room on his bed with a piece of tubing leading from the gas fire to his mouth. He had been dead for eleven days.

CHAPTER NINETEEN

AT HOME

Frank's death highlighted John's greatest worry—how to keep staff. Amazingly, the difficulty was not to find them; Langley had sometimes a waiting list of couples volunteering for the work—but in keeping them for longer than eighteen months.

That year and a half was to Langley what the sound barrier had been to aviation, apparently impossible to go beyond. One couple had stayed for three and a half years; but that had only been by dint of changing houses in midstream. It became a factor in John's life that after eighteen months or so his houseparents cracked up with mental and physical fatigue and had to leave.

It seems patronising to refer to grown men as children. But if you visit a Langley House and watch the men with the houseparents you just can't avoid the analogy. There are the sulks, the showings-off, the perpetual demands for attention. If you're a parent you are irresistibly taken back to when your children were young and being difficult. But here there are nearly twenty of them, most of them emotionally disturbed and with the physical prowess of grown men. Add to that the work of provisioning, feeding, laundering and administration and you almost collapse under the admiration for the tenacious Christianity which keeps the houseparents going at all.

What's more, being the sort of people they are, these couples are very vulnerable to emotional demands and under greater pressure than less sympathetic personalities.

It isn't all one way giving, of course. The men can have great charm and humour, which is presumably why more than one lady helper has ended up marrying one of them.

There's always more laughter in Langley than all the troubles and bickering put together. And I haven't met a Langley houseparent or helper who hasn't said that they've received more than they've ever given. As Trevor Dunkerley at Taunton said: 'These rejects of society have shown us aspects of character, love and tolerance, kindness, shrewdness and respect that could put many with far kinder lives to shame.'

But the constant strain of living without privacy, too long on a tightrope balancing the needs of their own family against those of their adopted one can be too much, and they break. In those days when money was extremely scarce and there were few staff to help, they broke much too frequently.

The Reverend Ron Smith, a very unconventional Congregational minister who for most of his life advocated—and demonstrated—the value of worker priests, stayed for two years, working with his wife for sixteen hours a day, sometimes more. 'The job is so great and useful,' he said, 'but eventually I had to give it up because I was in danger of losing my son as a son. In the nature of the work I hadn't been able to give him enough of my time.'

John sympathised; if he was Langley's general these were his front-line troops under continual fire. But the fast turn-over of staff broke the continuity of the work. Discharged offenders are the least adaptable of men and don't take kindly to losing a couple of whom they've become fond and being faced with strangers—it's too much like their childhood, the basis of all the trouble, when they were passed from hand to hand.

Even men who'd left Langley but still needed its support would feel bitterly resentful when they revisited it to find that the husband and wife they had come, literally, to call Mum and Dad had been replaced by strangers.

But in 1964 June and Arthur Baker applied for a post with the Trust.

They met the Trustees in the room in Whitehall Place where Langley House had its London headquarters, both small and slight with two young children. June was in her twenties, Arthur was a young-looking thirty-eight.

Nobody could help taking to June with her Yorkshire commonsense and *joie de vivre*, but Arthur, more retiring and reserved, would take longer to know. He told the Trustees frankly that he'd had his own emotional difficulties stemming from a disrupted childhood, and that their own son Andrew was autistic. But it was obvious that he had insight not only into his own problems but into other people's as well. Both he and June had a strong faith in God which demanded that they be of service.

'We want a job where we'll be extended to the limit,' they said.

That the Trustees could certainly offer, but was it fair to subject a family that had its own troubles to the strain?

John personally felt that it was, and that the Bakers were especially fitted to provide sympathy and understanding to other people.

In the end the decision was taken out of their hands;·the houseparents to replace the Smiths were suddenly unable to accept the post. The Bakers got a letter asking them to take over Elderfield at once... and Langley House got one of the best couples it has ever had.

After an early career in the R.A.F., Arthur had become an ordained Baptist minister and married June, but they both found their seven years in the ministry disappointing. They had started out with hopes of being useful, but instead found themselves bogged down in endless committees and meetings. Arthur echoed Ron Smith in believing that until the Church rolled up its sleeves and threw itself into work for the community, forgetting the mechanics of its own survival, it wouldn't get anywhere.

Eventually they were transferred to Shropshire where a feud in the parish meant that Arthur was giving communion to people who, he knew, nursed malice for each other, despite anything he could do. He went into retreat and made the agonising decision to leave the ministry.

Their first child, Andrew, had been born in 1958 and Rowena in 1959. When Andrew was two they realised something was wrong, although none of the doctors and specialists who saw him diagnosed him as autistic until he was six.

Arthur went back to engineering, but they both knew it was only a stop-gap. Their confidence might have been shaken but their faith had not and they knew, when they saw a Langley House advertisement in the *Baptist Times*, that they must apply. They arrived at Elderfield on a cold December day in

1964, never having met a criminal in their lives, to take over as parents a houseful of discharged prisoners.

Their experience during those first months is, as far as I can find out, typical of what almost every houseparent goes through.

At first they were both knocked sideways—June by the overpowering response of the men to her, Arthur by the lack of it.

As one of the youngest housemothers Elderfield had known, June found that some men regarded her as a mother, others as a sweetheart, others as a sister, while to the rest she was any permutation of the three. In her anxiety to offend nobody —all houseparents think like that at first—she found the men taking up all her time and leaving her none for Arthur.

Arthur felt a bit like Cinderella. He was working harder than at any time in his life, getting up first in the mornings, always last to go to bed, spending the day on correspondence, contact with employers and probation officers, budgeting, other men's problems, arrangements for new arrivals and for those moving on, shovelling coke into a voracious boiler. Yet, because he didn't 'go out' to work, all this was discounted by his residents, who did.

As one of them said patronisingly at the supper table where Arthur sat, almost too exhausted to eat: 'All right for you Arth, isn't it, staying home all day.' And Arth was amazed at how much he resented the remark.

Six weeks after their arrival there was real trouble. In their early tolerance June and Arthur had allowed some of the rules to be bent here and there—democratically-minded houseparents dislike the idea of imposing school-type rules on grown men. But that had been taken as permissiveness, especially by Patrick, a burly Irishman. He chose to come back late from the pub—not for the first time—one night when Arthur, having locked up at eleven-fifteen p.m. as usual, was very tired indeed. Arthur had to go down and let him in, there was a sharp exchange which ended with Arthur saying crossly: 'In future this door doesn't open after eleven-fifteen, so what are you going to do about it?'

He winces now every time he remembers it. 'Talk about asking for trouble; I wouldn't provoke a man with a question like that now.'

The answer was a swift cross to Arthur's jaw and June came running downstairs to find her husband crumpled on the floor and Patrick with his foot raised ready to kick him in the ribs. She flew at the Irishman like an angry wasp, which surprised him so much he went tractably to bed.

He was sheepish the next day, especially when he found he was allowed to stay on, but faded quietly away on his own accord at the end of the week. Later he sent Arthur his kind regards from court by way of a probation officer—he was up on a different account, Arthur having made no charges.

But he left behind him a highly-charged atmosphere that took weeks to fade. It was even longer before June and Arthur could treat their bigger lads without wariness. But it passed and the incident became part of their education.

While they were still unsure of themselves, Jimmy came to stay. There's always someone like Jimmy. He was forty-seven but looked sixty, as men with a long record sometimes do. His was the same old story, a loveless childhood, shifting from one home to another until, by adolescence, he had become a mental and physical vagrant. At some time there'd been a wife, but he'd left her as he'd left his jobs.

It was impossible to convince him that he was wanted at Elderfield. He needed to believe it, but couldn't. June, twenty years his junior, he called 'Ma' and kept testing her with a persistence which amounted to persecution. It was 'Ma, how about sewing on this button?' 'Ma, guess what happened at work today.' 'Ma, you got a minute?' every time she put her feet up. Realising he was really asking: 'Do you care for me?' June ran herself ragged to reassure him, hoping he'd feel more secure in time.

But there came a night when it was 'Ma, I want to talk to you,' and June was busy and didn't go quickly enough. By the next morning Jimmy had gone.

Two days later she got a letter from him, full of reproaches, accusing her of being responsible for his present loneliness and, because she was under strain, June reacted by suffering guilt.

Later there was a phone call from the police to say that

Jimmy had been arrested for falsifying his post office book. Arthur went to court to speak for him, which procured him a conditional discharge and another chance at Elderfield. He returned in an aggrieved manner as if he'd been affronted and went into the old routine of trying to monopolise June. Again, when she didn't jump quickly enough, he left.

The pattern repeated itself more than once during the next year until June was at her wits' end. It finished miserably one night when Jimmy had been particularly jealous of the listening time she was giving to another resident. They noticed smoke coming out of the garage where Jimmy had lit a bonfire on top of Arthur's car.

This time Arthur allowed him to be charged in order to get him away. June was upset and went around feeling responsible until, much later, she got a bright phone call from Jimmy asking to come to tea as if nothing had happened.

She let him come to tea, but from then on began to cultivate the 'detached involvement' which Arthur had been advocating for some time. It was difficult for her, but she recognised it as necessary for their survival; there are some neurotics who are still gaily suffering their neuroses while those who have tried to help them are in a nervous breakdown, and Jimmy, pathetic though he might be, is one of them.

Since a high proportion of Langley residents—like a high proportion of men in prison—have a drink problem, it's part of the houseparents' job to lessen the lure of the pubs by making home life as attractive as possible. Elderfield itself needed decorating from top to bottom and the men were careless, dropping their newspapers, orange peel and fag ends on the floor. June changed all that. The men became more co-operative and tidy and also more willing to stay in at evenings and weekends as long as she and Arthur stayed with them.

Their most drastic change came at the end of their first four months when the Bakers dropped the evening prayer and Bible reading which had been a part of Langley since its beginning. To Langley House, hewn from and for evangelism, it was a fundamental departure and it caused much discussion and heartsearching among the Trustees and others in the work.

But the Bakers had made their move because of their Christianity, not from lack of it. Arthur said: 'I came to my own conclusion that this was an imposition. I found myself inviting a man to make his home with me, then having to say to him in effect: "If you don't like prayer and Bible reading at the supper table—and surely it was his table as much as mine—then you don't have to stay." This was a denial of the love Christ commanded me to have; he never ordered me to read the Bible to men. To me it is more important to make his love real to men than to read to them about it. To force prayer on such men as these, who have suffered emotional damage in most cases effectively inoculates them against the real thing.'

Too often it was a reminder of institution life where prayers and hymn-singing are prerequisites to getting a bed and a meal.

John had seen the change coming; during his stay at Langley Ron Smith, minister though he was, had unrepentantly taken to 'squeezing in prayers during adverts on the telly'.

John's own faith had become more realistic. He realised now that, just as his own conversion had been triggered off by the example of Dr. Leonard Wilson, the men of Langley could most readily be reached by seeing Christianity work in the life of others.

By the end of eighteen months the Bakers were professional at their job, although it's difficult to define exactly a skill which is a combination of experience and intuition. They would become aware of an action which broke the pattern of a man's usual behaviour. He would come in by the front door, perhaps, instead of the back as usual and, almost without realising it, June or Arthur would chalk up 'Better have a talk with Charlie: something's wrong' on a mental jotter.

They were no longer gullible. In their early days Mack, one of the older men, came to them and explained he wouldn't be able to pay his rent that week because his firm had switched him from wage to salary, so he had to wait until the end of the month for his cheque. Since Mack was the most trusted resident they had, June and Arthur accepted his word unquestioningly.

When, telling John Dodd about it, he suggested they check

with Mack's firm, they refused. John, who tries not to inter-
fere with houseparents' decisions, left them to it.

At the end of the month Mack made another excuse and this
time a phone call to his firm established that he was on a
weekly wage and always had been. The money had gone to a
local bookmaker.

Petty betrayals and lies like these have been part of an
offender's make-up and they remain his first resort when he's
faced with a problem. But they always hurt. However, it was
a measure of Mack's love for the Bakers and Elderfield that
he gave his pay packet to June every week from then on
so that she could extract his rent arrears before he spent them.

The Bakers began to relax and no longer bent over back-
wards to get all the men to like them all of the time; they had
to be accepted by the men as they were, just as they had to
accept the men.

'At one time we used to keep a man's Sunday lunch if he
was late, for instance,' Arthur said, 'until it was borne upon
us that if we were a family we had a right to impose a family's
demands. I realised too that there was a place for anger. I'd
kept my patience under wraps at first but later, if a man was
consistently late or abusive, I'd blow my top. It often brought
a man closer to us and increased his security, showing he was
part of the family with responsibilities to it. It's one of the
advantages we have over a social worker.'

They relaxed to the extent of getting fun out of the job
even if some of it was only really amusing in retrospect; like
the time when one young man who had supposedly left them
for good in the morning turned up again in the afternoon,
drunk, in the middle of their Second Open Day. June laughs
now to remember him falling asleep on the lawn and the
superb indifference of the guests as they stepped over his legs.

They did their best to gain acceptance in the community;
they even put on a play in Otterbourne's village hall, an ambitious project since it demanded co-operation, which ex-offenders aren't very good at. Two local girls took the female roles,
and, despite some hairy moments, it was a success.

In 1966 a crowd of people coming out of that same village
hall after a Harvest Festival supper were mown down by a
ten-ton Army lorry which had gone out of control on the

hill. One woman was killed instantly and thirteen people injured. The residents of Elderfield heard the crash and screams and dashed out to help. They fetched blankets for the wounded and shocked, comforted the distressed and generally held the fort until police and ambulances arrived.

Later Arthur received a letter from the Parochial Church Council ... 'to express the council's deep admiration and gratitude for the help which was so readily forthcoming'.

Otterbourne was proud of them, June and Arthur were proud of them and, best of all, the men were proud of themselves.

But if, after eighteen months, the Bakers were experts they were also deathly tired. They could never sit alone in their room without a knock on the door from some man who had a problem. The only way to ensure a free day off was to take the children and go out for the day which, in bad weather, wasn't always a success.

(Outsiders are often concerned at the possible moral danger to Langley House children. But because of careful selection this danger doesn't really exist. The greatest threat to them is that they'll be spoiled—inadequates mostly have great sympathy for and fellow-feeling with children. The only sign that a child is living cheek by jowl with former malefactors is its tendency to use prison slang. Rowena and Andrew, for instance, always referred to tobacco as 'snout'. But any bad language has been picked up at school.)

June was exhausted and even Arthur, who had grown in stature in the job and gradually won the respect of the men, was talking in terms of only six months more. The only thing which kept them going was prayer, their own and other people's.

Commander Arthur Hague, then the Home Office adviser on voluntary work in after-care, once said: 'There's no doubt in my mind that it is the people with a religious motivation who keep the less attractive forms of voluntary social effort going. They provide a large proportion of those who are willing to offer their services and their life and who are least prepared to give in when the pressures build up. I have no doubt it is because of this that Langley House is conspicuous in the field.'

At the very beginning when Langley House was still on the drawing-board as it were, Bob Tullett had suggested prayer partners, men and women all over the country who would be asked to intercede for God's help in the work. The idea had been adopted and had grown; regular prayer letters high-lighting the difficulties of the work and the needs of the men went out—and still do—to 800 people.

Houseparents always acknowledge their indebtedness to these prayers. 'We were supported beyond belief,' Arthur says, and June took to crawling up to her room at odd moments during the day to pray for strength to go on. 'I'd go up knowing I couldn't, and come down knowing somehow I could.'

At the end of two years they had not only crashed the time barrier, they had got their second wind. What happened was a combination of the Bakers' own chemistry and a huge step forward in Langley's development. In 1966 a report of the Advisory Council on the Treatment of Offenders and the Organisation of After Care recommended Home Office grants to effective voluntary after-care hostels.

Up to then, I can't help feeling, and even for a time after-wards there had been a certain distrust between the probation service and Langley House; the old story of the professional versus the amateur. John's ethic demanded that if you were in the work you must give your life to it. He'd seen what could happen if it became just an eight-hour-a-day job when he'd made a tour of Canada and visited, among other places, a community pre-release centre where psychologists, socio-logists and psychiatrists studying men's behaviour abounded by day but went home at night leaving the men to their own devices.

The probation service in turn, not unnaturally, strongly dis-trusted the untrained. Over the years both prejudices have gradually broken down and the two forces work closely to-gether with mutual regard.

However, the closer links with the Probation and After-Care Service and especially the per capita grant for each Langley resident made an enormous difference. Langley could improve its houseparents' salaries, give them up to six weeks'

well-earned annual holiday as well as provide another couple
to act as deputies. On top of this each house was provided
with daily cleaners and a cook.

Langley House moved into the push-button age with oil-
fired central heating and modern kitchen and laundering
equipment. They still needed money—they will always need
money—but the shoestring days were over.

The Bakers finally reached exhaustion point after four and a
half years at Elderfield, establishing a record which has long
since been broken many times over, but which will never be
forgotten by Langley House.

The long-service record is now held by John Gadd who, in
1977, received the Jubilee Medal for his fifteen years' service
to Langley and who is still with the Trust, helping Elizabeth
and Peter Prior, who came soon after him, at Wing. And
after these three came a long succession of people from all
walks of life who have been and still are Langley staff. There
are clerks, steel-workers, builders, commercial executives,
agriculturalists, teachers, hoteliers, nurses, ministers of religion, social workers, military officers and other ranks, people
qualified in law, theology and science. All they have in common is that they are committed Christians (although even in
that they represent every possible denomination from Roman
Catholic to strict non-Conformists) and the fact that they
could not feel fulfilled in their faith or their life unless they
were helping others.

They are amazing people. Whenever I hear that religion is
in decline in this country I think of Langley House and know
it isn't. In fact, when I hear the words 'modern saints' I think
of the Langley staff, despite the guffaws of derision it would
bring from all of them. They aren't meek and mild, mind you,
but then the saints of old weren't either. To go round the
Langley houses and meet them is to be subjected to blasts of
personality so strong that it's like being blown about by the
various winds of the compass. There isn't one of them who
doesn't believe he or she is running their Langley house
better than it was run before and has taught John Dodd
something new about after-care. They may even be right.
John believes firmly in giving his staff enormous scope to run

their houses in their own way even if, occasionally, that way leads to mistakes.

Langley's greatest strength is this enormously varied flexibility. Because of it and because of the way the houses are now arranged, there is a niche somewhere in its set-up for nearly every kind of offender, even those which other agencies won't accept. They still can't and won't take cases of persistent violence and sexual offences. Alan Whittall, assistant general secretary and the man responsible for residents selection and staff in the southern houses, says: 'I'd never willingly put any staff at risk. But we still take people nobody else will. We're almost an appendage to the National Health Service, taking "grey area" men who really should be in mental hospitals if only the mental hospitals would take them, which they won't.'

The selectors know the different Langley Houses, the attitudes of their neighbours and staff very well. A mugger of old people would not be sent to Peter Prior at Wing, for instance, because he has, and quite openly says he has, an antipathy to such men. On the other hand the Priors will take difficult, footloose, ageing ex-cons and have considerable success with them. (They must have saved the public a fortune in stolen goods by building up a rapport with Bill, a professional cat burglar who, until he went to them at Wing, had never spent a Christmas of his adult life out of prison. Because of their friendship Bill spent the last years of his life going straight and, when he suddenly died, left them as grief-stricken as if they'd lost a close member of the family which, in a sense, they had.)

Some staff are geared for and prepared to take a minor sexual offender. Some houseparents find eneuretics distasteful, others don't mind them at all.

Over the last ten years the greatest change has been in Langley's switch of emphasis from halfway houses to fully-supportive communities. At first sight to a layman this might look like defeat; a recognition that the original purpose of Langley to establish men in jobs in society had failed. But it's not that. The main reason for the change was that the setting up of hostels by the Probation Service creamed off those offenders with the greatest potential for successful rehabilitation.

'More and more we were getting the very damaged men,' said John Dodd, 'men whose potential for coping in society was extremely limited, some who just obviously never could. It was clear we had to change our original thinking.'

Always adaptable, that's what they did. They established what Peter Spurgeon at the Home Office calls 'sanctuaries for non-survivors', a phrase which describes them perfectly.

First came Wing, setting with its market garden and workshops the pattern for the others, Forncett, Taunton, Otterbourne and Hanby House in Leicestershire.

Three houses, Bradford, Reading and Poole remain halfway houses and pretty well they're doing too. One house, which kept careful record, was able to show that 43 per cent of its men had settled down to take a stable place in society, some of them marrying or re-uniting with estranged families. Ten per cent had reverted to crime. Contact with 25 per cent had been lost and the remainder had gone on to some other kind of care.

Cheltenham, Lancaster and Strood have become retirement homes for older men or for those who have no further work expectancy.

All this has increased Langley's flexibility. If a man finds he can't fit in at one home he can be moved, without too much trauma or sense of failure, to another and still stay in the family. Also, as a man's work potential improves, he can move out of a fully supportive unit to a halfway house. Or, if it declines as he gets older, he can move to a retirement home.

Anthony Greenwood, an ex-Army major and former commercial export manager who joined Langley in 1972 to take over Hanby House in Buckminster, recently wrote an article for the *Prison Service Journal* which is one of the most comprehensive pieces of journalism ever written about Langley and from which I have borrowed heavily for this chapter. In it he describes once and for all what makes homeless offenders different from the rest of us: '... they don't belong to any network of people and associations which make up the "tribe" to which most of us belong. We have a mass of friends, relations and authorities who both bolster and chivvy us into keeping a stable position in society. There are the tribal taboos on the one hand and the rites and ceremonies on the other that control and fill our lives. Most important of all, nearly all of us have at least one person who fills a special place in our lives; someone for whom we feel responsible and whom we would not let down at any price.

'The homeless and rootless ex-offender has none of these supports and relationships ... Compared with the lot of the average man, when such a man leaves prison he is going into a world which is doubly hostile and unsympathetic because he does not bear the marks of the "average man". Lacking as he does the circles of support the rest of us have, he is destined to suffer continued rejection by his fellow men.'

When you think that Langley House takes on the greyest of these grey area men, the most damaged of the damaged, you can get some idea of how much more difficult even than it used to be the job is.

The staff at Langley used to be able to boast rather proudly that there was honour among thieves, that there was no internal crime during the time a man was with them. That's no longer true. It doesn't happen very often, but it does happen.

Only the other day Elizabeth and Peter Prior, who had thought themselves unshockable, were surprised at how appalled they were when one of the Wing residents broke into the office and absconded not only with the Langley money he found there but with his fellow residents' savings. 'And he *knew* it was their savings,' said Elizabeth. 'In the old days,' Peter said gloomily, 'the men would never have robbed us or each other.'

The man was caught and charged eventually, but the money was gone. The only saving grace was that the other Wing residents were as appalled as the Priors and even more angry. What they would have done to the thief if they'd caught him is not nice to think of.

On the other hand, Peter thinks that there is less violent and aggressive behaviour from Langley residents than there used to be, and this was echoed by other members of staff. Whether it's because the staff are more able to recognise a potentially dangerous situation and take action to stop it or whether the sort of men they're getting now are just more apathetic, it's difficult to say.

It's true that the men are mostly apathetic; as lethargic about their leisure activities as they are about work, and the most successful attempts to stimulate them into new activities are when volunteers come in from outside to interest them in something.

'One of the things we learned from our communities where we could get to know the men so much better,' says John, 'was how high a percentage of them were illiterate.' Now literacy classes, often held by outside volunteers, are a regular feature of the communities.

But if the potential of the residents is lower, their expectancy of material comfort is higher. Langley House has to be, and is, better fitted out and more smoothly run than it ever was. The ratio of staff to residents has improved so that it now works out at roughly eight staff to every twenty men.

Administratively it has been divided into two, with Keith Best responsible for the northern houses and Alan Whittall for those in the south with John Dodd as overall administrator. Both Keith and Alan are former probation officers, both Christians who separately gave up their job to take on the deeper commitment of Langley.

'I hope since our arrival,' says Alan, 'that professionalism isn't the dirty word it once was, and that professional and voluntary have married very happily. Most of the staff now have regular fortnightly in-training. Mind you, I'd still rather have a good social worker who wasn't a Christian than a bad social worker who was, but so far, miraculously, that hasn't happened. There's always a supply of people who are both.'

Between them the houses have places for 240 men. Allowing for the short stay of the men in the halfway houses and those who leave the communities for whatever reason, it means that Langley's intake is about 500 men a year.

But however streamlined and efficient the organisation of Langley has become, the job of its staff still remains one of the toughest there is.

It **was** Tony Payne, John's son-in-law, who gave me the sharpest subjective insight I've ever had into the tiny, everyday nerve-pricking irritations of the job. And it was odd that it should have been Tony because he's one of the new and attractive generation of Christians who so completely accept that every man is their brother they have no necessity to say so. He came to Langley after having worked with drug users and because, among other things, he's a skilled electrician drifted into the job of peripatetic helper, going round the houses to work with the men on projects, extensions, new buildings, etc. Two years ago he and Ros, the Dodds' eldest daughter, got married.

He likes his job. He likes the men. 'But every so often you find yourself getting irritated, you don't mean to, but you do. You've set up a job and all the bloke's got to do is drill a hole or something and he mucks it up, either because he didn't want to do it in the first place or because he didn't understand. Have you ever seen a man like that make coffee?' I hadn't. 'Well he pours the water on to his coffee until the mug's brimming, *then* he adds the milk and *then* he adds the sugar and *then* he trails coffee all over the kitchen floor.'

In cold economics alone Langley House makes sense. Despite the payments made by the Department of Health and Social Security to those men in the communities and any who are temporarily unemployed in the halfway homes, a resident at Langley still costs the country considerably less than half what it takes to keep a man in prison.

But there are other, less calculable benefits to us, society. If I haven't, to my shame, mentioned the offenders' victims it's not because Langley itself doesn't think about them.

To quote Anthony Greenwood again: 'A statement regarding the philosophy of the Trust is not complete without a word about the victims of crime. Although we address ourselves mainly to the deficiencies of the ex-offender, we feel very much for the victim and are working to bring about a reduction in crime by helping the offender to deal with his problems and become a useful member of society instead of its enemy. A man roaming the streets not knowing where his next meal is coming from or where he will sleep tonight, is a much greater threat to all our homes than a man who has his basic needs for survival.'

What it costs emotionally and physically to do a job that the rest of us wouldn't or couldn't do is something only the Langley staff can know. It's up to the rest of us, though, to be very, very grateful that it is a price they are prepared to pay.

CHAPTER TWENTY

THE NICE THINGS

Peter Spurgeon is the principal in charge of the Home Office section which looks after voluntary organisations helping offenders and ex-offenders in this country and, if he's anything to go by, his sort of Civil Servant is another thing that's changed, being younger, better-looking, less guarded and a good deal more committed than I remember them.

He attaches great importance to the Langley House Trust.

'We value it,' he said, 'not just because it's proved itself but because it's done a lot of thinking during its development. It's not a static body which set out with the Christian conversion ethic and never changed. It has adapted considerably and not only done its own thinking but contributed a lot to ours. I suspect it is dealing with the more inadequate end of the offending population and it has accepted reality, that a lot of its men cannot be rehabilitated back into society—when I see how damaged some of them are I wonder that they're still about—and that what is needed is a long-term sanctuary for men who can't cope with the pressure.

'Its Christianity is one of its strengths; there's an outside resource for the staff to draw on and, of course, it's lucky in John Dodd who's a man gifted with considerable presence. He knows his own mind and can be bullheaded about it. He is, of course, a born salesman who knows almost unconsciously all the psychological tricks to apply to selling. And above all he has that enormous capacity for survival which permeates all of Langley.'

John is all that and more, and the nice thing is that he is now being recognised. In 1968 he was awarded the M.B.E. He has become a valued adviser on his field to the Home Office. His knowledge is in great demand abroad so he travels a fair bit to share his experience and to evaluate any new methods.

The other day he was amazed to open a new book called *Twentieth Century Christians* by John D. Searle and find that he had been given a chapter to himself, in between one of Mother Teresa of Calcutta and another on Leonard Cheshire, V.C. The rest of us who love and admire him—and that's most of us who know him—weren't surprised at all.

'Touch a leper, touch him with love,' said Mother Teresa. Well, if the criminal is the leper of our society, then John Dodd has carried out that behest. If Winston Churchill was right and the attitude of the public towards criminals is a test of its civilisation, then John Dodd has helped us to become more civilised. He has talked and talked to any and every meeting that would hear him, pleading for understanding for the inadequate offender, explaining over and over again the pity and the waste in sending those damaged, incompetent men to prison.

If there is a more enlightened attitude towards them, and it's beginning to look as if there is—'it's only the lunatic fringe nowadays who believe that punishment or a kick in the pants can bring about any reform', said Peter Spurgeon—then it's John Dodd as much as anyone who has helped to bring about the change.

(John himself is never satisfied with what he's done. He's as restless as ever he was, wanting Langley to grow, expand, experiment, to take in more and more of the categories which at present it has to reject. Although he's a loved and loving husband and father, it's a restlessness which doesn't make him easy to live with. Alyson has always complained about him on holiday: 'Does the brute lie down on the beach like anybody else? No, he has to keep climbing the cliffs.')

But he's done more than change attitudes. As Peter Spurgeon pointed out: 'The thing about Langley is that it enables a lot of nice things to go on. It gives a human face, supplies a quality of mercy, in what would otherwise be a very depressing field.'

So that, in helping Langley to develop, John Dodd opened a sort of benign Pandora's Box and allowed a goodness to float out into the air for the rest of us to sniff and be heartened that the world isn't as bad as we thought it was.

It's a vital service to have performed. For it *is* a depressing field. If you go from Langley house to Langley house, as I have done, you could be overcome by it—the appalling deprivation which has produced these men is still going on for too many children who will grow up just like them.

As it is, the love which illumines each house allows not only the staff but the men themselves to make nice things happen ...

Perhaps one of the most positive of those nice things was the transformation in 1974 of Elderfield from a halfway house into a community. John and Alyson went in the summer to an auction and bought, on behalf of the Trust, the eight acres of farmland which adjoined the back of Charlotte Yonge's old house.

At first Otterbourne as a village disapproved, thinking that it meant Elderfield was going to increase its number of residents, but as the winter came on and it was possible to see what was really happening, it changed its attitude.

Neighbouring farmers especially looked on with increasing favour. Those eight acres had been in a pitiful condition, having been grazed for years without any proper fertilisation and the weeds and lack of drainage had been a nuisance to everybody around. Now, through sheer back-breaking work, it was being turned into a productive market garden.

The then housefather, Dick Bates, helpers and men got up every morning at 5.30 for the whole of that cold, rainy winter under the fanatical eye of Trevor Dunkerley who had been brought in as farm manager, to dig trenches, lay drains, spread topsoil, make fences, erect sheds, workshops and greenhouses. The women staff and helpers would come out into the dark in their wellies with relays of steaming tea for their frozen menfolk, before finishing the housework and coming out to help as well.

Men, women, staff, residents worked alongside each other so covered in mud, that you couldn't tell which was which. And when you remember that Elderfield was still a halfway house at that time and that many of the men were holding down outside jobs and coming back after a full day to start work in the mud, and that most ex-offenders aren't used to continuous hard work, then you can see that the transforming of Elderfield was nothing less than a sweated miracle.

People who went through it still talk about it as I've heard an older generation talk about wartime experiences, with that same affection for shared hard times.

It certainly won Otterbourne's respect and later, when the now thriving market garden set up a shop from which to sell its fresh vegetables and fruit, its gratitude. 'It's bridged a big gap,' says John, 'housewives with their children go in every day to buy and then stay to chat to the men who are selling.'

Graham Lockley who, with his wife Lorna, inherited Elderfield as houseparents, says that the men are so involved in the work that 'they don't resent the fact that we can take £60 to £80 a day on strawberries they've grown in the season, although they only get pocket-money left over when they've given us the rent from their D.H.S.S. payment.'

The greatest value to him is not in the end product but that the lads learn to work and even like it. 'One of those involved in the digging of trenches found he enjoyed digging holes and was good at it. He's since gone on to our house in Norfolk and volunteered to dig a hole they needed there. Come teatime he didn't turn up and eventually they found him down his hole—he'd dug so deep he had to be helped out.'

It was Graham who pointed out that the Latin root of 'rehabilitation' is 'habilitare' which means to make able. 'One of the great pluses of this job is in seeing a man get pleasure because, for the first time, he's grown something. That's success.'

In the pleasant tidy avenue of houses where he lives up North they don't know anything about his past, even his bright children who are doing so well at school don't know about it. But as he belongs in a list of Langley's nice things I'll call him Jim and camouflage him all I can.

He was orphaned very young and spent most of his childhood in a naval school where everything was geared towards his ambition to go into the Navy. But at fourteen he failed the all-important medical and hope of the Navy was over. Suddenly he was rootless, futureless and very much at risk. He graduated quickly from places of correction to prison, kicking bitterly against the pricks every inch of the way.

Oddly enough, even then when he was, as he says 'the

biggest thief unhung', he believed in a benevolent creator, 'even when I was on Number One, which is three days bread and water', even when the exasperated warders deliberately removed the glass from his cell window in winter, he believed in God. 'People say it's self-delusion. They say you shouldn't think of him as an old man with a beard, but I did. Why not? Jesus called him Dad.'

But he didn't believe much in man. When he first met John Dodd, after a spell in the punishment cell, he thought bitterly that here was a nice, middle-aged, middle-class man who knew nothing about life. 'When I read his story I realised I couldn't have stood what he had and got a respect for him.'

Anyway he went to Langley and there he met Mary, one of the helpers, who was about his own age of thirty-three. (I've seen a photo of him then; he looked older than he does now at forty-seven.)

He wasn't very much more impressed with Langley, Mary apart, than Langley was with him, and left after a while to take a job, but he developed back trouble, lost the job, stole and went inside again. But that was the last time. Langley heard about him and offered to have him back. 'There wasn't a word of recrimination.' He went back, proposed to Mary and looked round once more for work.

He went after a job at a very plush hotel in the nearby town while Mary waited outside. The manager was impressed by Jim's smart appearance—he was dressed in carefully-selected, carefully-cleaned jumble sale clothes. He didn't mention his record. 'They couldn't have taken me if they'd known.'

'You know the Kalamazoo system of accounting, of course,' said the manager. 'Of course,' said Jim, who'd never heard of it. He got the job. 'Do you know,' said the manager, escorting him to the door, 'the staff we get nowadays don't know an entrecote steak from an escalope of veal?' Jim, who didn't know either, laughed. 'Don't they really?' he said.

Within a couple of months he had saved the hotel so much money by the efficiency with which he ran the stores that they raised his salary. In the evenings he washed dishes, swept streets, all to get money to buy a house for Mary and himself and, eventually, managed it.

After eight years he decided he needed to earn more—hotel staff are badly paid. He wanted to go into transport but, because of his record, couldn't be accepted until John Dodd went on his behalf to the Traffic Commissioners and spoke for him.

He's bitter about that. 'Society gets its pound of flesh putting a man in prison, but it never lets him start afresh even after that.'

He's bitter about a good many things. Despite the happiness he's surrounded in now with his much-loved family and his books—he's become a well-read man—and despite his fourteen years of exemplary hard work, he still says *he'll* never get back the years the locusts ate when he was cold and hungry and desperate.

Like all self-made men he can't see why everybody can't achieve what he has if they would only pull themselves together. 'I think the trouble with Langley now is that it's a temptation for the men to stay still. They should be motivated to see something over the hill. Get out and get on. It's self-pity. The lost years. I know. You spend too much time banged up, thinking what's wrong with the world instead of what's wrong with you. But I've got to acknowledge my debt to Langley. It was a starting block, something to put my foot against and take off.'

For all the touches of bitterness, Jim is a lovely and charming man to meet. His wife says of him: 'He's the most honest man I know.'

'Well,' he said, 'with a record like mine you've got to have a different ethic. Not take a penny that isn't yours. People all around you can be fiddling in their job but you don't dare. You mustn't compromise an inch.'

It's obvious that the most important thing Langley did for him was to give him breathing space and introduce him to Mary. The moment those two fell in love was the moment Jim started his climb to get out and get on. As Mary says, echoing Anthony Greenwood: 'It's being needed. If every Langley man could be all-important to somebody, as Jim is to me, they'd never be inside again.'

It was Elizabeth Prior at Wing, one of the most kind and

tolerant women I've ever met, who said: 'I'll tell you a couple I really admire and that's the Tustians. I couldn't do the job they do. I just couldn't *stand* all those naughty old men.'

Jean and Eric Tustian are the houseparents of the Langley at Strood, Kent, one of the two retirement homes, which takes in fourteen men at any one time, some above retirement age, some below but all ex-offenders with no more work expectancy, 'no rehabilitative goal', as the current jargon goes. All of them draw supplementary benefit, some are listlessly apathetic, some are difficult, nearly all of them were adversely affected by the war.

'Our oldest resident is seventy-eight,' said Eric Tustian proudly, 'and he was on a man-o'-war in 1916 with Jellicoe at the Battle of Jutland.'

'Dear Sidney,' said Jean, 'best flaky pastry cook in England.'

'Then there's Harry,' said Eric, 'he was in the Merchant Navy all his life. Torpedoed six times. Both his parents were killed during the war and his wife died and he got into trouble after that.'

'But he's had a part-time job at a local garage,' said Jean, 'and his best time was when, not knowing he'd been in trouble of course, they showed their trust in him by sending him to the bank with the takings.'

The Tustians are incredible. Eric was a clerical worker, Jean a qualified nurse which, as she has to cope with a lot of illness and sometimes death among her residents, makes her ideal for the job. They are a devoted, middle-aged, childless couple, both Roman Catholic converts, who talk all the time, frequently contradicting each other, about their residents on whom they lavish all their considerable energy and love.

'There's a feeling that the elderly need less than the young,' said Jean indignantly, 'but they need more.' To see they get more she holds coffee mornings, saves waste paper, woollies, rags, milk bottle tops, postage stamps and even persuaded Radio Medway to appeal on her behalf for furniture, and got so much she was able to take her pick.

'Yes, I suppose they can be naughty sometimes. Geriatrics are only children at the other end of the scale. The difference is if a toddler has a tantrum you can smack his bottom. You can't smack theirs.'

It must be a temptation sometimes. One resident, in a temper, took all the house cutlery and hid it in various places, burying some of it in the flower beds. They still dig up the occasional fork.

'And we've got Albert. He has cancer of the throat. He's seventy and a dear, kind, pleasant gentleman some of the time, then at others causes havoc and throws his tea about.

'And when the Devil thinks we haven't enough complications he sends us somebody like David, who's fifty-seven, diabetic and ESN. You should try keeping David on his strict diet. He thinks I'm hard. He pinches anything in the food line when you're not looking and his unstable condition makes him cantankerous. I've spent a fair bit of my time resuscitating David from diabetic comas.'

'Still,' she added, 'I really do love them all.' And she means it. One of the worst times in her life was when she had to evict one of her beloved residents because he persisted in breaking the strict rule about bringing drink into the house. 'We'd given him miles more rope than anybody else because when he was sober he was lovely, so clean and smart. We'd warned him.

'And then, it was when Eric was away, I found him crawling up the stairs with a Tesco bag full of meths and red wine and out he went. But I wish I hadn't had to. I wish we had a place for our addicts. I felt inadequate, that I hadn't handled it right.'

'There wasn't anything else you could do,' said Eric, 'but I missed him.'

Drinking is as much a problem, if not more, among elderly Langley men as it is for the younger. While I was with the Tustians I heard a lot about Carlos, a Latvian, who'd fought with the Germans against the Russians who invaded his country, which must make a piquant situation in a house largely filled with British war veterans, Carlos, however, is a genius gardener, according to the Tustians, who's worth his weight in gold for the vegetables he grows for the house. I wanted to meet him. 'I'm afraid you can't,' said Jean, 'it's his vodka day.' One day a week Carlos stops being a gardener and goes out and blows his pocket-money on a bender.

People like Mary Biggart come in from outside to chat or play cards with the men. 'Sometimes you can make them laugh and that's a triumph,' she says. Mary is on Langley's central management committee, a young woman married to a company director, with four children under eleven, who works voluntarily in a psychiatric clinic and still finds time to help the Tustians in any way she can. 'I have so much, you see. I come from a totally secure background and I can't bear to see people unhappy and unloved. I'm lucky to have the privilege to be in on Langley.'

The Tustians welcome anybody and anything that will interest their residents. Despite their own personal energy, despite the outings, the dart tournaments, the snooker competitions, the men are on the whole too lethargic or too infirm to show much enthusiasm for anything. When I was there it seemed unnaturally quiet compared with other Langleys. Carlos was out on his vodka day, others were at the bookies, a couple had gone down to watch the boats on the Medway, Albert was in his room in one of his gentlemanly periods, another was lying on his bed reading, a couple were in the quiet room, talking quietly, when they talked at all.

'After all,' said Eric, '70 per cent of them have been in and out of prison for a very long time. They often say that if there'd been a Langley when they were young their lives would have been different. It's difficult for them to be part of a group. Because so many of them have been hurt they shrink from people. They come here and often three months of daily contact elapse before they even notice us, or allow themselves to—they're taking care not to be hurt again.'

It's no small thing to provide a refuge for battered men who have become old before their time.

All the Langley staff blast you with their personalities, but to meet Trevor Dunkerley, the housefather at Taunton, is like being exposed to a force nine gale. Physically, as well as in other ways, he's a very large young man. By profession he's an horticulturalist who writes poetry as a hobby. By vocation, he says, he's filled with an energy to transmit to sad people the extraordinary excitement he feels about everything. 'Life's so exciting,' he says, banging his desk, 'so exciting it's unbearable. Even depression is exciting.'

He'd know about that because, although there's no sign of it, he was disabled by chronic asthma for most of his youth.

Selectors often send Trevor cases they wouldn't give to anybody else. His motto, stuck up on his living-room wall, says: 'It's better to be stimulating than right.'

He worked for a time in a hospital for the subnormal teaching men and boys so severely disturbed and backward they could be classed as cabbages. But he left because he found the bureaucracy too confining.

He says God is the excitement that is with him all the time and which got him through the crippling asthma of his adolescence. He doesn't talk much about his faith and didn't think it showed until one day one of his ex-residents who, against all the rules, he'd metaphorically booted out into the big outside world, came back for a visit and said: 'Trev, I never asked, but what is it about you and God?'

'That was Dickie who was put away for incest while still a very young man. He's twenty-two now. Born illegitimate. Six brothers and sisters also illegitimate and all by different fathers. At two he was taken away from his mother because she beat him and put into care. At four she reclaimed him. She kept him locked up in the house for two years. There was no real emotional growth.

'The incest charge was for interfering with one of his younger brothers, a sort of immature sexual exploration, really. We took him back to early life. That's what you've got to do, go back to the moments of pain. They come in here and we talk and sometimes the emotion in this office gets so great I think the walls will blow out. But it worked with Dickie. He began to be an adolescent of fifteen. Five years late, but it was happening. Shirt open, all the gear, rock music thundering through the house, looking interestedly at fifteen-year-old girls. It was hell, but he was growing up.

'Now he's outside, got a job, got a wage. He rang me up— "They've actually given me a wage packet". Once when he was still here I had a terrible weekend with raging toothache. Patty, my wife, shoved a fiver in his hand and told him to rush to the nearest pub and get some brandy. Later he told us: "That's the greatest thing that ever happened to me when you trusted me with that fiver." Patty hadn't thought twice about it, but it had been of terrific significance to him.

'He was so institutionalised when he got here he'd call me sir. "What's my name, Dickie?" "Mr. Dunkerley." "What's my name?" Took him ages to say Trevor. You've got to put your arm round 'em. Suffer with them. Start them feeling emotion. Now he's thinking of having an affair with the boss's wife. I told him not to do it. "Find a good woman and get married." He will soon. He's nearly grown up.'

The Taunton Langley is now one of the prettiest houses in the Trust, with its old frontage looking out on to lawn and apple trees, and the extension and workshops with their own view of the Quantocks. Geese peer at you as you go up the drive and a cock crows in an enormous hen run.

'We try to be as self-sufficient as possible. Our men need wood for making things? Okay, we get off-cuts from the local timber-yard. Copper wire for the pin art pictures they make? Strip it from old T.V.s.'

Trevor also believes in testing his men, taking them on climbing holidays on Exmoor and deep-sea fishing in all weathers.

'Dickie came to me once and said: "I can't work with so-and-so, I hate his guts." I said he'd got to; it was a failure in him if he couldn't. "It's like climbing on Exmoor—he's the fellow holding on to your rope." '

Local relationships are good. 'The local bobby comes in regularly—the boys were a bit off with me at first, inviting the fuzz, but they get on fine now. And the local magistrates came and visited with the result that at Christmas a horse-box arrived carrying a billiard table and a T.V. plug-in game as presents to the men from them.'

He and Patty and the deputy houseparents live in two semi-detached cottages over the lane from the main house. 'We've done a lot of work here and we've only been able to do it because we've got a sound, happy marriage and family life.'

The Dunkerleys have two children, Martin aged eleven from Patty's previous marriage, and Paul aged three. Before her first marriage broke up Patty led a comparatively affluent life, 'all golf and cocktail parties'. She admits that she came into Langley for no better reason than that she wanted to share Trevor's work. Now she loves it for its own sake although it's meant that, first at Elderfield and now at Taunton, she's worked harder than ever in her life.

'It's so rewarding. If you can stand the pace you get so much out of it. I've matured a lot.' She's come to love all her men but has a special affection for Gordon, who's eneuretic, 'He's had a wretched life, but he's such a sweet person and I'm rather proud of the fact that he's wetting less and less. I've noticed it returns, though, if Trevor and I are away. He'll say, when we come back: "Bed's wet again I'm afraid, Patty." And I say: "Never mind, put it out to wash." I've given him a sleeping-bag, easy to slip into the machine. It doesn't worry me to handle it, although it does some people. You've got to do as a mum would do.'

It's a far cry from golf and cocktail parties but she seems to thrive on it. She's blonde, pretty and as petite as Trevor is large and it's a wonder half the residents aren't in love with her, but she says they're not. 'They know how Trevor and I feel about each other so there's no point. In fact if Trev and I have a row they get uncomfortable and say: "Made it up with Trev, yet, Patty?" They need security so much.'

Trevor has got large ideas for the Taunton house, wanting to make it more self-sufficient. To that end he's bought a second-hand Gestetner lithographic machine. It's already in business in a small way printing Langley stationery and even taking in outside jobs. He's very proud of the young resident who has shown an aptitude in using the machine. 'He's going places, that boy. I can leave him alone for two days at a time and he gets on with it, costing the jobs and carrying them out. He'll soon be going to technical college to get some qualifications I hope.

'That's what you've got to do, you see. My instructor at disablement college took me by the scruff of the neck and forced me to get better. I'm not going to build a wall round these men and tell them they're victims of society and protect them. That's rubbish. They're human beings and I'm going to make them demand the right to be normal. They're not criminals, they're little lads who somewhere along the line got it all blocked off. We're here to unblock it. Dickie may fall back some day. Okay. But we've sown something.'

Most of the residents at Taunton are young, in the eighteen-to thirty-five-year-old age range. They do take older men, but they're not really Trevor's material. 'They make me feel impotent; they're not going to change.'

Eight months ago Richard came to Taunton Langley. He is an ex-public schoolboy who, as a small child, was dumped on relatives in France for the duration of the war by his mother who cleared off to the United States. He managed for a long time and married. Then his wife left him, taking their three-month-old baby with her. After that it all went wrong. He became an alcoholic. In Wormwood Scrubs he had a nervous breakdown and was transferred to Broadmoor.

Trevor gives a graphic description of his arrival at Langley. 'He had his arms round his head, like a boxer being beaten on the ropes. For weeks he went round like that. You never saw his face. Now the defences are beginning to come down. He just keeps one hand constantly moving across the lower part of his face. But he's terrified of people. On Open Day when visitors were all over the house he went into Taunton and managed to persuade several doctors to give him barbiturates.'

On another public occasion he went off again, got drunk and Trevor received a call from the police to say that he was causing an uproar in a ladies' hairdressers. 'We went and collected him. There were all these ladies in rollers looking horrified. We took him to hospital to get him calmed down and all the way up the corridor he was pinching the nurses' bottoms.'

I met Richard. I walked through the sunshine up to the art and craft shop to buy some gourds which the men grow and then varnish, making a very saleable product.

It was quiet in the white-painted room, with a couple of men making pin pictures and another working on macramé. A thin, grave man, grey-haired at forty-one, greeted me courteously, picked out the best gourds, talking pleasantly all the time. It was difficult to think of him raving up that hospital corridor. Politely, he opened the door to let me out. From first to last his hand had been hiding his face; a pity, from the glimpses I got it looked a nice face.

'Yes, he's coming on,' said Trevor when I got back. 'The other day he said: "Trev, I'm terrified of being normal. And I can feel it happening." '

I had gone to Taunton with John Dodd and Alan Whittall who had business there. During a very good lunch I had sat next to Sid, the oldest resident who had been inherited from a time when the house had an older age group than it has now. For the whole of that lunch a dog, a nice-looking Labrador-Collie cross, sat between us, its eyes never leaving Sid's face. 'That dog loves you,' I said. 'That he does,' said Sid. It was obviously mutual.

Later, going back to Hampshire with John and Alan I listened to them talking about Sid who was, all unknowingly, causing them a problem. Obviously the time had come for him to move from Taunton where, because he can't or won't work as hard as the young men, he gets on their nerves. He had to go to one of the retirement homes, so much was obvious. The problem was the dog. All the retirement homes either had their quota of dogs, or kept cats and didn't want dogs.

'Well, he'll just have to leave it behind,' said Alan, uncomfortably. 'We'll explain to him.'

'Yes, we will,' said John.

There was a silence. We drove through sunshine along the A303, probably one of the most beautiful roads in England, going through Wiltshire past Stonehenge.

'What else can we do?' asked Alan.

'Nothing,' said John.

'What about slipping it a Mickey Finn?' I said, helpfully.

'Don't think,' said John, 'we haven't thought of that.'

There was more silence, more beautiful countryside.

'What about if,' said John, 'we leave him where he is for eighteen months and then when the houseparents leave Cheltenham we tell the new houseparents they've got to accommodate him and his dog.'

'Right,' said Alan. 'If Trevor will have him that long. Mind you, when he gets there he'll have to share a room, so it can't sleep by his bed any more.'

'Of course not,' said John. 'But I think there's a small room

at Cheltenham he could have to himself if we did it up ...'
It was a beautiful drive, and not just because of the
countryside.

In fact, in order to write this book I've driven hundreds
of miles along the roads of England which connect all the
Langley houses. And the one I remember best was the drive
to and from Forncett Grange, which is by the flat lands of
East Anglia, through isolated villages dominated by incon-
gruously large and beautiful churches, frozen with disuse.
It was a depressing journey, in the pouring rain. The news
on the radio was bad. The churches seemed to be asking why
they had been deserted. Perhaps nobody believed in God any
more. Just you and empty churches.
There was nothing special about Forncett, just another
community run by loving people, just another miracle—you
get used to them after a while.
There was a boy at Forncett who, of all the men I've met
in the Langley Houses, came the nearest to breaking me up.
We sat together at the lunch table, although he never saw
me because, like Sid's dog, his eyes were fixed on the face of
somebody else. This was Pam Carter, who was housemother
there then. She was a comfort to look at, was Pam; a large,
loving ex-farmer's wife who with her husband John had left
their farm because they didn't feel they were serving God
sufficiently.
The boy, his name was Dave if I remember, was twenty-
two although he looked younger and he watched Pam's
every move as if his life depended on it. His father had
dropped out of his life very early. When he was nine his
mother one day sent him to school with a note saying she
wouldn't be picking him up. When he got home the house
was empty and he never saw her again.
'He's a nice lad,' I was told. 'Below average intelligence.
Very willing. He makes up fantasies. He says he's been invited to his sister's wedding. He hasn't got a sister. He hasn't
got anybody.'
The question is not how Dave proceeded from orphanage
to foster parents to approved school to Borstal to prison, but
how society could expect him to do much else.

The drive back through a wet and medieval Norfolk was haunted by Dave, haunted by a lot of things. Sanctuary, the leper hospices of the Middle Ages, the monks who cared for the victims of that most dreaded disease and of whom the Langley House staff are the direct spiritual descendants, by Richard arriving at Taunton with his arms sheltering his head, by Sid and his dog, by Scouse, by Percy, by Terry Fenby, by the road that connected and bettered every one of us and which began a long time ago in Singapore.

'Oh cheer up, fellas,' I said to the churches.

After all, the faith that built them is still alive and well, and building something better than churches.